Consuming Desires

Consuming Desires

Family Crisis and the State in the Middle East

Frances S. Hasso

Stanford University Press
Stanford, California

Stanford University Press
Stanford, California

Printed in the United States of America on acid-free, archival-quality paper.

Library of Congress Cataloging-in-Publication Data

Hasso, Frances Susan.
  Consuming desires : family crisis and the state in the Middle East / Frances S. Hasso.
    p. cm.
  Includes bibliographical references and index.
  ISBN 978-0-8047-6155-0 (cloth : alk. paper)--ISBN 978-0-8047-6156-7 (pbk. : alk. paper)
  1. Marriage--Egypt. 2. Marriage--United Arab Emirates. 3. Man-woman relationships--Egypt.
4. Man-woman relationships--United Arab Emirates. 5. Family policy--Egypt. 6. Family policy--United Arab Emirates. I. Title.
  HQ691.7.H37 2010
  306.81095357--dc22   2010030287

Typeset by Bruce Lundquist in 10/14 Minion

To Jeff

Contents

Acknowledgments

THIS RESEARCH PROJECT would not have been possible without the kind and generous assistance of professors, religious scholars, researchers, policymakers, administrators, lawyers, court officials, other public servants, and activists in the United Arab Emirates and Egypt. While some of these individuals did not want their names acknowledged, they agreed to be interviewed, provided documents and other materials, mentioned events, people, and material I should seek at various points in the process, arranged or facilitated interviews, and diligently responded to my occasional e-mail queries. Most of these individuals are listed in the Bibliography. For Egypt, special mention is due to Heba Raouf 'Ezzat, Dina Magdi Taha, Hodda Elsadda, 'Abdul-Mon'em Al-Mashat, Buthayna al-Dib, Lamya Lutfi, Hoda Saadi, Hind Ibrahim, Ahmed A. Zayed, Huda al-Sharqawi, Mulki al-Sharmani, Nawla Darwiche, Martina Rieker, Ann Lesch, Helen Rizzo, Mona Al-Korashy, 'Ali Layla, Faysal 'Abd al-Qadir Yunis, Hala Kamal, Sulayman Khalaf, 'Ali Muhammad al-Makawwi, and Atef Sa'id. For the United Arab Emirates, I especially appreciate the assistance of May Seikaly, Rima Sabban, Mohamed Abdallah Mohamed Al Roken, 'Abdul Salam Muhammad Darwish, Amal Bachiri, Widad Naser Lutah, Ahmed Saif, Sulayman Khalaf, Mona Al-Bahr, Maryam Sultan Lutah, Ebtisam al-Kitbi, Mohammad 'Obayd Ghubash, and Ahmad al-Kubaysi. I am also grateful to the many unnamed students and other young people in both countries who took the time to share their concerns, analyze the present and future, and debate with me and their peers on the issues that were the focus of this project.

This project has benefited from presentations and intellectual exchanges at the University of California, Riverside (2004); the University of Illinois,

Champaign-Urbana (2004); the annual *Critique* Symposium (2006, St. Paul); the Second World Congress of Middle Eastern Studies (2006, Amman); Rice University (2007); Dartmouth College (2007); the Social Science Research Council Inaugural Conference on Inter-Asian Connections (2008, Dubai); the Institute for the Study of Islam in the Modern World (2008, Leiden); the University of Michigan, Ann Arbor (2009); and Duke University (2009). Especially important has been the intellectual and professional support offered by Leo Chavez, Parama Roy, Jenny Sharpe, Ken Cuno, Marilyn Booth, Annelies Moors, Amaney Jamal, Aya Ezawa, Lila Abu-Lughod, Nadine Naber, Rhoda Ann Kanaaneh, Elora Shehabuddin, Moulouk Berry, Khalid Medani, Zeinab Abul-Magd, and Anuradha Dingwaney Needham. I am grateful to Emory Elliott, who sadly passed away unexpectedly, for offering me the opportunity to participate in a Rockefeller Residency Fellowship on "Global Migration, Social Change, and Cultural Transformation" in 2004 at University of California, Riverside. Lila Abu-Lughod and Amira Azhary Sonbol were superb readers and critics of the book manuscript; their support was crucial and their questions and suggestions helped me to refine my arguments.

Research and writing would not have been possible without the recognition and financial assistance provided by an American Sociological Association Fund for the Advancement of the Discipline Award (2003), funded by the ASA and the National Science Foundation; a Rockefeller Foundation Residency Fellowship (2004) at the University of California, Riverside; and a Residency Fellowship at the Institute for the Study of Islam in the Modern World (2008), Leiden, Netherlands. Research, writing, and translation were also supported by an Oberlin College Powers Travel Grant (2003), an Oberlin College Research Portfolio Grant (2008), funded by the Andrew W. Mellon Foundation, and additional funds provided by the Oberlin Office of the Dean of Arts & Sciences. Duke University faculty research funds covered costs related to the final stages of book production.

Special recognition is due to Oberlin colleagues Gina Perez, Gillian Johns, Meredith Gadsby, Grace An, Eric Estes, and Kimberly Jackson Davidson, who offer the invaluable gifts of friendship, moral support, and levity while we manage busy professional and personal lives. Oberlin students, most notably those who have taken my advanced seminar, "Gender and the State in the Middle East and North Africa," have made important contributions to the development of my ideas. They (and sometimes their parents!) have been enthusiastic supporters who were often to be found in the audience when I presented research in distant venues. Suha Qattan-Walsh was an excellent translator of a number of Arabic documents analyzed in this study. Linda Pardee, the department secretary for the Institute for Gender, Sexuality, and Feminist Studies at Oberlin, provided varied and crucial assistance with dispatch whenever I asked. Mudd librarians, especially Jessica Grim, Allison Gallaher, and Alan Boyd, went to significant ends to provide access to needed materials during the research process.

Kate Wahl, executive editor at Stanford University Press, was an extraordinary advisor, reader, and sounding board from the early stages of this book project. I am grateful for her calm, intelligence, and efficiency at every step.

Last but not least, I acknowledge my immediate family, especially Jeffrey Dillman, who in addition to cooking wonderful dinners every week could be counted on to keep distractions at bay, the house running, and the kids on track when my work on this project consumed too many evenings and weekends. He also provided close readings and useful editorial comments and questions on sections of the manuscript when I urgently needed them. Our sons Jamal and Naseem kept things real, asked interesting questions, and provided title and subtitle suggestions (and vetoes) that I could not always dismiss. I love all of them.

Consuming Desires

Introduction

IN EARLY 2004, in a case that received extensive coverage in the Egyptian media and on Arabic satellite channels,[1] Hind al-Hinnawy, a twenty-six–year-old Egyptian set and costume designer from a well-to-do family in Cairo, secretly married twenty-four–year-old television actor Ahmad al-Fishawy in a *'urfi*, or unregistered "customary," marriage contract. Unlike most such relationships, however, al-Hinnawy revealed the relationship to her parents because she became pregnant, although she waited until the second trimester so they would be unable to pressure her into having an abortion. The relationship between al-Hinnawy and al-Fishawy had fallen apart over the pregnancy, and al-Fishawy and his parents, well-known actors themselves, were unsuccessful in their attempts to convince her to have an abortion.[2] Al-Fishawy, who had become famous as the host of a television program "dispensing advice to devout Muslim youth," which was subsequently canceled, denied that the marriage had occurred or that they had had sex, reportedly telling al-Hinnawy that he "would never marry an unveiled woman."[3]

After having the child, al-Hinnawy filed a lawsuit against al-Fishawy in Cairo Family Court in December 2004, requesting he be compelled to submit to a DNA test in order to validate her daughter's biological paternity.[4] While uninterested in continuing a relationship or his money, she wanted to provide her daughter with legitimacy and Egyptian citizenship, which require a birth certificate that includes an Egyptian father's name.[5] Al-Hinnawy reported that in spring 2004, when she informed al-Fishawy of the pregnancy, he "nicely asked for both copies [of the marriage contract] so he could make the marriage official by registering it" but never returned her copy.[6] Al-Hinnawy recognized that she went against the social grain in Egypt by preferring what most consider "public disgrace" to "hypocrisy."[7]

Al-Fishawy refused to take the DNA test ordered by the court in February 2005.[8] In January 2006, a lower Egyptian family court denied al-Hinnawy state recognition of the legitimacy of the customary marriage on the basis that the witness testimonies were insufficient, no documents of proof were proffered, and "formal paternity could not be granted to children conceived out of an illicit relationship."[9] In March 2006, the Cairo Family Appeals Court overturned that ruling, recognizing the marriage and the young child as Ahmad al-Fishawy's legitimate daughter, based on testimony from neighbors, witnesses, and other evidence.[10] Al-Fishawy divorced al-Hinnawy following this ruling.[11] In late November 2008, al-Fishawy admitted during an Egyptian television talk show (*al-Bayt Baytak*) interview that he had taken a DNA test that affirmed he was the biological father of the child, named Lina. He shared that he and his parents were now on friendly and respectful terms with Hind al-Hinnawy and maintained a loving relationship with Lina, and he provided video and picture evidence attesting to this relationship.[12]

Al-Hinnawy is unusual in that her parents, an economist and a psychology professor, publicly advocated for her and their granddaughter after recovering from their shock.[13] In a telling Arab satellite televised interview, Hinnawy's mother criticized "boys and girls" who engaged in such relationships but challenged males: "The world is changing and the boys need to know that they cannot get away with everything. They need to take this issue seriously and ethically. The contract is not just a paper."[14] Hind al-Hinnawy viewed the publicity of the case as important for other Egyptian women in her predicament and had a similar message for men: "You are not always going to have [sexual] relations and run away."[15] By insisting that her intimate concerns had political and social dimensions that require public address, al-Hinnawy encouraged collective claims-making—many women, as well as human rights and women's rights organizations, advocated for "Hind" and her daughter at all stages. The case encouraged such organizations to examine the widespread problems Hind's situation illustrated with respect to gendered citizenship rights.

Al-Hinnawy's case highlights some of the central and related concerns of this book, including the nature of emerging marital and sexual practices, values, and desires; pervasive "family crisis" discourse; transformations in women's gender ideologies; and the wider political and social implications of postcolonial legal and pedagogical projects absorbed with managing, defining, developing, and protecting the "national family." The principal sites of this transnational and comparative research are Egypt and the United Arab Emirates (UAE), although many of the phenomena examined can be found in other parts of the Middle East and North Africa.

Marriage, Divorce, and Weddings in Historical and Social Perspective

The conflict between al-Hinnawy and al-Fishawy about sex and the character and essence of marriage, paternity, and citizenship is only unusual in the notoriety that came to be attached to the couple and their situation. It unfolded not merely in private relationships and Egyptian courts, as would usually be the case for most people in similar positions, but in the limelight of new and old media. Customary marriage is one form of contemporary relationships among Muslims in a history of contestation and multiplicity as to the definition of licit marriage. Rather than being a static institution, marriage is regularly buffeted by legal, political, social, and economic developments in the Middle East and North Africa, as it is everywhere.[16] Not surprisingly, cultural norms, practices, and traditions related to marriage, divorce, and weddings in the UAE and Egypt are plural. To be married is often understood as following the example of the Prophet Muhammad and completing half of the religion's requirements.[17] Marriage is also often understood to provide a licit framework for male sexual drive, especially given the likelihood that heterosexual activity might lead to offspring.[18] The most common terms used to refer to marriage, *nikāḥ* and *zawāj*, are deployed in different ways in various contexts. For example, *nikāḥ* can refer to legally contracted marital sexual cohabitation, the marriage contract itself, heterosexual sex, or any type of sexual activity as, for example, in *nikāḥ al-maḥārim*, or incest.[19] The term *zawāj* is agreed by Islamic jurists to include "all the aspects of marriage."[20]

Muslims have engaged in a range of marriage practices that have been endorsed as orthodox by Islamic theorists and jurists. Muslim marriage is normatively understood to require a husband to provide material maintenance (*nafaqa*) at a level appropriate to the wife's class, housing for the wife and child(ren), and maintenance and housing for his children in case of divorce. In return, a wife is expected to provide her husband with exclusive sexual access and to be obedient, if her Muslim husband is righteous. The Qur'an states that in addition to obedience to the husband, the virtuous Muslim woman is modest (as is expected for men) and exhibits motherly love.[21] This economic and social contract of exchange is premised on a gender complementarity framework that assigns a husband to lead or have guardianship (*qiwāma*) over the household, wife, and children.[22] Classical Islamic traditions did not recognize a shared matrimonial regime, sometimes characterized as communal property.[23] Ottoman court records indicate that judges always buttressed a wife's right to secure her material support from the husband, and "[b]y repeatedly raising this issue," as Judith Tucker convincingly argues, "women also contributed to its centrality in the discourse on marriage."[24] This understanding of husbands as the normative breadwinners and social leaders of the household and wives as separate economic entities was incorporated into the rationalized family law of most postcolonial Middle East and North Africa states and is most relevant during a divorce, when the husband and wife are each supposed to leave the relationship with the property, gifts, and earnings they brought into or accumulated during the marriage, with the exception of what the husband spent for maintenance.

Different types of divorce and annulment can be initiated by Muslim men and women, and scholarly research on these issues in various Islamic traditions and historical and geographic settings indicate that the Arabic terms used to describe them do not imply the same conditions or circumstances: one cannot simply trace consistent genealogies and meanings for marital dissolutions called *khul'* or *faskh*, for example. The easiest divorces then and now are those that are mutually sought and where the couple has no disagreements about the rights and obligations that follow, including child custody and support for the wife. Male repudiation of the wife for any reason has also been an easy (although often economically and emotionally costly) and unilateral prerogative for Muslim husbands and usually occurs out of court. Women have been unable to initiate divorce as easily, although they often successfully resorted to Islamic judges or courts for a divorce judgment or to sue for a husband's material obligations if he initiated the divorce in the Ottoman period.[25] In Sunni Islam, the Maliki jurisprudence tradition was the most liberal in allowing women to obtain a divorce, followed by the Shafi'i and Hanbali schools.[26] Wife-initiated divorce was particularly difficult in the Hanafi tradition since it provided limited valid grounds of "harm" for women and made it the most difficult to prove such grounds to a judge.[27]

One type of divorce initiated by women that did not depend on any male failure to fulfill a contractual obligation, termed *taṭlīq* through *khul'*, was often recorded in Ottoman court registers in Syria and Palestine; women needed to offer no valid reason in such cases although the husband typically had to agree and the wife usually had to forfeit her delayed dower and possibly give the husband other compensation.[28] Such divorces were also common in the court records of Ottoman Egypt,[29] although Abdal-Rehim Abdal-Rehim found no records in which the judge denied a wife's request for *khul'* divorce even when the husband did not agree to the divorce. Moreover, in some of the *khul'* cases, the wife did not pay the resistant husband compensation or forfeit dower.[30] In unhappy marriages in which divorce is sought by the husband in contemporary Egypt, he will egregiously violate marriage obligations to force her to ask for a divorce but is nonresponsive to court requests to appear so as to pressure the wife to renounce or reduce economic obligations required of him if the divorce is determined to be his fault.[31] Typically, when a wife claims she wants a divorce on the basis of being harmed, a husband accuses the wife of disobedience without justification (*ḥaq al-ṭā'a*), opening the possibility that a court could find her guilty of such and rule that a husband does not have to provide her with the delayed dower or alimony support required if she was divorced through no fault of her own.[32]

Although men have this right, native women in Trucial Oman (the previous name of the territories currently designated the United Arab Emirates) and the UAE were rarely repudiated (unilaterally divorced) by a husband. As Linda Soffan writes, "Divorce in tribal society is usually for reasons of barrenness or incompatibility."[33] Girls and women who found their married lives unbearable usually behaved in such a manner that men were compelled to divorce them, usually before the birth of children.[34] Married men with children typically did not prefer divorce because they lost contact with their children and had to pay the delayed dower in addition to major expenses required for any new marriage.[35] Christine Eickelman similarly found male-initiated divorce to be rare in nearby inner Oman in the late 1970s because of "its repercussions upon the complex, interlocking ties within the family cluster." Men were more likely to marry "an attractive, younger second wife."[36] Polygyny in Trucial Oman was generally limited to wealthy and politically influential men until the arrival of social and economic changes introduced by oil, gas, and other wealth. State elites distributed some of this wealth to natives, allowing Emirati men of more modest means to marry a second, younger, woman and to have additional children rather than to divorce a first wife.[37]

Divorce and remarriage were relatively common and considered socially and religiously unproblematic in Trucial Oman/UAE and Egypt. Ken Cuno writes that before the twentieth century, men and women in Egypt experienced little stigma as a result of divorce and remarried easily, which often elicited condemnation from European Christian observers. In the first half of the twentieth century, Egypt had the highest divorce rate among countries reporting data,[38] with one in three marriages in the 1930s ending in divorce.[39] Similarly, both partners easily remarried after divorce or widowhood and divorced people experienced little stigma in Trucial Oman/UAE.[40] Indeed, widowed or divorced native women rarely had "to look far for a new husband" since "women of the tribe were in high demand" given high maternal morbidity rates during the birth of a second child.[41] By the late 1970s, however, Soffan notes that divorce was "increasingly frowned upon by the younger educated couples."[42] Emiratis I have interviewed since 2003 agree with this assessment. The increased censure of divorce is part of a newly dominant definition of the good modern family that frames divorce, male polygamy, and marital seriality as threatening to the well-being of the nation-state.

Guardianship power (*wilāya*) over the marriage of daughters differs in Muslim jurisprudence traditions. In the Hanafi tradition, Muslim women of majority, a status based on reaching physical or social maturity (*bulūgh* or *rushd*), had the legal right to refuse a marriage offer made through a male guardian (*walī al-nikāḥ*); it was forbidden for women to be married against their consent;[43] male guardians were required to be present and approve the marriage of any minor girl, usually below the age of fifteen; and females of majority could contract their own marriages. However, judges had the power and often did annul a marriage if the male guardian could show that the groom was not suitable to the woman's status (lack of *kafāʾa*),[44] was dishonest about his or his father's lineage or occupation, or the dowry's value was deemed inappropriate to the socioeconomic background and status of the woman's family.[45] The Maliki and Shafiʻi jurisprudence traditions, by contrast, considered a female to be a minor and thus unable to contract her own marriage without male guardian permission *unless* she had been previously married. They also allowed a father to give a daughter in marriage, conclude a marriage contract on her behalf, and consent or object to her choice of a husband if such decisions are based on her best interests, take "her wishes into consideration," and do not prevent her from marrying "without proper justification" ("improper" including status inequality or inappropriate dowry).[46]

Amira Sonbol's research demonstrates, nevertheless, that actual rulings within a given juridical tradition in Ottoman Egypt were inconsistent and contingent on the historical moment, the judge, and the local precedents that took into account the social status, "family, money, beauty," or level of male protection for the bride.[47] She found examples of Egyptian Hanafi judges validating forced marriages, marriages in which a father arranged a match with a man not of the bride's status, and marriages in which the potential husband was the "guardian" giving the bride in marriage (to himself). Sonbol also found that an adult woman in late Ottoman Egypt could rarely "transact her own marriage against the wishes of her family," even when she had been previously married.[48] Ron Shaham's analysis of Egyptian *shari'a* court records for the first half of the twentieth century similarly found that adult women rarely married without paternal permission and were "often" married by their male guardians "without being notified about the marriage or against their will," usually to control property or reinforce social or familial ties.[49] By contrast, Sonbol found contracts in which women (1) married themselves to men even in traditions that do not allow them to do so independently and (2) were the only witnesses to a marriage.[50] Sonbol reinforces a point also made by Annelies Moors that normative religious texts, laws, and requirements must be compared against practices.[51]

In contemporary Egypt, codified law based on the Hanafi tradition allows a woman "with full legal capacity," which is determined as sixteen years or older, to marry without male mediation or permission, "whether she be virgin or previously married."[52] Egyptian legislators have recently attempted to codify the Maliki tradition in order to invalidate marriages that do not have guardian approval.[53] In the dominant Maliki and Hanbali traditions of the UAE, if a woman has not been previously married, the legal male guardian of the bride must approve of the match.[54] If parents arranged a marriage, a "girl was always asked for her consent to the marriage in front of the [local religious leader], another trusted and well-known male witness or before a group of people," although she was unlikely to withhold such consent to a guardian.[55]

An Islamic marriage ceremony typically begins with recitation of the opening passage of the Qur'an (not required), the *fatiḥa*, followed by completion of a witnessed and consensual contract that includes a verbal offer and acceptance between the two parties to the contract or their representatives.[56] Marriage registration requirements were instituted at different points in the twentieth century by most Middle East and North Africa states and have no bearing on whether a marriage is licit in Islamic terms. Sonbol makes the point that the formula of offer and acceptance is not specific to marriage contracts or even religious in nature; it is present in all contracts of exchange between "two parties with conditions for continuation and a legal system that determines how the contract could be terminated."[57] The marriage contract is required to be undertaken verbally in front of witnesses who can repeat and verify the details in case marital conflicts emerge, accusations of adultery are made, or either party does not gain their rights or fulfill their obligations.[58] Marriages in which a groom asks witnesses to keep the marriage secret have been considered invalid, although the Hanafi and Shafi'i jurists have held that failure to announce a marriage beyond the minimum of two upright witnesses and the two parties to the contract does not make the contract secret or invalid.[59] Normatively, the Muslim marital contract requires a gift for the bride from the husband. While usually substantial, the material value and payment conditions of the dowry have always varied for differently situated women.[60] Similarly, the period preceding the sharing of a home by the married couple is marked by a range of ceremonies and celebrations that differ by class, ethnic, regional, and religious differences and are "subject to the historical transformations of the region."[61]

Marriage in Egypt is usually a series of events that may or may not occur in stages that are distributed over days, months, or years.[62] Initial discussions between families are followed by research, if needed, on the backgrounds of the potential bride and groom by the family of the other side. If all goes well, there is a *shabka*, considered the beginning of an engagement period, in which jewelry (at least a pair of gold bracelets) and other gifts are given to the bride by the groom.[63] It is quite common for engagements to be broken off as this is the most acceptable period for a couple to get to know each other, especially among working-class women.[64] A marriage contract is completed and signed by the couple, two witnesses, and a religious official or registrar during the *katb al-kitāb* (writing of the contract) stage. The marriage may be celebrated and consummated before the couple lives together, in a ceremony called the *zafāf*, *dukhla*, or *gawāz*.[65] Money is saved by all parties as the marriage stages are combined.[66] Egyptian custom includes an additional written contract that lists the furniture and other gifts given to the bride (from both sides of the family) for the marital home, with the often inflated value of each item and a stipulation that they "are the sole property of the bride."[67] Any lawsuits related to these items, their value, and ownership in situations of divorce are addressed by criminal rather than civil courts.[68]

As a large body of research on contemporary Egypt has demonstrated, including the important work of Diane Singerman, marriage is typically the point at which the largest "intergenerational transfer of wealth" occurs for most people.[69] From a parental perspective, the goal is to assure that the bride and groom have as much as possible of the resources required for a successful marital life, so that "they are only responsible for eating and living."[70] Poor and working-class women begin saving and working from a young age to purchase a trousseau (*gihāz*).[71] The major costs related to marriage remain the responsibility of the groom and his family,[72] although they are increasingly split between the two families.[73] The higher the contribution of the bride and her family to the trousseau and furnishings, the more prestige and negotiating power she enters the relationship with.[74] In 2006, the bride's side in Egypt on average paid about 31 percent of marriage costs while the groom's side paid the remainder.[75] Material contributions toward marriage and thus parental influence on a son are the highest among the richest and poorest parents.[76] The main area of significant parental support for many married couples is in housing.[77] In urban contemporary Egypt, a symbolic amount of dower is registered in the marriage contract by an increasing number of couples,[78] and in recent years, a husband's contributions in furniture, appliances, and "key money" (a down payment to rent a place) are more valued than any dowry, a high dowry, or jewelry.[79] Ostentatious wedding practices have increased in urban Egypt among the wealthier classes, sustaining a "wedding industry" that includes planners, DJs, "decoration specialists, video film specialists, flower decorators, light system suppliers, fancy wedding dress designers, makeup specialists, wedding magazines to advertise hair dressers, dress makers, [and] photographers."[80] These products and services, which are unaffordable to the vast majority of Egyptians, constitute new desires for the thousands who attend or view lavish wedding celebrations on streets, television, or as poorly paid hotel and service staff.

Marriage has become increasingly expensive in the UAE as well. Contemporary UAE weddings are highly elaborate, with families often incurring great debt to pull off what Jane Bristol-Rhys calls "truly spectacular" events in an effort to have "the wedding of the year."[81] Most couples have wedding parties in hotels and take a honeymoon abroad.[82] The weddings she attended averaged eight hundred guests, four hundred from each side of the family, easily reaching approximately US$250,000 for each wedding's event expenses alone.[83] 'Abdul Salam Darwish, a high-ranking official in the reconciliation section of the Dubai courts, contends that weddings have indebted 90 percent of Emiratis at an average of "40 million dirhams per young man, the equivalent of 12 million [U.S.] dollars."[84] Bristol-Rhys interviewed forty women from Abu Dhabi who were between sixty-two and seventy-five years old about the weddings of their youth. They reported that weddings were celebrated over three or four days and were cooperative endeavors held at tent encampments with temporary abodes assembled by extended family groups as they arrived for the occasion.[85]

Marriages in the UAE are usually arranged by mothers, sisters, and aunts who find potential partners, research possible brides or grooms and contact their parents, purchase gold for the bride, and make economic arrangements, although the male guardians are technically in charge.[86] The marriage contract in the Emirates is typically completed in a ceremony called *al-milka* that is officiated by the *muṭawwaʻ* (also referred to as *al-millik*), requires at least two witnesses, and precedes the wedding.[87] The *milka* ceremony usually occurs at a mosque or the bride's home and the conclusion of the contract is often "announced by firing a number of shots."[88] Heard-Bey stresses that no matter how close the premarital familial ties (for example, in cases of cousins marrying),[89] at least an oral contract was "almost certainly worked out" and its safeguarding rests largely in the fact that "everyone in the community is told [its] details."[90] The "most important" part of the marriage contract is usually the money, livestock, or real estate given directly to the bride as a dowry and expected to be kept by her in case of divorce.[91] A delayed dowry must also be stated and paid in case of divorce or other conditions specified by the wife.[92]

Secondary sources and field research support the dominant accounts that immediate and delayed dowry expectations have regularly increased since the 1970s in the UAE. Soffan writes that even "before oil wealth" men sometimes had to wait until "late in life" before they accumulated the necessary funds to marry, although the situation seemed difficult in a different way in the 1970s, as parents of daughters increasingly vied to "set the highest possible dowry."[93] Emirati women complained to her of feeling as if they were being sold and worried that native men were "marrying girls from outside the Emirates (many Indians and Egyptians, especially)." Legal attempts by the federal government in the 1970s to limit dowry amounts were unsuccessful.[94] More recently, UAE rulers have ineffectively decreed limits on dowry requests.[95] Religious leaders in the UAE and Egypt have, in turn, promoted the idea that marriage only requires token dowry, although this idea has not taken hold.[96]

Consummation of the marriage usually occurred in a number of stages in Trucial Oman/UAE, beginning in the bride's home and bedroom assisted by a midwife (who may have circumcised the younger girl) or a hairdresser. After about a week, the couple moved to the home provided by the bridegroom.[97] Until the 1980s, an Emirati bride rarely interacted with a groom until the marriage was consummated.[98] Today, brides and grooms regularly visit, although usually in chaperoned or group situations.[99] In a 1986 study of the UAE, Malcolm Peck notes a weakening of patriarchal authority as members of extended Emirati families increasingly lived in separate abodes, facilitated by government money for housing. Emirati men and women expected to exercise "greater choice" in marriage partners and partners were increasingly of "similar age" because of the high number of native women who complete university first. Moreover, greater leisure time had led to expectations of shared interests and recreation by the married couple, strengthening companionate bonds.[100]

People in the UAE, Egypt, and other places contract customary marriages of the sort engaged in by Hind al-Hinnawy and Ahmad al-Fishawy in order to avoid the elaborate rituals, significant material costs, parental control, and complicated social expectations attached to engagements, weddings, and marriages, as well as to bypass cultural and social restrictions on heterosexual relations outside of marriage. Unlike regular marriages, most customary marriage contracts are not widely publicized by the couple, are short-term in practice, and do not require men to provide women with housing and economic maintenance. These contracts are also used in many instances to bypass the requirement in some of the classic Islamic legal schools for permission to marry from a girl or woman's male guardian. As the al-Hinnawy case illustrates, when a woman citizen in such a relationship becomes pregnant and a man denies he is married to her, significant legal, political, and social dilemmas result because in Egypt and the UAE that child's citizenship status depends on the mother being *licitly married to a male citizen*. In both countries, 'urfi paper contracts have a voilà! quality of protection to them in that they can easily be waved in front of disapproving family members, the public, or the decency police after sexual partners have been caught or must reveal a relationship.[101] The contracts also provide social flexibility if they are dated inaccurately, for example if a pregnancy results from a sexual relationship that must be legitimized post facto.

In avoiding states, families, and established religious authorities, customary marriages in their contemporary forms can facilitate nonheterosexual marital unions. Sexual and gender-"queer" practices and identities are recognized as indigenous, contrary to moralistic rhetoric emanating from conservative circles that condemns them as signs of Westernization or cultural invasion, and they are facilitated by gender segregation in some communities.[102] One can assume that the oral or written customary contracting of marriage was part of the plan for a November 2005 mass wedding ceremony for male couples (in male and female dress) in a hotel along the Abu Dhabi-Dubai highway in the

UAE. Newspapers reported the arrest of twenty-two of twenty-six men present, most of them from the Emirates, and an Indian disc jockey. Similar arrests at mass male wedding ceremonies had occurred in the previous few years in other emirates, such as al-Shariqa.[103]

Misyār, or ambulant, marriage contracts are another relatively recent phenomenon in parts of the Middle East and North Africa region. Unlike *'urfī* marriages, *misyār* weddings are registered in state courts in a number of countries, including the UAE, and on their face appear to be regular marriage contracts with the appropriate number of witnesses and a dowry. But men involved in them usually do not provide women with housing or maintenance if women concede these rights. Most male practitioners do not inform a first wife of the *misyār* relationship and thus, like *'urfī* contracts, *misyār* is often referred to as "secret marriage." Also, like customary contracts, *misyār* relationships clearly benefit men by allowing licit sexual relations without the same material investments and support required of regular marriage. But such relationships can also benefit, for example, divorced or widowed women who do not want a child, or who have a home, custody of children, and resources (either provisioned by the state or the previous husband/husband's family) that they do not want to lose with announcement and registration of marriage.[104] The perceived Islamic licitness of such contracts, however contested and stigmatized, allows women of all ages to engage in private sexual and marital relations, and even to have a legally sanctioned child in the case of *misyār*, while avoiding a range of rules, traditions, and sanctions.

In their contemporary uses by Sunni Muslims, these forms of secret marriage legally differ from but can resemble in social and cultural terms temporary marriage contracts made by Shi'i Muslims. The Shi'i *ṣīgha* contracts, also known as "pleasure" marriages, were studied by Shahla Haeri in Iran in the 1980s.[105] The contracts are based on a widely accepted logic among Muslims that the sexual needs of men and women are rooted in nature and must occur in the licit context of marriage or they will produce social chaos.[106] The temporary marriage contracts are privately negotiated, must precisely state the duration of male sexual access and payment to the woman (*ajir*), usually involve women who are widowed or divorced, and do not require permission from a male guardian.[107] Significant proportions of Muslims in the Arabian Peninsula are Shi'i and follow the instructions of their religious authorities with respect to marriage. According to a married Shi'i woman from the UAE, temporary marriages are used by divorced and widowed women largely as polygynous relationships with Shiʻi men. An Emirati Shiʻi man does not usually contract such a relationship with a native Emirati woman, but rather with a Syrian, Lebanese, or Iranian woman. If a woman in such a relationship becomes pregnant, the marriage may be made regular.[108]

National Families in Crisis

Because men and women involved in secret marriages selectively comply with religious, social, and legal norms in their marital, gender, and sexual behavior, the relationships elicit great anxiety and commentary in Egypt and the UAE. I examine such relationships within larger family crisis discourses absorbed with a number of additional issues widely understood to be sources of social instability and moral dilemmas, including singlehood, marriage delays, divorce, and exogamy.[109] Family crisis discourse is produced by state institutions and functionaries, intellectuals, court officials, social workers, religious leaders, editorialists, and community activists. This discourse is often conveyed in morally sensationalist terms that encourage "religious adherence as a remedy for social and moral disintegration."[110] This discourse has led to a proliferation of pedagogical instructions produced by state organizations, religious officials, social scientists, and others aiming to "develop" or "improve" families. States in particular bolster their legitimacy with projects and narratives claiming to assist and defend the family and protect morality, and they regularly remind citizen-subjects of their willingness to act in these paternal capacities. Among the paradoxes addressed in this book is how family crisis, in its lived and perceived dimensions, has encouraged the expansion of state intervention and regulation in biopolitical domains, often prodded by feminist or women's organizations, despite male dominance in judicial, legislative, and executive apparatuses and the authoritarianism of ruling regimes. I contend that women more than men are made further dependent on undemocratic states by the expansion of state power and influence over sexual and family life, although the targets of these governance projects are men more than they are women.

The postcolonial Middle East and North Africa states that emerged or were remade in the twentieth century were concerned with rationalizing and regulating family life, as well as reconstituting sexual and marital norms and behaviors. Such state-initiated marriage and family projects are typically examined through reform or modernization lenses, or they are understood as primarily motivated by the patriarchal agendas of states. I view such projects, in contrast, as largely functioning to manage life and resources for the purposes of efficient rule. The rulers of these largely undemocratic states often represent a stable nation-state led by them as a harmonious patriarchal family and the modern, yet culturally authentic, family as crucial to national health and security. One of my unexpected findings in this research is that while feminist scholarship on the Middle East and North Africa region has largely focused on the patriarchal nature of family legal systems and the regulation of women and their sexuality, it is men's unregulated marital and heterosexual practices that are often assumed by elites to be disorderly and thus threatening to social stability and resources.[111] Men are often constructed as unruly and poorly educated in their willingness and skills to center the nuclear family as the basic unit of a stable modern *national* order. State and religious authorities—and very often, women—understand this unruly behavior to threaten the "national family." I began to understand these states as acting on behalf of women in their family politics and policies—in paternalistic terms—more often than is usually recognized. It follows, I argue, that citizen women may need authoritarian states more than men do, not least for their ability to police men and extract resources from them within a corporatist family framework that requires men to provide for wives, children, and parents. The terms "corporatism" and "corporatist" refer to a vision of families, states, or communities that is worth defining since I use them at various points. There is frequent slippage between normative (how things ought to be) and descriptive (how things are) understandings in this vision, which posits families, states, or communities as naturally hierarchical systems in which members harmoniously play their assigned roles. In such an understanding, social formations are in metaphorical terms seen to work like the human body, where organs have different levels of power but function smoothly and interdependently. For example, men rule and financially support and protect the home and its members; women rear children, nurture, and maintain the household; and children obey in return for protection, financial support, and nurturing. From a corporatist perspective, conflict or resistance in families, communities, or states is typically understood as "dysfunction," "crisis," or "disease."

In Egypt and the UAE, the characterizations of perceived family crisis and the objects of blame for crisis are plural. Women criticize men and the gender inequalities that limit their sexual and marital options. Young people blame elders for being too restrictive and picky with respect to gender relations and marriage partners. Elders accuse young people of deficits in self-control and responsibility. In addition, particularly in Egypt, high marriage and housing costs and the decreased ability of many families to meet the marriage needs of their children are understood to have made it more difficult for many to accumulate the resources necessary to marry. New media and communication technologies such as the Internet, mobile telephones, and satellite television are seen to undermine traditional norms in both countries. Foreign and Western "invasions" are also blamed for family crisis: sexual unrestraint, light-hearted marriage commitments, alienation within the family, lax commitment to parental obligations and responsibilities, and consumerism are widely assumed to be unwanted imports that threaten less powerful cultures' sexual and marital values.[112]

The marital and sexual behaviors examined in this book are not the results of imported or "invading" ideas and practices, however, but of dynamic interactions between indigenous experiences, beliefs, and desires, modern state requirements, and the less bounded flows of people and ideas made possible in the late twentieth and early twenty-first centuries.[113] Even the indigenous has always been less static and insular than it is often represented in hegemonic discourse. In a comment about the Arab Peninsula that is also applicable to Egypt, Mawadi al-Rasheed reminds us that narratives of a golden age of indigenous cultural coherence and purity are "too rigid to account for the historical and contemporary manifestations of Gulf cultural, ethnic and religious diversity, on the one hand, and ancient economic connections with the outside world, on the other."[114] Not surprisingly, privileged narratives of moral and cultural malfeasance focus almost exclusively on violations of dominant gender norms, sexual behavior perceived to be inappropriate, and challenges to traditional family authority, notably avoiding issues such as legalized gender inequality, exploitative labor standards, abusive treatment of the impoverished sector of foreign laborers (in the UAE), state corruption, torture by police and intelligence services, or state restrictions on expression and political association. In response to perceived threats to authentic values and mores, UAE rulers have invested in museums and architecture that reconstitute "tradition," working to at once feed into tourism and "preserve [their] traditional legitimacy," writes Christopher Davidson.[115] Rulers in some emirates have also introduced restrictions on alcohol drinking, dress practices, prostitution,[116] and "public indecency," and police occasionally target violators.[117] Regional regimes, writes Scott Long, are caught in the tension between widespread access to a range of "consumer goods and dreams" in late neoliberal capitalism and legitimating themselves "by controlling—and being seen to control—the cultural changes those economic changes put in motion. They must both stimulate desire and suppress it." In Cairo, for example, a "duality" distinguishes the attitudes of officials who want to facilitate foreign tourism and mitigate the impact of foreigners on culture.[118]

Changes are undoubtedly occurring in individual subjectivities, desires, and practices with respect to marriage, sexuality, and gender. Women in both countries seem increasingly impatient with stark gender inequality in marriage and less willing to marry for the sake of marrying. While material factors make marriage more difficult for many, especially in Egypt, overreliance on economic explanations miss the obstacles posed by cultural norms and state laws and policies that support conservative gender and sexual relations. Economic explanations also underestimate ongoing changes, sometimes inchoate and thus more difficult to articulate, in gendered, marital, and sexual subjectivities and desires. Family crisis discourse typically reinforces hegemonic values and inhibits discussion that reflects the complexity of the actual changes and their sources. Across gender, consumerism, new communication technologies, and the multidirectional flow of ideas through satellite television and the Internet have facilitated individuation, emerging emotional and sexual appetites, and new marriage desires. The subjectivities and practices encouraged by transnational Islamic discourse and neoliberal globalization, moreover, paradoxically appear to be mutually sustaining in that both rely on individualism and thus undermine the corporatist authority of states, families, and the religious establishment. Thus while changes cannot be reduced to cultural, ideological, and economic "invasion," less bounded processes that challenge dominant family, gender, and sexual ideologies are indeed at work.

Situating the UAE and Egypt

Definitions of the national subject, citizenship, and belonging are ongoing rather than complete in the UAE and Egypt and national subjectivities are often structured by other formations—sectarian,[119] regional, ethnic, pan-Islamic, and Arab, among others. In the UAE, the most salient division is between the well-resourced minority "native" citizens (*muwāṭinūn*) and the more than 80 percent who are long- and short-term resident workers (*wāfidūn*) of different job tiers from South Asia, Southeast Asia, Iran, the Arab world, and Africa.[120] The very presence of these nonnationals substantially impacts "native" fears and anxieties related to sexuality, citizenship, and the makeup of the "national family." While most UAE citizens are Sunni Muslims, possibly as many as 41 percent of them is Shi'i Muslim,[121] some originally from Iran.[122] Shi'i citizens experience discrimination at cultural and institutional levels, as do Sunni Muslim citizens of Persian origin.[123] Ahmed Kanna contends that discoveries of petroleum in the UAE required ruling elites to delineate the "national" subject (*muwāṭin*) in order to determine which residents can legitimately draw on some of the wealth these elites controlled. Before these resource discoveries in the 1950s and 1960s, differentiations between Arabs, Indians, and Persians—or Sunni and Shiʻi—"were far less rigid" and intermarriage was common. Thus the economic and political rationalization attached to building a modern state required the "naturalization" of Arabness "as the authentic identity of the nation-state."[124] Nevertheless, as Maha Khatib found during her early 1990s fieldwork in the UAE, definitions of who is a "national," "local," or "native" (and who is not) are socially and culturally situational and contested among Emirati citizens.[125]

The contemporary UAE and Egyptian states repress the civic sphere and rely on patrimonialism to varying degrees to consolidate and maintain the economic and political power of ruling regimes. Egypt is nevertheless a country of institutions, including a complex and to some degree autonomous judicial system that provides openings for activists and lawyers of a range of political persuasions.[126] Both states license and subsidize Shiʻi and Sunni mosques and their imams, and distribute weekly sermon themes, although the control is less porous in the smaller and wealthier UAE; there is a large informal mosque sector in Egypt.[127] Azza Karam argues that the civil and political spheres in Egypt rely on "similar discourses of political power and legitimacy" and "the state's use of particular laws (e.g., Law 32 of 1964, the Law of Association) renders state control a defining aspect of the articulation of civil discourses."[128] Egypt experienced popular revolts in 2004 and the spring and summer of 2005 that challenged authoritarianism and "crony forms of neo-liberalism that had come to define the contradictions of a new, globalized Cairo."[129] The often-violent responses of state authorities further mobilized activist energies and helped establish alliances of opposition that crossed some of the usual ideological boundaries.[130]

Nothing close to this level of activism or differentiation between state and civil sectors exists in the UAE, although this should not imply that resistance to ruling elites has been or is nonexistent. Opposition to ruling family dominance and British colonial rule in the twentieth century has come from sectors of the male merchant class, divided between those from non-Arab (for example, Indians, Persians) and Arab ethnicities; Arab teachers (most of them imported) influenced by Arab nationalist ideologies, especially Nasserism; and individuals from nonruling Emirati families.[131] The rise of oil and other wealth from the 1960s, Davidson argues, allowed ruling families to establish "new forms of rentierism" that distributed natural resource-based wealth in a manner that tamps down both resistance and calls for political reform.[132] Most Emirati civic organizations today are apolitical education and service-oriented entities affiliated with ruling families in some manner. Such organizations must be approved and licensed, ruling families provide them with significant funding, and they are usually led by members or allies of these families.[133] Emirati authorities actively repress criticism of the state and ban independent social movements and political parties.

The first UAE women's association was established in 1973 in Abu Dhabi.[134] Early in their histories, the women's association in each emirate financially depended on "personal contributions" from women affiliated with ruling families, although by 1980, "all of the chapters submit[ted] annual budgetary requests to the Ministry of Labor and Social Affairs" and were partly "subsidized by the federal treasury."[135] Each association is nevertheless under the patronage of a first lady from an Emirati ruling family.[136] From their inception, these associations shared with the state a "national development" agenda of women's improvement and empowerment framed by Islamic idioms and values.[137] An early 1990s study found that religious, health, literacy, and social awareness programming were the dominant activities of these associations.[138] In the contemporary period, these organizations heavily depend on state subsidies and are banned from receiving any "grants or donations from abroad."[139] A critic argues that the associations suffer from "inaction and ineffective managements," have "failed to attract university graduates," and avoid "any involvement in political issues concerning women."[140] Interviews with Emirati women involved in these organizations and a review of their publications and brochures reinforce this assessment. The organizations are committed to sustaining families in which Emirati men marry Emirati women, are concerned with divorce rates, and stress that native girls and women should stay close to the Qur'an and Islamic values in their lives, relationships, and child-rearing practices. Other biopolitical concerns of these associations include mother and child health and general hygiene.

In contrast to the UAE, the Egyptian political field is crowded with women's organizations with a range of ideologies and strategies.[141] Most receive project-oriented financial support from external funders associated with the United Nations, the European Union, wealthy states, or private Western foundations. In comparison to other Middle East and North Africa states, Egypt did not establish "state feminist" apparatuses until relatively recently, driven largely by the "human development" and "women's empowerment" discourses dominant in the logic and funding priorities of transnational governmentality.[142] The formal positions of the Egyptian National Council of Women are conservative on gender and sexual issues perceived as socially sensitive in a patriarchal society. The most persistent organizational narrative is highlighted in *Women in Egyptian Legislations*, a booklet written by the lawyer Dr. Fawziya Abdul Sattar: women's political rights and participation, and recognition of their involvement in the history of modern Egypt, are crucial to the nation's "development." Gender equality in political participation, which includes women running and being elected to high office, is framed as Islamically licit. Women's political inclusion is represented as the "fruit of a bitter struggle [by] Egyptian women."[143] Predictably, NCW documents include no criticism of state authoritarianism.

Egypt and the UAE are patriarchal, corporatist societies, although norms, practices, and opportunities within particular families—structured by class, rural/urban location, education, and values—seem to matter most for individual life trajectories. In the UAE, broad differences also exist regarding marriage and gender expectations between different emirates: northern/southern, coastal/inland, Dubai/'Ajman.[144] Based on her field research with hundreds of Emirati women in the early 1990s, Maha Khatib found that women from Shariqa are reputed to be the least conservative in their gender norms, followed by women from Dubai, with 'Ajman as the most conservative.[145] Unlike in Saudi Arabia, native women throughout the UAE drive,[146] are not legally limited from working outside the home in a broad range of occupations, and can be found in most public spaces, especially the ubiquitous and luxurious mega-malls. Indeed, given that Emiratis are a small proportion of the country's population, women are crucial to the state's aims to nationalize ("Emiratize") the workforce.[147] At the same time, widespread social stigma remains attached to national women working in mixed-gender occupations in the private sphere or outside professions such as "school teaching, nursing, and some civil service jobs."[148] Native teenage girls and women are generally expected to veil their hair (with a *shāyla*) and to wear an elegant long black coat (*'abā'*), although they are not legally required to do so.[149] Unaccompanied heterosexual dating remains socially restricted for most Emirati girls and women, as it is for most Egyptian girls and women, although girls and women in both countries violate these restrictions. State-sponsored schools are segregated by gender in the UAE and Egypt, while universities are gender-segregated only in the UAE. It is notable that girls and women outnumber boys and men in secondary and postsecondary education in the UAE.[150]

While gender and sexual understandings are often couched in an Islamic idiom in both countries, it is not the only or even most important framework. People selectively employ religious, culturalist, nationalist, psychological, biological, anti-imperialist, liberal rights-oriented, and radical class discourses to challenge *or* support particular gender-sexual regimes. Regular people, scholars, and religious activists, for example, not infrequently argue that the often deeply gender unequal rules of marriage (and in the Gulf, gender segregation) merely reflect the natural psychological and physical constitutions and needs of men and women. However, it was impossible to avoid the conclusion, especially during fieldwork in the UAE, that such rules radically *constitute* a particular gender order, upheld by women as well as men, and attenuated by regional customs, resources, and religious beliefs. Gender-segregation rules eroticize and gender subjects and spaces in ways that are difficult to ignore and yet appear to be unintended.

Notes on Genealogy and Methodology

This research is shaped to some degree by lessons learned from my preceding book, *Resistance, Repression and Gender Politics in Occupied Palestine and Jordan.*[151] In that book, I argue that the different strategies and outcomes of Palestinian nationalist and gender politics in places such as Jordan, the Occupied Territories, and Lebanon are significantly informed by the dynamics of their political fields, including state policies, national repertoires of resistance, and national experiences of repression. I also demonstrate how less bounded transnational dynamics at different scales (Arab, regional, Western, third world) interact with these political fields to impact Palestinian nationalist and gender politics. *Consuming Desires*, by comparison, emerged from my interest in examining gender, sexuality, and politics in the Arab world in a manner that highlights interactions between transnational processes and quotidian life. It seemed to me that the emergence of customary marriage among Sunni Muslims, which I understood was a significant phenomenon in Egypt but present elsewhere in the region as well, would allow me to ask such questions because the practice challenged both state oversight and family control. I suspected that these relationships were linked to and facilitated by the less regulated circuits of new media and communication technologies. As I became more involved in the research, I learned that these customary marriage contracts were only one kind of secret relationship and one dimension of broader changes and anxiet-ies related to gender, sexuality, and marriage. While at the outset I was largely concerned with the transnational aspects of these dynamics and the manner in which they are often blamed on Western cultural "invasions," during the re-search process it became increasingly clear that the nation-state remains the most relevant force in its effect on the biopolitical domains of sexuality and marriage, especially in its legislative, judicial, and policing capacities. This led me to significantly engage with Michel Foucault's "governmentality" approach in order to understand how state laws and policies impact people's desires and actions with respect to marriage and sexuality and the intended and unin-tended workings and consequences of "family crisis" discourse.

Examining these issues in two nation-states draws attention to the relevance of local histories, cultural norms and contexts, and political fields.[152] Given the proliferation of national discussion focused on young people's emerging sexual and marriage practices, it was clear that Egypt should be one of the field sites for this research project. The choice of the United Arab Emirates emerged first from my interest in a culturally, historically, and legally contrasting Arab and Muslim case and second from discussions with colleagues working in the re-gion who informed me that issues related to marriage and sex were dominant concerns. As a secular and feminist Arab-American woman, I had more than the usual fieldwork misgivings and anxieties regarding research in the socially conservative Gulf region, and as a result chose to avoid the most politically sig-nificant of these countries, Saudi Arabia. I chose the UAE because a number of colleagues assisted me with contacts and facilitated entre into various settings. When I arrived in Abu Dhabi to conduct interviews, it serendipitously turned out that I shared a last name with a second cousin who had been a well-liked undergraduate professor at UAE University in the late 1970s and early 1980s and had taught a number of the native intellectuals and professionals I met.

The contrasts are sharp between the UAE, a relatively new and wealthy nation-state in the Arabian Peninsula with a small population comprised pre-dominantly of noncitizens, and Egypt, an older, populous, and much poorer state of lengthy urban history and ancient civilizations. At the same time, the pervasive relevance of Islamic idioms and the circulation of competing defi-nitions of the licit life in both countries afford similarities in the discussions and debates regarding gender, sexuality, and the family. In both of these post-colonial states I found a family crisis discourse that differs in degree rather than kind; a dominant understanding that national well-being requires family stability; changes in sexual, gender, and family values and practices that are widely blamed on foreign invasions; and significant concern with cultivating appropriate values and subjectivities that support the "national family."

This multisited ethnography employs a research approach grounded in the relevant histories and cultural and political dynamics of Egypt and the UAE. It also applies a lens that recognizes how these national histories and dynamics interact with transnational formations and processes. These interactions often occur across scales.[153] Rather than examining them as separately existing, even opposed, entities, I highlight "interdependencies" between what Richa Nagar and coauthors term "formal and informal spheres."[154] As Nathan Sayre and other geographers have noted, there are always "methodological trade-offs" in research choices.[155] By their nature, the often informal and under-the-radar phenomena examined in this book, such as secret marriage and other sexual practices that violate dominant norms, offer nonsystematic information that is less amenable to definitive evidentiary claims, the typical expectation in the social sciences. Many feminist scholars have argued, instead, for epistemologically recognizing that all knowledge projects are situated and partial.[156] In comparison to a strictly positivist, objectivist research method, discourse analysis informed by ethnographic and feminist research approaches encourages attention to gaps, hesitations, silences, narrative framing, and language use in all offered accounts, whether they are produced by individuals or institutions, irrespective of the legitimacy, power, or status of the narrator. Such approaches to knowledge and research also facilitate reading all information in a double manner—at its face and against its grain.

I conducted fieldwork stints in Egypt and the UAE in 2003 and 2008, interviewing young people, state officials, religious authorities, intellectuals, leaders in women's associations, and social movement activists. The research depended on the generosity of a few colleagues in each country whom I contacted through e-mail, telephone, and in-person meetings. The project quickly evolved in response to the many suggestions of friends, respondents, and informants, who triggered ideas during interviews, proposed other useful contacts, and brought relevant documents, materials, newspaper stories, and events to my attention. Group interviews with university students at Cairo University, al-Shariqa Arab University (UAE), UAE University (al-'Ayn, Abu Dhabi), and 'Ain Shams University (Egypt) depended on the willingness of faculty members and administrators to provide access to students in their courses and on their campuses. In addition to analyzing interviews and English-language scholarship, I examine family status laws and government-sponsored and independent social science research produced by scholars in the region on various dimensions of "family crisis." I also examine books and other material (cassettes, brochures, and so forth) produced by intellectuals, religious authorities, and state officials and organizations. These materials, I argue, reflect pedagogies designed to cultivate subjectivities and behaviors considered appropriate to sustaining national family life. Finally, I examine newspaper and magazine articles and programming from Arabic satellite television programs concerned with marriage, divorce, and sex. I conducted fieldwork in Arabic and translated and transcribed all recorded interviews. Suha Qattan-Walsh and I divided translation of Arabic-language documents.

1 Legal Governmentality and the National Family

Men and women are constructed as different entities under [Islamic] law, particularly in the sphere of family relations, where male privilege is undeniable. For as long as the law remained uncodified, the interpretations of the meaning of these differences retained some fluidity and flexibility. . . . But as soon as the law is codified, gendered right and gendered duty became incontrovertible points of law, brooking no adjustments or modifications except from on high.

Judith E. Tucker, *In the House of the Law* (1998)

LEGAL RATIONALIZATION has been central to consolidating complex societies into modern nation-states in the Middle East and North Africa (MENA) since the nineteenth century. In the process of creating their secular legal systems, these states also established institutionalized forms of gender inequality less subject to negotiation. God's law, or "shari'a" for believing Muslims, differs from these modern legal systems in that it was historically uncodified and thus more flexible, heterogeneous, and at times even idiosyncratic in its application. The shari'a, a noun referred to frequently in the Qur'an, is the ideal "path" for human behavior: "Muslims understood this to mean that God had established a body of rules and recommendations and that human salvation depended on their ability to identify and obey these. Over time, Muslim legal thinkers came to conclude that God had placed every conceivable act in a five-part moral scale" that ranged from mandatory to prohibited.[1] The Islamic jurisprudence (*fiqh*) that developed over time to determine and clarify God's rules, however, was always based on hybrids of sacred, secular, and customary sources, methodologies, and concerns that coalesced in specific contexts. Despite the instability and plurality of its deployments and meanings, the term shariʿa is unlikely to be forfeited by political, religious, or other social actors given its cultural significance and association with sacred and thus legitimate authority. Modern legal codes related to "personal status" or family domains continue to be the most likely to maintain Islamic idioms (such as referring to them as drawing from "shariʿa") in MENA states. While these projects are often defended as necessary to improve social well-being, I argue that codification of law, rationalized legal procedures (such as minimum age requirements for marriage), registration requirements, and other state-initiated changes with respect to birth, marriage, inheritance, guardianship, and divorce are largely designed to expand state power. These projects are often "successful" because access to rights and resources controlled by the state is usually attached to compliance with state rules. These projects are most important, I contend, in their ability to reshape norms and subjectivities, although they do not always work in the intended directions.

Legal rationalization has existed for well over 150 years in Egypt and is more recent to the United Arab Emirates (UAE), although the ability of these laws to penetrate daily life and establish preferred norms of behavior has always been uneven. In other words, there is a historically contentious relationship between people's actual marriage, sexuality, and other practices and the "national family" agendas of most modern states. I use the term "national family" as a metaphor for a modern, consolidated, cohesive nation-state (the postcolonial state as family writ large) *and* for actual families understood in instrumentalist terms as social units that either weaken or strengthen the nation-state. People in the UAE have more insistently than Egyptians resisted governance projects designed to mold their identities, norms, and family practices. They have also significantly hindered the consolidation of a federalized nation-state. This resistance does not stem from their more democratic and antipatriarchal orientations but rather because the governance agendas of the UAE as a federal entity compete with the still relevant values and norms associated with shariʿa and tribal authority systems, themselves often in tension with each other and responsive to sociohistorical conditions. Moreover, not all ruling families in the UAE are equally interested in the establishment of a unified nation-state—a "national family"—that supersedes their regional sovereignty.

In both Egypt and the UAE, legal rationalization is often attached to modernization goals and has typically been encouraged not only by state authorities but also by nationalist, liberal, women's rights, and many Islamist activists given its potential to displace existing sources of authority. That is, nonstate actors do not uniformly reject "reform" projects that consolidate state power. Indeed, as Liat Kozma shows for late nineteenth-century Egypt, there is often "interaction rather than mere domination" between state apparatuses and people. In the virginity cases she studied, Egyptians who perceived that their young charges were sexually violated often appealed to new civil courts and police authorities for intervention—including inviting them to examine young girls' bodies and encouraging them to close brothels to "protect" girls and women—for a "plethora of reasons." These interventions, she argues, "enabled the state to increase its hold on the population."[2]

Some relevant observations are in order on what is signified by the Arabic words (signs) "*usra*" and "*'ā'ila*" as references for "family." *Usra*, the preferred term in postcolonial MENA states and the one most often used in the contemporary UAE and Egypt, means "family, household, house." It comes from a modern *spatial* understanding of confinement and implies a nuclear family of parents and children in an architecturally bounded, private household. Indeed, *asīr* (masc.), from the same root formation, is the Arabic noun for "prisoner" or "captive." *Usra*, moreover, is usually deployed in a manner that conceptualizes the family as a foundational unit of the state, an understanding that facilitates the governance and management of individuals and collectivities. In contrast, *'ā'ila* is an older *social and relational* rather than spatial way of referring to family as a wider and more powerful network of people who depend on each other for "sustenance, support, food." *'Ā'ila*s can compete with states for sovereignty, control over economic resources, and legitimacy, which is why states typically choose to weaken them through co-optation/absorption or exclusion. While both *'ā'ila* and *usra* are hierarchical and patriarchal in their hegemonic forms, family as *usra* makes women more socially, materially, and emotionally dependent on their husbands or fathers, or on states in lieu of these individual men.[3] I contend that the "modernization" of family and other laws in the MENA region has primarily been motivated by the desire to shift family norms and structures from *'ā'ila* to *usra* arrangements to better serve the interests of the nation-state. This formula is more complicated in the UAE, where sovereignty over territory and people at the emirate and federal levels was secured (but is nevertheless always insecure) by the most powerful *'ā'ila*s. These ruling families are no less concerned with the sexual and marriage practices of subject-citizens, noncitizen residents, and migrants.

Governmentality, Law, and the Family

This section provides an overview of what may be called postmodernist and postsovereigntist approaches to the state, law, and family. While Michel Foucault understood power and resistance as "immanent in our social practices and conduct" rather than objective things lodged in state or other apparatuses,[4] he considered the state to be the most important "form" and site for "the exercise of power" and argued that "in a certain way all other forms of power relation must refer to it."[5] Nevertheless, the state "has no heart in the sense that it has no interior"; it is, rather, an effect.[6] Derek Sayer similarly understands the state to be a discursive mask of unity, what Philip Abrams calls a "collective misrepresentation,"[7] although to rule, states must use domination since they are often unsuccessful in thoroughly constituting the "subjectivities and socialities" of the targets of rule.[8] From such a perspective, the purpose of the modern state is to legitimate and mystify what would otherwise be considered "unacceptable domination," although "armies and prisons" are critical "backup instruments."[9] Rather than assuming states to be complete except at revolutionary or other moments of rupture, such approaches consider all states to be ongoing projects.[10]

Foucault's essay of the same title explains governmentality as a "complex form of [modern state] power" comprised of practices that began to develop from the middle of the eighteenth century.[11] Government in this use "designated the way in which the conduct of individuals or of groups might be *directed* [emphasis added]: the government of children, of souls, of communities, of families, of the sick. . . . To govern, in this sense, is to structure the possible fields of action of others."[12] Modern governmentality creates "new institutional and discursive spaces (themselves not immutably fixed) that make different kinds of knowledge, action, and desire possible."[13] The goal of governmentality is to integrate people into "a totality" in a way that individualizes them while augmenting the state.[14] The techniques of modern governance are sometimes coercive and sometimes seek consent, although neither are their "essential form,"[15] since they aim to constitute subjectivities that are self-regulating and self-managing.[16] Alan Hunt and Gary Wickham stress that "all instances of governance" include failed attempts and "elements of incompleteness (which at times may be seen as failure)," although these become grounds to design new projects that aim to succeed where previous efforts foundered.[17] The practices of governmentality occur "at once internal and external to the state, since it is the tactics of government which make possible the continual definition and redefinition of what is within the competence of the state and what is not, the public versus the private, and so on."[18] Civil society, then, is a "transactional reality" that like others (sexuality, madness) is "real" and yet "born precisely from the interplay of relations of power and everything which constantly eludes them, at the interface, so to speak, of governors and governed" in liberal political systems.[19]

Biopolitics is a form of productive power that is essential to governmentality and targets subjectivities and bodies. It describes power that "exerts a positive influence on life, that endeavors to administer, optimize, and multiply it, subjecting it to precise controls and comprehensive regulations."[20] Biopolitical methods are concerned with the "welfare" of a population and improving "its condition," which Foucault argued was the nature of modern "pastoral power."[21] Biopower requires the development of relevant fields of knowledge, "technologies of government,"[22] such as statistics, and experts to study "biological processes: propagation, births and morality, the level of health, life expectancy and longevity."[23] *Stati*stics and other information provide comparative knowledge of "different states' respective forces" and are necessary because "government is possible only when the strength [and 'capacity'] of the state is known."[24] Working with other entities,[25] states use such information to undertake "large-scale campaigns," not always with "the full awareness of the people," to stimulate "birth rates," direct populations to live in "certain regions," or have people engage in particular "activities."[26] Talal Asad affirms that for colonizers and even "more strongly" for modernizing states in the Middle East and North Africa, statistical practices enumerating "births, deaths, diseases, literacy, crimes, occupations, natural resources, and so on [were], from a governmental standpoint, not merely a mode of understanding and representing populations but an instrument for regulating and transforming them."[27]

Indeed, rather than using "laws, decrees, [and] regulations" to exert control,[28] the modern arts of government rely on discipline and "regulation of conduct."[29] Foucault maintains it is not that "law fades into the background or that the institutions of justice . . . disappear," but rather that norms and normalization become more important than a "juridical system" that threatens with a "sword those who transgress."[30] Modern governmentality, with its attention to efficient human conduct, "must discover its own instruments and ways of reasoning that are distinct from patriarchalist models of the household and family." It aims to avoid "subtractive methods" that threaten to take things away from those who do not obey.[31] This orientation breaks with the previously dominant political rationality since the goal is "not to reinforce the power of the prince" but rather "the state itself,"[32] even as mechanisms of sovereign power continue to exist.[33] Mitchell Dean usefully distinguishes the objectives of sovereign, disciplinary, and governmentality rationalities in Foucault's work: "The object of sovereign power is the exercise of authority over the subjects of the state within a definite territory, e.g., the 'deductive' practices of levying of taxes, of meting out punishments. The object of disciplinary power is the regulation and ordering of the numbers of people within that territory, e.g., in practices of schooling, military training or the organization of work. The new object of government, by contrast, regards these subjects, and the forces and capacities of living individuals, as members of a population, as resources to be fostered, to be used and to be optimized."[34]

On what basis can one argue, as I do, that *legal processes* are at the core of the governmentalizing practices of states such as Egypt and the UAE given that Foucault is understood to have focused on *discipline* and *normalization* rather than the sovereign power of modern states? Kevin Walby contends that Foucault's early work "creates an unjustifiable binary between sovereignty/law versus discipline/norm."[35] Walby argues for "retrieving" law and analyzing it as a "mode of regulation" with intended and unintended consequences.[36] Others argue that while Foucault did not systematically study legal systems in his major research projects and had no theory of law, he richly considered law using a nonessentializing approach that treated it as "uncontainable" and "illimitable."[37] François Ewald contends that Foucault did not understand the *juridical power* ["law as the expression of a sovereign's power"] of premodern monarchical states as synonymous with our general understanding of *law*. Rather, Foucault perceived juridical forms of power to be dominant in premodern states and normalizing forms of power to be dominant in modern states, *but both forms can be expressed in law*. Indeed, Ewald argues (as does Foucault),[38] that "normalization tends to be accompanied by an astonishing proliferation of legislation."[39] Thus, while there is a "regression of the juridical" that "accompanies the rise of biopower," this does not "necessarily signal the disappearance of the law."[40] Postsovereigntist approaches examine law as the formal expression, derived in time and place, of different political rationalities.[41]

How does the codification of family and other law in the MENA region relate to normalization and modern governance? In addition to its rationalizing and regulatory purposes, law constitutes and expresses "norms," or normalizes particular behaviors, especially through the power to "qualify, measure, appraise, and hierarchize . . . [which] effects distributions around the norm."[42]

This normalization for political purposes requires the development of "common standard[s] of measurement,"[43] as illustrated by the postrevolutionary "introduction of the metric system, the institution of a truly national language, calendar reform, [and] the creation of the Civil Code" in France.[44] Similarly, I examine codification, other forms of legal rationalization, and regulation in the UAE and Egypt as *normalizing* techniques that reconstitute relationships between rulers and ruled, sexual possibilities, and family relations and that do so in order to consolidate state power and resources.

How can one apply a governmentality approach to nonliberal, largely authoritarian states in the Middle East and North Africa? Foucault insists that governmental practices be examined for how they articulate in the "specificity" and "actuality" of particular states, which he recognized to differ in their "forms," "roots," and "origins."[45] While he understood this approach to apply to modern European regimes of different forms and ideologies, he elaborated his ideas most thoroughly through historical analysis of liberal and neoliberal capitalist states.[46] Such states were historically concerned to accentuate their "self-limiting" practices: they allowed capitalism to flourish and "limited the exercise of government power" over individuals, developing "the art of least possible government" or "frugal government."[47] In MENA states, in contrast, top-down rule by sovereigns, policing in the negative sense,[48] and penal power work hand-in-hand with biopolitical and governmentality techniques. Dean provides some useful direction in this regard using Foucault's distinction between the "deductive power" of sovereignty, which seizes "things, time, bodies, and ultimately life itself" to "imped[e], mak[e] them submit, or destroy them," and the productive "life-administering power" of modern pastoralism, which concerns itself with "generating forces, making them grow, and ordering them."[49] *All states*, Dean argues, rely on a balance between both types of power to different degrees.[50] Even in liberal governmentality, authoritarian forms of rule can be found in "practices and rationalities" that are "applied to certain populations held to be without the attributes of responsible freedom."[51] Liberal forms of government, moreover, "can never fully check" their "deductive" or "demonic possibilities," such as eugenics, racism, cultural genocide, and war, often undertaken in the name of the victims' "own well-being."[52] Although they rely on internal political repression much more than liberal states, modern "non-liberal forms of rule," in turn, use biopolitical techniques and pastoralism to "optimiz[e] . . . the processes of life." That is, authoritarian states are like nonauthoritarian states in that they "must find ways of articulating elements of sovereignty and biopolitics," which is simply the "condition of all forms of government of the state in the twentieth century."[53]

In the contemporary UAE and Egypt the methods and technologies of governmentality, including assessment and study of population, territory, and material capacities; regulation of conduct; rationalization; individuation; and discipline are largely put to the service of maintaining and defining the power of the prince in the Machiavellian rather than "pastoral" sense. Nonetheless, these methods and technologies are also framed by pastoralist, social welfare discourses. In Egypt, this discourse includes Islamic, republican, and constitutional idioms. In the UAE, where there is genuine, even paternal, concern for the small proportion of the population considered to be nationals, modern governmentality practices are undertaken within a shared understanding that Emiratis live in a state whose rulers grant few political rights but are invested in increasing "national" well-being and wealth and distributing a significant proportion of the latter. There is little interest among most citizens in undermining the political rationality of this system so long as it continues to work for them.[54] In both countries, discussion of well-being that centers on family and sexual practices is ubiquitous and saturated with Islamic idioms in ways specific to their historical, cultural, political, and legal contexts.

Within a governmentality orientation, the family becomes an "element within the dynamic field of force that is the population," an "instrument and objective of government."[55] In his study of nineteenth-century France, Jacques Donzelot highlights how the postrevolutionary state's agenda was attached to charitable (or modern pastoral) concern with respect to families.[56] The goal was for families to manage themselves, to have "government through the family" as people privately pursue "well-being."[57] The family thus conceived provides a haven and release from the political and economic regulations and requirements of the "public sphere" and facilitates a stable social order.[58] While families were often troubled by "adulterine children, rebellious adolescents, women of ill repute—everything that might be prejudicial to their honor, reputation, or standing," states were in contrast concerned with "the squandering of vital forces, the unused or useless individuals."[59] Reducing the costs to the state of "illegitimate children" was a fundamental motivation for "campaigns for the restoration of marriage in the poorer classes" undertaken primarily by "a multitude of [moralizing] philanthropic and religious associations."[60] State budgetary concerns also produced laws that encouraged "legitimate families" not to abandon children and the "easing" of laws and administrative rules for marrying and certifying marriage, especially for working-class men whose marriages brought in little dowry and had few attached incentives.[61] Some of these techniques required the collusion of women. Working-class men were encouraged to marry in return for a woman's domestic labor, but "only to the extent that he deserved" this labor by his behavior. In return, wives received "exclusive control" over the interior "domain." As housewives and "attentive" mothers, women came to be seen as "the privileged instrument for civilizing the working class," or subordinating unruly men so that they pose no threat to state power or coffers.[62] Such "corrective interventions in family life" often had unintended consequences.[63]

In her research on Hawai'i, Sally Merry Engle likewise demonstrates how from the mid-nineteenth century, law was used "to construct new regimes of family life" that encouraged marriage and the preserving of a stable nuclear families understood to exist in a private sphere "under paternal authority." In this vision, married families were only to experience state intervention in "cases of severe injury," usually of the wife.[64] Hawai'an laws on "marriage, divorce, and adultery" and lower-court interventions in cases of domestic violence promoted marital norms that served the sociopolitical, religious, and economic interests that were dominant in different times.[65] Family was understood, addressed, and constituted by law and the courts as a private, bourgeois space (even for the poor) in which husbands provided economic support and wives had a duty to obey, following Christian missionary understandings.[66] This vision is remarkably similar to the one promoted by family modernizers in most Middle East postcolonial states.

Governmentalizing Islamic Legal Institutions and Discourse

> Part of the strength of the hold of Islamic law in Muslim societies arises from its being embedded in the very norms of behavior; the price, which did not appear exacting until the rise of the modern centralizing state in Islamic lands, is the law's impregnation with the multiple and differential values of Muslim culture and forms of life, leading to the absence of a single, unified legal canon, with differences and disagreements over many points of law.[67]

Over time, MENA states have considered it necessary to control and delimit Islamic juridical processes, experts, and discourses given their relevance to everyday life and potential as competing sources of authority. To accomplish these goals, state authorities have primarily used rationalization of legal systems and law, always considered "eminently political" projects.[68] Specifically, the flexible and decentralized nature of classical Islamic jurisprudence, governed by methodologies and rules developed outside of state auspices over generations, had to be standardized and turned into positive or human-made laws that could be revised as needed by state authorities. Expanding state control over the realms of daily life often required authorities to redefine or challenge definitions of the Islamically licit, historically recognized as plural and contextual by scholars, producers, and analysts of shari'a.

Changing the status of written and printed words, axiomatic to legal codification and positivization, was crucial to legal governmentality in the MENA region. Brinkley Messick, studying twentieth-century Yemen, stresses the "cultural and historical variability" of writing in Islam and how modern relations of domination required a new understanding that authorized written words and documents irrespective of who produced the words and in what context they were articulated. In classical Islam, oral and embodied recitation and witnessing were privileged over documents, especially in religious communication and transactions such as marriage contracts, and handwriting was privileged over print.[69] Writing was viewed as unreliable, unstable in meaning, and reductive in comparison to spoken transmission, preferably from a source considered to be truthful and faithful.[70] As a consequence, although written material was very important in everyday affairs, "legal documents remain 'ambiguous'" in classical shari'a, with a "structural tension in the sphere of evidence between testimony and text."[71] Timothy Mitchell notes how government and government-sponsored education in late nineteenth-century Egypt demanded "a precise system of signs, in which words are handled as though they were the unambiguous representatives of singular meanings." Such a "linguistic transformation was part of the process of ordering," a system of producing "what seemed a structure [the state] standing apart from things themselves."[72] In such a light, modern state requirements that attach the licitness of a marriage with its written documentation and registration with state officials can be contested. The difference between classically Islamic understandings of licit marriage contracts and the documentary practices and legal requirements of states facilitate contemporary innovations in which marriages and sexual contracts that may violate state requirements can be categorized by lay practitioners as "customary" ('urfi) for Muslims and thus licit.[73]

In most contemporary Middle East and North Africa states laws are codified and/or applied according to state-sponsored procedures in state-sponsored or supervised institutions, rather than interpreted in relation to a particular situation based on the relevant methodologies, hermeneutics, and epistemologies of a Sunni legal tradition, as was the idealized case of classical Islamic shariʿa. The *madhāhib* (sing: *madhhab*, "path"), or independent legal traditions of Sunni Islam, were named after exemplary (the meaning of "sunna") male leaders whose authority "was both constructed and augmented" after they died, Wael Hallaq argues.[74] In each tradition, generations of jurists established and passed on interpretative methods and "accepted substantive doctrines."[75] Over time, the schools of jurisprudence developed differences in epistemology and method, leading to competing interpretations about God's command, but these were mutually recognized as orthodox, allowing Muslims to "choose from several possible rules of behavior."[76] These interpretations at times differed even among the followers of a Sunni tradition since decisions about licitness arose out of particular contexts. Applying the principles and methods of their school (*uṣūl al-fiqh*), jurists "contributed to an evolving body of classical Islamic *fiqh*— legal rulings that represented their [fallible] understanding of God's law, or the shariʿa."[77] Trained Muslim jurists (not courts) interpreted and "extended" the "law of God" to "cover new legal problems" rather than creating "new rules."[78] Messick notes, "In this gap between divine plan and human understanding lay the perennially fertile space of critique, the locus of an entire politics articulated in the idiom of the shariʿa."[79]

Legal flexibility was facilitated in Islamic jurisprudence, historians argue, by fatwa opinions issued throughout the Muslim world by religious scholars (muftis) in response to the queries of believers. These fatwas remain dynamic and better reflect the practices and beliefs of Muslims in their various contexts, particularly with respect to gender, sexuality, and marriage.[80] Judith Tucker has shown how in Ottoman Syria and Palestine such opinions were sometimes incorporated into the doctrines of particular Sunni guilds, arguing that muftis served as the crucial link between Islamic legal thought and practice.[81] Since the late nineteenth century, rulers intent on controlling this arena for granting an Islamic imprimatur have installed muftis and elevated them into positions of hierarchical authority over other muftis.[82] Even classical (medieval) Islamic jurists allowed political rulers to "impose their preferred understanding of God's law as the law of the land" and later Sunni theorists argued that subjects were required to obey state law (*qānūn*) that fell within the domain of "*siyāsa shar'iyya*," or policies that advanced the welfare of the community but "did not command Muslims to sin."[83] While *fiqh* was as a result no longer the sole source of "positive legal norms in an Islamic state, it remained a crucial source of negative restrictions on the state's legislative powers."[84]

The governmentalizing agenda was furthered by a broad set of legal trans-formations introduced by the Ottomans between 1839 and 1876, the Tanzimat, which have been translated as "reforms" but are better understood as "order-ings," whose "guiding ideas" were "central control, conciliar bureaucracy, the rule of law, equality," as well as communicating to European powers that Europe was "the exemplar of modern civilization and . . . the Ottoman Empire [was] its partner."[85] Centralizing and governmentalizing techniques by Egyptian rul-ers predated and continued following the Tanzimat years and were applied by new institutions that surveyed, mapped, studied, coordinated, schooled, engi-neered, and disciplined (especially militarily) the "productive powers" of the country.[86] An essential aspect of the Tanzimat was the "shariʿa"-derived civil code (majalla) produced between 1869 and 1876 by a "new breed of public offi-cials constituted as a drafting committee," and approved by the Ottoman sultan (for the first time in Egypt giving such power over shariʿa to a head of state) before promulgation.[87] Talal Asad notes that while the code had "jurisdiction through the empire," it was never applied in Egypt.[88] The majalla, modeled after the French Civil Code of 1804, compelled articulation of the "related concep-tions of the state and of individuals as responsible legal subjects"; thus, it was foundational for regional modern states and state identities.[89] In order to be accessible, the code had to be, in the words of Brinkley Messick, "built in an orderly and regular fashion, ideally of conceptual units that could stand alone, equivalent in their logical self-sufficiency and in their independence from any need of interpretive clarification. In selecting ʿonly the least contested and least controversial opinions' from the fiqh manuals, the drafters took an important step toward silencing the open-ended argumentation of shariʿa jurisprudence."[90]

Other utilitarian legal innovations in nineteenth-century Egypt enlarged the domain of state authority and facilitated governance. In classical jurispru-dence, ijtihād referred to "the personal endeavor by the scholar to arrive at a ruling (ḥukum) in accordance with the principles of fiqh,"[91] premised on a ranking system to assure that "only the most qualified jurists should gain their information about God's law through direct engagement with the texts that re-corded God's revelation to the Prophet."[92] Sunni jurists rarely used this method but rather derived law by imitating or extrapolating from the rulings of leading jurists of earlier periods, reasoning that jurists with sufficient skill in religious hermeneutics no longer existed. Mohammed Fadel argues that Sunni taqlīd ("imitation") was not the opposite of ijtihād, but included debate and legal transformations, although taqlīd was more structured in its reasoning and thus narrowed "interpretive discretion." This structuring allowed *taqlīd* rulings to be more easily codified.[93] Beginning in the late nineteenth century, modernizing Islamist intellectuals in Egypt redefined *ijtihād* to refer more broadly to "independent legal reasoning on the basis of the Koran and the Sunna," argues Jakob Skovgaard-Petersen.[94] The most well-known of these intellectuals, Muhammad Abduh and his disciple Rashid Rida, deliberately circumvented the teachings and methodologies established by the classical Sunni Muslim traditions in order to reduce the power of reigning Islamic jurists.[95] This redefinition of *ijtihād* allowed for more utilitarian, even sociological, interpretations of Islamic licitness on the basis of new analyses of the sacred text of Islam and the transmitted behaviors, sayings, and silences of the Prophet Muhammad.[96]

While all the long-term consequences were likely not envisioned, these changes facilitated the instrumental and even cynical use of religious idioms by state apparatuses and the later proliferation of unorthodox notions of the Islamically licit by nonstate groups and actors. In the contemporary period, for example, the term *ijtihād* is frequently used to explain how a contested practice is determined to be Islamically licit by individuals not necessarily trained in Islamic methods of reasoning. Just as the nature of *ijtihād* was destabilized, rulers in nineteenth-century Egypt redefined the notion of *ijmā'*, or Islamic juristic consensus,[97] allowing for radical reconstruction of principles and practices whilst shari'a as a metadiscourse and idiom was maintained by the state.[98] With the establishment of modern states, the domains addressed by positive laws and regulations expanded, although the popular understanding of "shari'a" as a superior form of governance has not been stamped out. Indeed, this understanding has encouraged postcolonial campaigns to "Islamicize" state legislation in an effort to repudiate Western social, legal, and political hegemony. Nevertheless, it should be stressed that these projects conflict with the norms of classical shari'a and undermine its doctrines.[99]

Governmentalizing Marriage, Divorce, and the Family in Egyptian History

Lisa Pollard traces the manner in which "caring for the nation as a family had become the sine qua non of modern Egyptian politics by 1919."[100] She argues that largely because it was constructed so by British colonial elites, "progress" in domesticity increasingly became a "measure of modernity" for elite Egyptians who accepted a framework that linked self-governance to "transformation of the household."[101] From the mid-nineteenth century to the revolution of 1919, the "monogamous couple, their children, and the reformed, modernized do-micile" became the ideal of Egyptian nationalist discourse.[102] The opposition to this formulation was polygamy, harem life,[103] and other familial examples of the nonmodern. As discussed by Lila Abu-Lughod, the companionate nuclear fam-ily, which required "informed child rearing" by educated mothers, was promi-nently articulated as a national necessity at the turn of the twentieth century by the Egyptian intellectual Qasim Amin. The aim of this "domesticating" project "was for a liberation of women that would make of them good bourgeois wives and mothers in a world where state and class ties would override those of kin, capitalist organization would divide the world into the distinct spheres of pri-vate and public, and women would be subjected to husbands and children, cut off from their kin and other women."[104]

Foundational to this modern family was marriage, whose stability was framed as urgent to national health.[105] Representations of the married couple as a "nucleus" of society requiring state protection are thoroughly modern in Egypt, argues Amira Sonbol.[106] This point is reinforced in Talal Asad's examina-tion of an 1899 report to reform the shari'a courts in Egypt. The report was au-thored by the Islamic reformer Muhammad Abduh, who by this time had been appointed as chief mufti (a new state position) of Egypt with British colonial support, and illustrates the degree to which family modernization goals were shared among elites of different ideological persuasions, including Islamists. Abduh wished to use the courts to "restore" the family, "especially among the lower classes," stressing its national importance by conceptualizing the "people" (sha'b) as composed of "families" ('ā'lāt) who are the "basis of every nation" (umma). He viewed the courts as protectors of a "social life [that is] . . . in danger of moral collapse," exemplifying the lengthy history of family crisis dis-course in Egypt. Abduh argued that "since the welfare of families is connected in its most detailed links with the shari'a courts—as is the case today—the de-gree to which the nation needs the reform of these courts becomes clear. It is apparent that their [the courts'] place in the structure of Egyptian govern-ment is foundational, so that if they were to weaken, the effects of this weakness would be evident in the entire structure."[107]

Beginning with their 1517 conquest of the country, the Ottomans reorga-nized the Egyptian legal system, opened many shari'a courts staffed with Is-lamic jurists, and applied "either qadis' [judges'] fiqh or statutory law that had been examined and approved [as Islamically licit] by jurists serving as official legal advisers."[108] People in southern Egypt largely followed the Maliki legal tradition and those in the Nile Delta the Shafi'i school, while in major cities such as Cairo the Hanafi school was dominant because it was privileged by Ottoman authorities throughout the empire.[109] Thus one finds a range of possibilities and combinations in customs and codified laws historically and in contemporary Egypt.[110]

In 1880, two years before the British occupation of Egypt, "a code for shari'a courts was promulgated . . . and substantially amended in 1887."[111] After 1882, most laws in the partly autonomous Egyptian state were codified and secularized, with a few areas still governed by "unwritten *fiqh*" applied in shari'a courts.[112] The jurisdiction of shari'a courts was gradually restricted by Egyptian and colonial officials, climaxing with an 1897 law regarding evidence and procedure that (1) limited such courts to addressing issues of family or personal status and religious endowments,[113] the last arenas for which shari'a court judges in the Ottoman Empire made legal decisions by relying on the compendia of the Sunni legal traditions, although they were required to apply codified procedures;[114] (2) introduced a system of hierarchical appeals by establishing three levels of shari'a courts, the first two levels of which were distributed throughout the country; and (3) privileged "nonsuspect" documents over orality in court practices.[115] Criminal and commercial cases involving Egyptian nationals went to National Courts established in 1883 and if they involved at least one foreign party to Mixed Courts (established in 1875) administered by European judges. Both National and Mixed courts used civil codes derived mainly from the Napoleonic Code.[116] The system of hierarchical courts and appeals is a radical one from a classical shari'a perspective, as the Sunni schools of jurisprudence generally consider decisions by an Islamic jurist to be binding unless he was incompetent or he improperly used independent reasoning.[117] Even when laws were argued to be "shari'a-derived," codification, new procedures, and new institutions established by the state to train judges to simply apply written rules, even in shari'a courts, transformed the legal system.[118] Jakob Skovgaard-Petersen contends that Egyptian rulers by the late nineteenth century believed that "Islam had to be controlled, not only for the sake of control, but also because the question of legitimacy of rule had arisen. By gradually institutionalizing the religious field, the Egyptian state demonstrated a commitment to preserve and encourage a correct Islam."[119] Moreover, positivization was associated with the modernity of European colonizing states from which nationalists of all stripes wanted to be liberated and was seen as effective for imposing "top-down reform on a society."[120]

State jurisdiction increasingly expanded over sex, birth, marriage, divorce, and paternity. Egyptian laws promulgated in 1880 and 1897 "made civil registration of marriages and divorce all but mandatory" through procedural changes that did not allow courts to hear a case unless a marriage or divorce was registered with the state.[121] A 1910 procedural law restricted the ability of shariʿa judges to try a lawsuit where one party denied the marriage and there were no witnesses or trustworthy documents, or where one party (usually the man) died and no official documents existed establishing paternity for a child.[122] Classic Islamic precepts, in contrast, not only did not require state registration of marriage or documents but also assumed a child to be the product of the "marriage bed" of a married couple and ruled such a child to be fathered by the husband even when he denied paternity or no physical contact occurred between the couple (according to Hanafi doctrine).[123] Notwithstanding the legal changes, and as a corrective to assumptions that such campaigns are always effective, Ron Shaham's study of court decisions by shariʿa judges in the first half of twentieth-century Egypt found examples of judges who ruled a couple married with no proof of marriage;[124] continued to assume that denial of a marriage and/or a child was a tactic used by men to evade maintenance obligations;[125] flexibly applied Hanafi precepts that fixed the minimum duration of a pregnancy during marriage to six lunar months and the maximum to two lunar years to minimize illegitimacy and adultery accusations, even if scientific or medical evidence indicated otherwise; and used these precepts to allow paternity to be established by a married man's acknowledgment.[126] Lower courts in postcolonial Egypt (after 1952), by contrast, have been less willing to place the state's imprimatur on marriages undertaken in the "customary" (not registered with the state) manner, "considering this to be part of the public order legislation."[127] The consequences of this state unwillingness are important when the husband in an unregistered marriage disappears, denies a marriage (making the wife adulterous if she remarries), or where such unions have produced a child denied the status of being the legitimate issue of a "marriage bed" and thus maintenance, inheritance, and citizenship rights.[128]

In 1917, Ottoman rulers established the first standardized Islamic family code (the Ottoman Law of Family Rights) for use by shariʿa courts in the empire. The code selectively incorporated Sunni rulings, especially from the Hanafi and Maliki schools. This law was the first to "introduce stipulations in marriage contracts by way of statutory legislation,"[129] allowing an Egyptian woman to divorce *only* if she could show the court that her husband was imprisoned,

could not "consummate the marriage, was missing, refused to pay her maintenance," suffered from a range of infectious diseases, "went insane after marriage," was a source of "bodily harm" to her, or "there was continuous fighting
in the home."[130] Earlier contracts negotiated "harm" and "good treatment" on a
case-by-case basis between the parties. In all Sunni Islamic traditions in Ottoman Egypt, if women demonstrated harm based on that tradition's criteria to a
judge's satisfaction, they typically received a divorce and did not lose resources
such as dowry and alimony support.[131] Sonbol makes clear that women's "flexibility and agency" deteriorated with the development of "narrowly defined legal
control and structures first in the late Ottoman Empire and more so under a
centralized nation-state."[132]

The Egyptian Ministry of Justice established a Personal Status Law in 1920
(No. 25), expanded in 1929, using the 1917 Ottoman family code as its basis. State
committees agreed on lists of harming situations that would allow a woman to
gain a divorce in the shari'a courts if she could "prove that one of the codified
reasons was applicable to her case."[133] The 1920 law allows a woman to be judicially divorced from a husband who is "insane" or afflicted with "the two kinds
of leprosy." The law makes a husband responsible for maintenance of the wife
even if she is "wealthy," not Muslim, or ill, and defines maintenance to include
housing and medical treatment.[134] In a change that reified unequal marriage
relations, for the stated purpose of "family welfare," the law codified a "shari'a
requirement" that a husband maintains his wife and children "in return for" her
obedience, which included "not leaving home without his permission," writes
Amira Sonbol. In this new formulation, so "long as her husband was willing to
support her financially, [a wife] had to stay married to him and obey him."[135] The
language in early Egyptian marriage contracts, by contrast, did not constitute the
marital relationship as an exchange of womanly obedience for husbandly economic support.[136] Egypt's personal status codes, moreover, defined a marriage
contract as making a woman "lawful to" a husband "with the object of forming a family and producing children." Before this, marriage was seen to make
licit sexual "relations between men and women and give legitimacy to children."
Moreover, marriage permanency was not assumed, and couples even married
"with the expectation that the husband will be in town temporarily," an arrangement that was acceptable in customary and legal terms and "widely practiced"
in Ottoman Egypt.[137] Thus, although permanent patriarchal marriage is often
ahistorically understood as authentically Islamic, Egyptian, or Arab, this "ideal"
is often motivated by the biopolitical considerations of modern states.

The 1920 law states that a wife loses maintenance "if she apostatizes or . . . refrains by choice from submitting herself [sexually] without justification or is forced so to refrain by circumstances which are not the fault of the husband, or if she leaves the matrimonial home without the permission of the husband."[138] The 1929 revisions of the code selectively use Maliki and Hanbali rather than Hanafi doctrine on harm to recognize four new conditions that allow women to be divorced by judges, including a husband having a "chronic or incurable disease," not providing a wife with maintenance, deserting her for a year or more, and physically or mentally abusing her. Article 6 requires judicial determination as to whether treatment is abusive or inappropriate to the status or class of the wife.[139] The law also calls for judicial arbitration and empowers the judge to dissolve a marriage if reconciliation does not occur, although he cannot divorce the couple if the wife is determined to be at fault.[140] While unilateral divorce remained a husband's prerogative, the 1929 version of Law No. 25 restricted it based on "the sources and rules of religion and in accordance with the imams and the jurists, even if these [be taken from] other than the adherents of the four schools. . . . There is nothing that forbids this [selective codification]," particularly if it resolves "social ills."[141] In response to elite perceptions that divorce rates were high, the law also made unilateral divorce less "capricious" by invalidating a husband's repudiation of a wife if he was deemed to have done so while angry, intoxicated, or swearing an oath.[142]

Legal, social scientific, and demographic discourses were fixated on marriage, family life, and reproduction as national concerns during this period. Hanan Kholoussy argues that the laws and policies of Egypt's monarchical government (1919–52) aimed to assure that marriage served the nation-state, constituting "a nationalist, nuclear, and 'modern' family,"[143] by, among other things, establishing minimum ages for marriage, limiting divorce, and challenging polygamy.[144] State authorities often allied in this agenda with Egyptian women activists and male modernizers of secular, nationalist, and Islamic persuasions. Codification also strengthened conjugal over extended kin relations, which not incidentally decreased the power of leaders of larger family units as arbiters of economic resources and political power, as Mounira Charrad found was the case for postcolonial Tunisia.[145] State officials instituted various requirements to weaken possible antistate activities from extended family politics and increase the state's ability to monitor and control the population.[146] Kholoussy contends that state interventions in family life generally enforced in new forms rather than challenged male privilege,[147] limited women's and men's access to divorce, and facilitated "medico-legal state intervention and control."[148] Omnia El Shakry argues that social science and demographic discourses in interwar Egypt encouraged "population quality" and "normalized monogamous sexuality within the parameters of modern family life—bourgeois companionate marriage, small family size, and middle-class hygiene."[149] Laura Beir's examination of the move from "birth control" (implying individual action by rational individuals to stem reproductive rates) to collectively oriented "family planning" in state population discourse in Republican (post-1952) Egypt also illustrates the attention to the family as a national concern and the plural forms of modern subjectification projects.[150] Contraceptive use was represented as "the duty of citizenship" by "exemplary maternal subject[s]," not as a choice, a right, or "an aspect of personal freedom."[151]

Law No. 78 (Article 99) of 1931 established the legal age of marriage at sixteen for girls and eighteen for boys;[152] created a standard marriage contract form; required a completed contract to include information from official birth certificates for the bride and groom; required that such a contract be approved by a state notary (ma'dhūn) or shari'a judge; and made it clear that for marriages contracted after August 1, 1931, attempts by parties to take legal action in shari'a courts in situations where the marriage is denied by one party would not be heard if these conditions were not met.[153] However, the law did not challenge the Islamic licitness of marriages that violated these requirements; continued to allow the use of oral testimony from witnesses, hearsay evidence regarding their life as a couple, and circumstantial evidence of transactions and behaviors indicating married life between the couple (such as letters), for example in cases of denied paternity; and did not prohibit or delimit the jurisdiction of shari'a courts if such marriages were not denied by one party.[154] From the state's perspective, controlling marriage continued to be a problem following the 1931 law because many Egyptians were without official birth certificates, little state supervision over marriage notaries actually existed, and criminal sanctions against lax notaries were not strong.[155]

By 1931, the Egyptian Shari'a Court Ordinance required such courts (which primarily focused on marriage, divorce, and guardianship issues) to be bound by statutes rather than edicts from religious scholars, disempowering muftis completely within the court system.[156] Immanuel Naveh argues that criticism from "Muslim religious circles" to the gradual procedural and legislative expansion of state organs into the arenas of family law was surprisingly weak, partly because they had "difficulty . . . criticizing legislation that incorporates the shari'a."[157] I would add that lack of strong resistance to such changes can also be attributed to a history in which Islamic reformers in Egypt were often willing participants in governmentalizing processes and state institutions. Moreover, the language and rationalizing methods of modern order and efficiency are compelling not only to political elites, who on the face of it seem to benefit most from them, but also to many regular people, activists, intellectuals, and professionals.

In 1955 and 1956, after the promulgation of Law 462 following the Free Officers Revolution, all shari'a and denominational courts (the latter for non-Muslims) were abolished.[158] From then, family cases in Egypt were heard by national civil courts focused specifically on personal status issues at the district, primary, appeal, and cassation levels.[159] These courts used codified statutes and policies based on "shari'a norms as an interpretive yardstick" and "Western-inspired regulations of evidence and procedure."[160] Naveh writes that where there are "lacunas in statutory provisions, the Egyptian national courts, headed by the Court of Cassation [or Supreme Court] (*Mahkamat al-Naqd*), adopt traditional *shar'i* norms in accordance with the most approved opinion of the Hanafi school of law," although legal reforms are also influenced by "local customs and ongoing power struggles . . . between those who favor . . . western, secular legislative patterns and those who support the direct and precise application of the shari'a as the only source of legislation."[161] Laws were not required to be checked against shari'a for faithfulness until the 1980 amendment of Article 2 in the Egyptian Constitution declaring that "the principles of Islamic shari'a" would be "the" rather than "a chief source of legislation,"[162] opening the way for challenges to laws that could be argued to contravene Islamic law.[163]

In 1979, the Egyptian Personal Status Law (PSL) was controversially reformed by a presidential decree from Anwar Sadat (Decree Law No. 44) that required a Muslim husband to notify his first wife in case he married, eliminated his right to prohibit her from leaving the house, allowed her to petition for divorce without losing alimony or child support if she could prove that a plural marriage harmed her mentally or materially, and allowed a judge to order a man to make a (*mut'a*) payment to his former wife if he was to blame for the divorce.[164] Using Maliki discourse, the decree also broadened the definition of "harm" so that a husband taking a second wife on its face harmed a first wife. If she produced evidence of the second marriage, she was automatically entitled to a court divorce.[165] This decree was annulled by the Egyptian Supreme Constitutional Court (established in 1979) in May 1985. While the forces challenging the decree argued that it violated Article 2 of the Egyptian Constitution requiring all laws to "not transgress the foundations and general principals of shari'a," the court chose to overturn it on the basis that it violated the constitution's requirements for when the president is allowed to use his emergency legal powers to bypass the legislature.[166]

In a palliative to women activists seeking an improvement in divorce rights, the Egyptian legislature amended Law No. 25 of 1929 with Law No. 100 of 1985 to require: men who initiate a divorce where the wife is not at fault to provide former wives with alimony (*mut'a*) based on Hanafi principles;[167] a groom to indicate whether he is already married in a new marriage contract; and a groom to list in the contract the name and address of an existing wife so she can be informed of the additional marriage by registered letter. In such cases, the existing wife could receive a divorce if she effectively demonstrates to a judge that she is "harmed" within one year of learning of the second marriage. The law also cancels "the [state] provision which forced a woman to return to her husband and considered her disobedient if she did not return to the matrimonial house upon request by the husband" and requires the husband to pay for housing a divorced wife and their children if/while she has custody of them.[168] Deploying Maliki discourse, the law allows a judge, following arbitration, to issue a compulsory *khul'* divorce for a wife who wants to be divorced and is determined to be at fault if she returns the marriage dowry to the husband.[169]

Despite legal revisions over time to Law No. 25, Egyptian women seeking judicial divorce or the implementation of court rulings in maintenance and child support cases continued to experience difficulty. They often could not prove "harm" to a judge's satisfaction.[170] Such divorces reportedly took "decades" for some women to receive, and five to seven years for most.[171] Court rulings requiring the husband to provide alimony and child support were often difficult to "implement because of corrupt and poorly trained law enforcement authorities as well as lack of effective sanctions against husbands who failed to comply with court orders."[172] A radical shift in the Egyptian legal terrain occurred in 1993, when the Constitutional Court decided that abiding by shari'a in Egypt required them, based on ninth-century Shafi'i methodology, to give priority in their rulings to the scriptural texts of the Qur'an and the Prophet Muhammad's verified actions and statements, overriding the legal doctrinal traditions of Sunni Islam. At the same time, the court allowed the state to regulate human behavior that had no clear scriptural guidance using the overarching Muslim principle of community welfare,[173] taking for granted that codified law would result. This decision had significant impact on the development of Law No. 1 of 2000 regarding personal status.

The Marriage Contract
as a Technology of Governance

A historical examination of state marriage contracts illustrates their development into what Michel Foucault terms a "technology of power," or a means to "determine the conduct of individuals and submit them to certain ends or domination."[174] Amira Sonbol insists that marriage contracts be understood as products of "historical conditions and processes." Marriage in Egypt was seen as more of a civil contract between two full Muslim persons until the beginning of the nineteenth century, when there was a shift to "privileging the religious side of marriage at the cost of the contractual."[175] As in France, marriage contracts in Egypt were not treated as fundamentally different from other contracts, separated, or given special dispensation. However, from the nineteenth century, marriage contracts were "placed together in separate volumes and classified under the name of the notary for France and the ma'dhūn (government assigned official who transacts marriage and divorce) [in Egypt]. . . . The notary and ma'dhūn's job was to register marriages in the residential quarter in which they were assigned. The rules they applied were [the] new rules and regulations of centralizing modern states toward achieving homogeneity and bureaucratic rationality."[176]

From pre-Islamic to Islamic times, marriage contracts in Egypt largely focused on "financial transactions and conditions," including the wife's property, gifts from the husband, his commitment to support her and their children, and a range of other "promises that differed from one contract to the other." The contract was not a basis for determining a marriage's legitimacy, but rather "a written record of a transaction" usually made later than the union itself.[177] In comparison to the later "standardized 'fill-in-the-blank' official document which is given a serial number and . . . date," the Ottoman marriage contract was written on a blank sheet of paper "in which the basic marriage formula changes significantly from place to place and marriage to marriage."[178] "Premodern" contracts were more likely to include free-ranging conditions and provisions constituted by both parties in comparison to later more rationalized and formalized contracts.[179] The most common condition Egyptian brides included in a contract delimited a man's right to polygamy and the next most common restricted wife-beating, with previously married women more likely to include such conditions in a contract and to insist on receipt of full financial rewards at the outset of marriage.[180] Early contracts indicate that dowries could be negotiated to be due at any time and not be subject to a husband's dispute.[181]

Notations in Egyptian marriage contracts registered in Ottoman courts researched by Abdal-Rehim Abdal-Rehim include dowry amounts, conditions of payment, and the judge's observations of social parity between the bride and groom as demonstrated, for example, by the Islamic guild they followed and the occupations of the groom or his father and the bride's father.[182] Abdal-Rehim found "great diversity" in these contracts based on "time, place, and social conditions of the parties involved," including situations where the wife's right to certain support from the husband, such as food, housing, and clothing, was amended or waived with her agreement or a man's right to take up to four wives was nullified.[183] Abdal-Rehim and Nelly Hanna also found, especially in large Egyptian towns, marriage contracts that delineated additional specific conditions that safeguarded the wife's interests, including requiring a husband to provide security and support for her children from a previous marriage and live in a place the wife prefers. If such conditions were broken, the woman could receive a court divorce without having to fulfill other obligations or lose material support.[184]

The different Islamic schools disagreed as to whether and which marital rights and obligations can be negotiated between the couple or are infallible aspects of Islamic law that could not be superseded in a contract.[185] The Hanafi tradition was the strictest regarding contractual stipulations, only allowing them when they emphasized already required spousal rights and duties.[186] Ottoman Egyptian judges, however, treated polygyny restrictions in marriage contracts as valid because this condition was allowed by the Hanbali tradition,[187] the most "lenient" of the Sunni schools on the use of stipulations in marriage contracts.[188] Women and their families often insisted on spelling out maintenance expectations in the marital contract because the Hanafi guild did not treat failure to provide maintenance as a sufficient basis for women to receive a divorce, while detailing such a requirement made it indisputable.[189]

After the Ottoman codification of family law in 1917, courts in Egypt usually refused to recognize "prenuptial conditions added to marriage contracts," finding the contracts to be "correct but the conditions invalid," including those restricting plural marriage, stating a wife's preferred living location, restricting a husband's ability to travel for extended periods of time, insuring "that he would treat her properly," and making it easy for her to end the marriage for any reason.[190] A 1925 amendment reintroduced women's right to include unilateral dissolution as an option in the marriage contract, referring to it as *'iṣma*, a practice found in the Qur'an.[191] If written into the contract, this allowed a woman to receive a divorce unilaterally and without judicial intervention, although wealthy, upper-class, experienced, or famous women were more likely to insist on it, since men who allowed this option were belittled and women's use of it was stigmatized. While this deployment of *'iṣma* was constructed by Egyptian religious scholars in the modern period as *a delegation of the right of divorce from the husband to the wife*, Sonbol argues that "the Qur'an does not say so,"[192] providing another example of the unstable and plural meanings of such terms. In a study of Egyptian shari'a court decisions from the first half of the twentieth century, Shaham found that in response to restrictions on women's divorce rights, women-initiated marriage stipulations often occurred as "informal documents signed by the husband before or concurrently with the signing of the formal marriage contract, or in the course of conjugal life."[193] This indicates that at least some women found ways to circumvent increasingly formalized and restrictive contracts before and during marriage.

Women's groups in Egypt, sometimes in collaboration with the state and other modernizers, have at various points attempted to include printed stipulations in state-issued marriage contracts that, for example, allow a bride to choose to restrict polygyny in the marriage or make judicial divorce easier in such cases. In 1926, a committee—including the Egyptian minister of justice, the Shaykh of al-Azhar University, and religious scholars considered to be disciples of the Muslim modernizer Muhammad Abduh—was appointed by the government to "prepare amendments to the 1920 family law," among them some that would permit "a wife to include in her marriage contract stipulations that supported her interests and that did not contradict the purposes of the contract." The King of Egypt vetoed the proposal in response to "public turmoil,"[194] although the term "public" masks which social sectors were upset. Similarly, in 1964, the Ministry of Social Affairs adopted a proposal to expand stipulation rights, specifically mentioning a "wife's right to work," but dropped the idea due to "public opposition."[195]

Women activists continued to challenge the nature of the marriage contract. In the late 1980s, the idea of expanding stipulation possibilities in marriage contracts was revived by a group of activists, lawyers, and intellectuals who called themselves "the Communication Group for the Enhancement of the Status of Women in Egypt," also known as the Group of Seven and led by lawyer Muna Zulfiqqar.[196] They published an Arabic-language booklet, titled "The Legal Rights of Egyptian Women in Theory and Practice," which included information for women on "how to formulate stipulation questions that were to be asked by the [marriage registrar] to the husband, who had the option to accept or reject them." These questions asked a potential husband's opinions on his potential wife's right to work, pursue education, travel without restriction, make claims on the conjugal home and furniture in case of divorce, initiate divorce, and restrict plural marriage.[197] During the September 1994 UN International Conference on Population and Development in Cairo, a document presented by a coalition of Egyptian nongovernmental organizations recommended that a marriage contract including such questions be legally required. This proposal was eventually "adopted by the Ministry of Justice and presented to the Grand Mufti of Egypt for review."[198] Zulfiqqar and historian Hoda El-Sadda drafted a standardized marriage contract that listed such optional conditions.[199] The religious establishment and Islamist organizations contended, however, that this idea "forbid the permitted and permitted the forbidden," and such stipulations would lead to distrust among married couples and "discourage young men and women from getting married."[200] The proponents argued that contractual stipulations are based on the Hanbali idea of 'isma allowing a married woman to divorce herself unilaterally if stipulations are violated. The executive branch dropped the idea in response to conservative resistance, but it reemerged in the early twenty-first century.[201] Zulfiqqar argues that allowing only a husband to break the marriage contract "contradicts [its] essence" as a civil document that is entered consensually by two parties. In the 1990s, Zulfiqqar and other feminists unsuccessfully proposed that the government give only Egyptian courts the power to resolve disputes or end marriages, following Tunisian family law, taking away the male unilateral right of divorce but further empowering the state.[202]

Politics and Government in Trucial Oman and the UAE

The UAE is a loose federal entity of tribal shaikhdoms (emirates) led by the ruling clans of al-Shariqa/Sharjah (al-Qasimi family), Abu Dhabi (al-Nahyan), Dubai (al-Maktoum), Ra's al-Khayma (al-Qasimi), Fujayra (al-Sharqi), 'Ajman (al-Nu'ami), and Umm al-Quwayn (al-Mu'alla), although the ruler of Ra's al-Khayma originally resisted joining the federation.[203] It should be stressed that the concept of "tribe" in the UAE is not reducible to male patrilineality and tightly regulated marital genealogies. As Paul Dresch emphasizes, a given tribal name includes people "adopted by the tribe" (for example, of slave origins), people with mothers of less "noble" local origins than their fathers, and many ethnicities and nationalities absorbed through intermarriage, reproduction, and alliance. In addition, naturalized foreigners often have more political access and influence in ruling family circles (in Abu Dhabi, for example) than locals with "impeccable descent on both sides" (mother and father).[204] Claiming affiliation with a respected or powerful family has become more important given its attachment to modern political power. Illustrating the social construction of tribal affiliation, in 1999, a local notary was imprisoned for "selling false certificates of tribal membership," significant in urban contexts where people are less likely to personally know who is related to whom.[205] The hierarchy of citizenship in the UAE is locally understood to be comprised of Abu Dhabi citizens at the top, followed by the citizens of other emirates, with the bottom rung occupied by those who are naturalized, whose citizenship and the citizenship of their wives and children can be revoked across generations if they are deemed a threat to security or order.[206]

The rulers of Abu Dhabi and Dubai hold disproportionate influence within the UAE because their families are the wealthiest.[207] The president of the federation is from Abu Dhabi and the prime minister from Dubai (the largest emirate in population). The ruler of each emirate is its "supreme authority," governing largely by decree, although he is technically subordinate to federal executive authority on foreign affairs, defense, health, and education.[208] In fact, both Dubai and Ra's al-Khayma, the latter the poorest and northern-most of the emirates,[209] are independent of federal authority on a number of dimensions. Application of the Federal Law of Civil Procedure (Law 11/1992), for example, has been resisted in the emirate-level courts of these two emirates, which do not have federal court branches and do not consider federal law to be binding on them.[210] Emirati rulers have historically been in conflict or competition with each other over international investments, business, borders, budgets, and political power.[211] Most UAE federal ministries are funded by the rulers of Abu Dhabi, who use the vast hydrocarbon resources they control in that territory to buy influence and power in Abu Dhabi and nationally.[212] Although each emirate is supposed to contribute 10 percent of its revenues to the federal budget, this expectation has been resisted by Dubai and Shariqa as relatively wealthy emirates.[213] Of the emirates, Dubai has the longest history of ethnic pluralism, the largest proportion of migrant workers, and has traded with India and Iran for hundreds of years.[214] Dubai is a "global city" whose existence and identity is intimately linked to this history of mercantilism.[215] These and other reasons explain why Dubai has resisted federal governmentalizing projects more than the other emirates.[216]

As Frauke Heard-Bey makes clear, sovereign territory-based state power was not the dominant form of rule in the eighteenth and nineteenth century in the lower Arabian Peninsula, and when it existed, it was recognized as relatively fragile and subject to challenge. Governance was local, mobile, and more likely to be negotiated as tribes competed for resources on land and sea, rulers engaged in wars, and family members challenged each other for dominance. It was penetration by colonial powers (especially British India) that required and established clearer lines of sovereign authority in the region by the nineteenth century. Much archival and social research remains to be done on the United Arab Emirates, which exhibits significant and continuing tensions between centralized state power and rationalized legal systems on the one hand, and local tribal and Islamic norms on the other.

Among the principal legal events that anticipated the establishment of the UAE is the 1820 British-imposed agreement that followed its successful military attack on the Qawasim tribal forces at Ra's al-Khayma. This "general treaty" was comprised of separate treaties signed between the British government of India and various shaykhs. Muhammad al-Musfir argues that the treaty "set the stage for the fragmentation of the Coast of Oman."[217] Eight shaykhs signed this "Cessation of Plunder and Piracy by Land and Sea" in order to be recognized by the British as having "the right to rule." The treaty prohibited African slave trading and threatened confiscation of property and capital punishment for the ruler if "piracy" or other "hostile acts" were committed against "tribal members or foreigners" in their jurisdictions.[218] As a result of ongoing struggles for power that disrupted navigation, the pearl industry, and the livelihoods of many people, in 1835 a number of coastal tribal rulers signed a maritime peace agreement with the oversight of the "British Local Resident Agent."[219] Al-Musfir argues that the British persistently used their "oversight" to actively discourage unification and weaken stronger emirates such as Shariqa.[220] The 1853 "Perpetual Maritime Truce" between some of these shaykhs made the 1835 treaty permanent and explains the word "Trucial" in Trucial Oman, the entities that preexisted the United Arab Emirates. This truce required the shaykhs to agree to a "'complete cessation of hostilities at sea' between them, their dependent subjects, and successors forever," and empowered British imperial authorities, through the

Resident Officer, to intervene in case of breaches.[221] In response to competing ambitions in the region from the German and Russian empires, as well as from Persia and France, in 1892 Britain imposed the "Exclusive Agreements" on rulers in the region, restricting them from making political or economic agreements with other governments without British approval.[222]

Ali Khalifa contends that although they controlled foreign affairs and defense in the region, British forces minimally interfered in the "tribal structure and pattern of rule," doing so only "to keep internecine tribal hostilities to a minimum" because their main concerns were mercantilist and thus focused on control of sea routes until the discovery of oil.[223] In contrast, Hadif al-Owais argues that it is the British government of India that "recognized" each ruler as a legitimate authority "over the internal affairs of his territory," encouraged each of them to "exact strong control," and gave them, their families, and allies "many privileges."[224] These nineteenth-century agreements, Christopher Davidson writes, meant that "the centuries-old ebb and flow of tribal power [was] frozen in time, as Britain signed treaties with whichever family happened to hold the reins of power at that time."[225] In 1922, the rulers of the Trucial States pledged not to give concessions for oil resources except through the British government.[226] From the 1930s, British representatives established various apparatuses in fits and starts designed to unify or efficiently divide-and-rule (depending on one's vantage point) the emirs and consolidate administrative operations across their territories.[227] The main British concerns remained strategic between the two world wars.[228] Through the 1960s, British officials aimed to protect their economic, political, and military interests in the region, with ebbs of power and conflicts with local rulers at various points.[229] Despite the "Trucial" designation, conflicts (sometimes violent) between and among ruling families over borders, jurisdiction, succession, and resources in harsh environments where most lived at subsistence levels continued through most of the twentieth century.[230]

Early in 1968, the British Labour government announced its intention to relinquish the imperial relationship with the Trucial rulers in three years' time.[231] In December 1971, after "difficult negotiations" among themselves, most of these tribal emirs used a "Provisional Constitution" (renewed as provisional five years later) to declare a sovereign federal nation-state, the UAE, with Abu Dhabi as its temporary seat of government.[232] During the three years of discussion, which included treaties that did not last, rulers heatedly debated whether representation on the Supreme Federal Council should be proportional and whether council decisions should be unanimous, with smaller, poorer emirates having equal influence.[233] Rulers were and remained conflicted: while they preferred to preserve the status quo, many believed that sovereignty in the modern sense required them to consolidate their limited human, financial, military, and administrative resources.[234] Given differences in territorial and population size, wealth, and access to natural resources among these emirates, as well as the related unwillingness of many rulers to cede authority to a federal entity dominated politically and economically by the ruling family of oil-rich and territorially large Abu Dhabi, the main impetus for federation came from a shared goal to discourage external territorial and military threats, for example from Iran and a liberation movement in western Oman that was supported by South Yemen and Iraq.[235]

Despite federation in 1971, the originating tensions and others continue to mean that the UAE's federal authority in juridical terms is not unequivocally recognized across the emirates. It was not until May 20, 1995, that the Supreme Council of the Federation "approved an amendment to the provisional constitution that deleted the term 'provisional' from its clauses" and declared Abu Dhabi to be the permanent seat of government.[236] While the constitution lays out a system of checks and balances in which judicial bodies are independent of the executive and National Assembly, it allows the president and his Supreme Council (comprised of the ruler of each emirate) to impose decrees and enact the laws they prefer.[237] Thus the National Assembly, which proportionally represents citizens of the different emirates, exists in form rather than substance, with no binding power, no ability to propose bills (generally the domain of the Council of Ministers), and its members appointed by the ruler of each emirate.[238] According to the constitution, at least five of the seven rulers on the Supreme Council must agree for substantive decisions to be valid, with Abu Dhabi and Dubai among them, thus giving the latter emirates veto power.[239] Moreover, the most important federal ministerial portfolios are controlled by Abu Dhabi and to a lesser degree Dubai, whose leaders appoint members of their ruling families to the most powerful posts in emirate and federal governments: foreign and domestic policymaking, the oil and gas industry, finance, military, and police and security apparatuses.[240] To convince rulers of the poorer emirates to cede some authority, Abu Dhabi is compelled to leverage its great wealth and offer services such as education to them.[241] As a consequence of this economic relationship, al-Musfir argues that the poorer emirates ('Ajman, Umm al-Quwayn, Fujayra) are more tightly integrated into the "federal" system.[242]

Given its economic independence, Dubai extracted further concessions that allowed its ruler to have supreme authority over its territory, resources, and citizens in a number of economic, legal, and political realms before agreeing to join the federation.[243]

"Nationalizing" the UAE Through Law

As in other Muslim-majority societies, principles of shari'a defined in multiple ways were fundamental in Trucial Oman. But tribal customs and forms of rule were probably more crucial. Legal disputes were much less likely than in Egypt to be in the domain of a sovereign ruler or a state in the nineteenth and twentieth centuries. Overall, systems of rule were porous, not regularized, and quite decentralized. Heard-Bey writes that the heads of "families, tribal groups and communities" dealt with most disputes without resort or reference to "the Ruler," involving him only if parties could not come to resolution.[244] If needed, parties consulted with an *'ārif*, or "someone well versed in the customary law of that community," or requested the intervention of "a powerful, wise, and popular shaykh." Judgments were based on "common sense" and local custom, "which developed within a particular group of tribes, was known to and recognised by its members," and whose legal principles were "moulded by Islam" but usually not based on particular Sunni legal traditions unless a *muṭawwa'* was asked to intervene.[245] This local personality was usually a man who had studied the Qur'an and a few other sources, was known to be pious, and was sometimes called a "qadi" (judge).[246] Most villages had a *muṭawwa'*, financially supported partly by the ruler and partly by private fees paid to him for "officiating marriages and certifying divorces."[247]

In the early twentieth century, rulers of some of the regions, such as Abu Dhabi, began to import and appoint judges with some formal training in Islamic law. This allowed a ruler, after hearing the disputants in his ruling court, to "send for the qadi to deal with the case, or . . . send the parties away to consult the qadi in his house."[248] These judges, trained in *fiqh*, were Sunni Arabs who came from Morocco, Bahrain, Tunis, Najd (Saudi Arabia today), Dubai, the (Iranian) Port of Linga, and (Iranian) Qishim Island, although they settled, married, and remained in their positions for decades.[249] The judges would have studied in Islamic schools or centers such as "al-Mubarak School in Al-Ehsa (Saudi Arabia) for Maliki, Sultan al-'Ulama School in Linga for Shafi'i, or Al-Mani' School in Qatar for Hanbali *fiqh*."[250] For the vast majority of Sunni Muslims living in the Trucial States at the turn of the twentieth century, the "finer points of difference between these schools [of jurisprudence]" were not important given the low level of formal training of most *muṭawwaʿīn* and that most disputes did not reach a ruler.[251] Rather, each community typically accepted "most readily the judgments which were in conformity with earlier judgments in identical or similar cases. These judgments, which were thus bound to take precedents and analogies into account, almost inadvertently perpetuated the adherence to a particular *madhhab* [Islamic school of law]."[252] Butti Ali al-Muhairi, by comparison, contends that especially in coastal towns, tensions existed even in the early twentieth century between the two most influential systems in the region: Islamic legal approaches and tribal customs.[253]

Within commercial sectors, such as the early twentieth-century pearling community in coastal towns, "matters . . . were tried by respectable members of that community, merchants, captains, and divers alike."[254] Disputants were most likely to engage higher levels of judicial authorities outside of local family circles—using "the universally acceptable interpretation of shariʿa"—when at least one of them was an immigrant in conflicts about property, money, fraud, and theft; or alternatively, when marital disputes occurred between "non-related families."[255] Thus law was not systematized or overseen by state authorities to the degree normalized in Egypt by the same period. British influence was most prominent in the laws of the Trucial States in international domains, such as the postal service and air traffic, which had little impact on daily life.[256] By the 1920s, mixing between desert migrants, locals, and various foreigners including Iranians and British-protected Indians,[257] led to a "less cohesive society" and more complex legal and policing needs in coastal towns.[258] From the 1930s, "the dualism" between tribal and shariʿa jurisdictions sharpened, as did an awareness that "not everyone should be subject to traditional jurisdiction." In the 1940s, the jurisdiction of shariʿa was delimited through the development of separate regulations that applied to foreigners and the introduction of laws to "deal with novel offences such as traffic accidents, labour and contractual disputes." By the late 1940s in Dubai, the shariʿa court established a "register of marriages" and "became the authority which handled all matters relating to personal status, family affairs and inheritance, both local and British. Regulations were devised for new situations by way of Rulers' decrees and His [British] Majesty's Order in Council."[259]

The legal system in the contemporary UAE has become much more formalized and includes vast areas of codified law and procedure in commercial, civil, and criminal realms that incorporate a range of sources and methods. Despite this proliferation of modern law codes, in situations where there is no provision "the Islamic principles of shariʿa as found in the Islamic shariʿa textbooks are applied" by state organs. Article 1 of the UAE Civil Code instructs, for example, that, "if there are no applicable principles in either the Maliki or Hanbali [*fiqh* compendia], then the Judge must turn to the Shafiʿi or Hanafi school."[260] Law in the UAE remains less rationalized and more flexible than in contemporary Egypt because of significant and continuing tensions between (1) federal versus local authority, both of which are "tribalized"; (2) classical shariʿa versus "Islamized" legal codes; and (3) the "developmental" needs of a unified nation-state versus clan, regional, and Muslim traditions that are more fluid and plural. It is worth noting that the "tribalism" I refer to in the first point is modern given its attachment to territorial, sovereign, and *rentier* forms of rule. As a result of the tensions enumerated above, the jurisdiction of different legal traditions is often unclear and contested on the ground in the UAE.

The Provisional UAE Constitution of 1971 gave the state the sole right to create law, in violation of classical shariʿa,[261] and promulgated the establishment of federal governance institutions.[262] The constitution also required that local laws not conflict with federal laws in "principle legal areas" and empowered the Federal Supreme Court to examine local laws and determine whether they conform or conflict, giving its decisions binding power.[263] Al-Muhairi contends that the UAE Constitution has conflicting ends: to constitute through legal mechanisms both an "Islamic" and a "united/modern" state.[264] Specifically, Article 7 of the constitution (the "Constitutional Clause") declares, "Islam is the official religion of the Union. The Islamic shariʿa shall be a main source of legislation in the Union." This formulation contradicts the nonrationalized, plural traditions of shariʿa.[265] The clause nevertheless has been interpreted to require "reinstatement of traditional Islamic criminal law, under which the principle of legality in its narrow modern sense does not exist."[266] Unlike in Egypt, where the debate has been over whether Islam would be "the" or "a" main source of law, in the UAE, the "Islamists," or advocates of Islamically informed codified law, stress the term "main," arguing that Article 7 requires Islamic values to supersede all others in the creation of legislation. In the Islamist reading, laws that violate Islamic values, such as those legalizing interest levied by banks, are unconstitutional and the constitution itself is subordinate to shariʿa jurisprudence according to its own wording. By contrast, the "liberals" stress the term "a" in the Constitutional Clause, contending that Islam is *one* of the legal traditions that can be taken into account in making legislation and only codified Islamic precepts are relevant in any case. From the liberal perspective, a law can conflict with Islamic values but be considered constitutional.[267] UAE Federal Supreme Court decisions have been ambiguous on this issue. The court has ruled that all federal legislation should be derived according to shari'a precepts *and* has ruled that the federal legislature should decide whether shari'a precepts should apply in particular cases. The Federal Supreme Court has hesitated to find laws unconstitutional if they violate these precepts.[268]

Al-Muhairi contends that the legal specialists who formulated the Provisional UAE Constitution had no shari'a training, came from Arab countries whose legal systems were highly influenced by Western norms, and supported pan-Arabist secular ideologies committed to the idea of a sovereign nation-state "as the sole source of authority."[269] For example, the Egyptian jurist Wahid Ra'fat authored the UAE Constitution, which was adapted from the Kuwaiti Constitution of 1962, itself drafted by the Egyptian jurist al-Sunhoori. Thus the UAE Constitution is "significantly influenced by the Egyptian Constitution of 1971 and by Egyptian constitutional writings."[270] More generally, most codified laws and procedures at the emirate and federal levels in the UAE borrow heavily from the Egyptian legal system, which relied on French legislation and procedures to a significant degree.[271] Like the judiciary, the UAE federal legislature is primarily comprised of noncitizen men who are Arab Muslim lawyers. Many members of the Emirati intelligentsia believe that these foreigners do not trust the "technical competence" of UAE citizens to make laws.[272] More important, I contend, is the logic of the rulers who appoint these foreign judges and legislators. The fact that foreigners dominate the legislative and judicial bodies means they cannot become independent or powerful enough to threaten the executive branch, where power is concentrated in the hands of the most powerful ruling families.

The Provisional UAE Constitution was concerned with consolidating the emirates socially and politically by fashioning new norms and a national identity that superseded local orientations.[273] But it also reflects contradictions and ambiguities that defeat the goals of national unity, argues al-Muhairi. For example, while the constitution encouraged the transfer of authority from the emirate to the federal level, it allowed this transfer to occur "at the request of the Emirate concerned."[274] UAE federal legislation has similarly been unsuccessful because in some respects it was too radical in trying to transform local norms and in other places it was "ambiguous and equivocal," with unclear or contradictory wording that allows selective rejection of laws by local leaders.[275] For example, while Federal Law No. 6 and Federal Law No. 10, both of 1978, replaced some local courts at the emirate level with federal courts, they did not enact laws explaining how to organize and administer these bodies; they allowed local codes to apply; and they did not clarify the role of shari'a.[276] The term "law" in the constitution, moreover, is not clearly defined and in the UAE context can refer to the constitution, Islamic codes, shari'a jurisprudence, presidential decrees, local laws, and federal legislation. As a result, courts throughout the UAE have interpreted "the principle of legality" (Article 27) of the constitution in widely divergent ways.[277] The vague wording of Article 27, the delays in the promulgation of federal laws in many civil and criminal areas, and the lag in establishing federal courts and a federal prosecution department are partly related to debates regarding Article 7,[278] the Constitutional Clause.

These legal ambiguities and delays are also evidence that the more powerful and wealthy of the ruling families never intended the UAE as a federal entity to supersede their respective emirate-level power, an argument made by Hendrik Van der Meulen.[279] Van der Meulen contends that the UAE federal government has not used the most common mechanisms for undermining "tribal" norms: establishing a national military that recruits and promotes irrespective of kin origin; allowing ideological political parties to exist; building a meritocratic bureaucracy; articulating Islamic norms everyone must follow regardless of kin affiliation; and cultivating an urban class of Islamic scholars who "provide legal and scriptural resources" that legitimate the consolidation of federal power.[280] While Van der Meulen does not use this language, such projects would facilitate federal governmentality. There is significant evidence, then, that the interests of ruling families, framed in tribal idioms, are more powerful than Islamic norms in UAE government. While differences between ruling families have been overcome enough to maintain a federal entity, this federalism largely "confirms and extends" kin-based rule.[281] The UAE federal system has been effective, however, in distributing resources to residents of the resource-poor emirates. The resources come in the form of employment for citizens in the wealthier emirates, federal-level military and security jobs in the poorer emirates (financed by Abu Dhabi), and investment in health, education, and so on. The federal system has also expanded the sovereign influence of the Abu Dhabi ruling family over the people and territories of Abu Dhabi and the poorer emirates.

Legal unification at the federal level in the UAE is complicated by codes and judicial systems developed in different emirates that predate the establishment of the UAE. The emirs invited Egyptians, Sudanese, and other Arab legal specialists to help them design these systems as it became clear in the late 1960s that British rule would come to an end.[282] The specialists devised secular criminal codes and procedural rules adapted from the British Indian Penal Code for each emirate.[283] Because of the disconnect between imported norms and local realities and values, after a "short time" neither local governments nor "ordinary citizens" followed the new codes and procedures. Rather, they became "voluntary arbitrational rules and institutions," a loss of legal force that was especially apparent in Abu Dhabi's civil courts, where people respected neither the courts nor the laws. In fact, they insisted that local authorities allow them to use the shari'a courts, leading to informal decisions by the ruler of Abu Dhabi agreeing to this even in a range of criminal matters.[284] More broadly, emirate-level codes and judgments can significantly diverge from each other given differences in the origins of Arab judges and local conditions.[285] It took sixteen years of debate for the Federal Criminal Procedure Law to be ratified in 1992 because local governments resisted ceding their authority and the law challenged tribal loyalty systems on issues such as pardons and capital sentences.[286]

Dubai has the most influential emirate-level legal system in the sense that the structure for its lower level courts was adopted by a number of the northern emirates. The Dubai system is highly secularized, with laws that are substantially codified and an appeals court and a cassation court that are final arbiters on judgments in its civil and shari'a courts and whose judgments are not accountable to federal high courts. Shari'a court jurisdiction in Dubai is limited to "personal status" cases, but the court applies both civil and shari'a rules. When Dubai officials worried in the early years that the proposed system violated shari'a, they were assured otherwise by the Egyptian legal advisor to the local government, Udi al-Betaar, who argued that much of the legislation is "derived from Islam" and delimiting shari'a court jurisdiction to personal status matters allowed for the maintenance of "justice."[287]

Shari'a courts in all the emirates have "exclusive jurisdiction" over divorce, inheritance, child custody, and guardianship issues involving Emiratis,[288] and until the July 2005 passage of a unified code of personal status promulgated later that year,[289] these courts relied on the compendia of various Sunni guilds and local customs to make rulings on such matters. Even before passage of the personal status code, in order to receive state recognition and resources, all marriage contracts that involved Emirati citizens had to be on file with a marriage registrar in these courts.[290] It is widely accepted in the UAE that government registration of marriage protects women as the weaker party in sexual interactions in societies in which "men are protected by their maleness." In such situations, women will pay a disproportionate social price, "squandering" their rights and those of possible children if they are accused of sexual misbehavior and documentation cannot demonstrate otherwise.[291] Registration is seen as especially important in more urbanized contexts where "marriage . . . might occur in a room in which only five or six individuals know about it."[292] It is also understood to be crucial for inheritance in cases where a husband who passes away married more than one wife and had progeny, but had not informed the first family of the relationship.[293]

While the UAE legal system has civil, criminal, and shari'a courts at the federal level, and in most emirates at the emirate-level as well,[294] shari'a courts can be involved in the other courts' jurisdictions in some of the emirates. For example, local shari'a court jurisdiction is not delimited to personal status issues in Abu Dhabi, Shariqa, and Ra's al-Khayma; these courts also address minor civil matters between Muslims, although "there is no guide for such an application under the applicable laws."[295] Civil courts are primarily for non-Muslims, who are not required to appear before shari'a courts in any civil matter.[296] Porousness and flexibility are nouns that also apply to criminal law, since where no emirate-level criminal courts exist, local shari'a courts hear criminal cases, although they apply the Federal Criminal Procedure Law combined with "shari'a principles."[297] All of this is to reinforce that the line between secular and shari'a jurisdiction is ambiguous in the country. Federal legal provisions do not always clarify this distinction and laws are contradictory in places such as Abu Dhabi, where at least until the 1990s shari'a courts could hear and decide on nonpersonal status matters if both parties agreed.[298]

Codification and other government requirements in the UAE are defended on the Islamic jurisprudential precept giving a head of state (*hakim*) the right "to add conditions to protect the general good."[299] Elites in modern Muslim-majority states in the region often contend that laws of Western origin are necessary in many spheres of life, such as commerce, because they facilitate economic development and modernization, presumed to increase the general good in the pastoral sense of state power.[300] For example, UAE development goals economically rely on and encourage foreign tourism as a source of pleasure, and thus some emirates allow the selling and drinking of alcohol in certain venues. The state has also branded itself as a site of commerce and finance and thus has not punished banks for levying interest, which is banned in Islam.[301] By contrast, at least as of the mid-1990s, Dubai did not have written law as to whether bank interest was allowed, leaving uncertainty in commercial law.[302] Indeed, given the ambiguities and dualities discussed, there are conflicting legal judgments among the emirates and between local and federal bodies on commercial banking, alcohol drinking, nonmarital sex, and other matters.[303]

For shari'a purists, even when a code is inspired by Islamic tenets, as is the case in the UAE Federal Penal Code of 1987, which allows some offenses (alcohol, "unlawful sexual intercourse," blood money payments) to be dealt with according to classical shari'a jurisprudence or Islamic codes,[304] its very rationalization as well as the inclusion of Western procedures and traditions makes it secular.[305] From this perspective, the Federal Penal Code is contradictory because it aims to establish one federal "Islamic" system for crimes committed throughout the country despite considerable variance in the orthodox traditions of the Islamic schools of jurisprudence.[306] Ultimately, "Islamisation of law" projects are trying to balance the popular legitimacy of shari'a, which does not accept human supremacy over God's law, with the paradoxical interest of consolidating state sovereignty.[307] These and other conflicts explain why rulers at the federal and emirate levels regularly use wealth to build institutions that promote hybrid Islamic-"national" authenticities.

. . .

Political and cultural factors explain the different evolutions of and social responses to legal governmentality and rationalization in Egypt and the UAE. The establishment of Egypt as a modern state depended on the systematic disempowerment of independent Islamic authority and institutions. In the UAE, projects of legal governmentality that attempted to supersede local, religious, or tribal sources of authority and norms met more resistance from regular people and from competing Emirati rulers. While in both countries the legal changes examined often incorporated religious idioms, they nevertheless fundamentally transformed Islamic institutions and jurisprudence norms and made them less relevant. Egypt has a much longer, and arguably more effective, history of state-sponsored legal and procedural interventions designed to reconstitute sexual and family values and norms in order to better serve state interests and increase the efficiency of rule. In both cases, however, state projects and interventions often had unintended social responses and consequences.

2 National Families in "Crisis"

It has become an essential ritual of our societies to scrutinize the countenance of the family at regular intervals in order to decipher our destiny, glimpsing in the death of the family an impending return to barbarism, the letting go of our reasons for living; or indeed, in order to reassure ourselves at the sight of its inexhaustible capacity for survival. Far removed from the immediate rationality of political discourse, it appears to constitute the other pole of our societies, their darker side.

Jacques Donzelot, *The Policing of Families* (1979)

PEOPLE FREQUENTLY USE THE FAMILY to reflect on a range of existential concerns, uncertainties, and anxieties. While the family is often evoked in "mythical" and ahistorical terms, Michael Shapiro reminds us that the institution is often "manipulated by nationalistic reasons of state and then moralized as being in crisis."[1] In placing scare quotes around the term crisis, I do not intend to undermine the evidence of turbulent change in family structures and sexual practices in the United Arab Emirates (UAE) and Egypt or the Middle East and North Africa (MENA) more generally. This chapter examines some of these changes and highlights causal attributions that are culturally and socially national or domestic rather than transnational. It also demonstrates that differently situated groups disagree as to the nature and sources of the challenges to the hegemonic family, and the possible solutions. Indeed, one person's solution to a problem—such as marrying secretly to avoid difficult-to-acquire guardianship approval or to assuage desire—is often another person's crisis. While economic, historical, cultural, political, and demographic differences between the UAE and Egypt guarantee some divergence in emphases and concerns, remarkable similarities are nevertheless apparent.

A common narrative in the UAE is that many of the country's indigenous young people are materialistic, superficial, immature, naive, and do not have the tools to deal with the freedoms and resources they have available to them in a wealthy country that encourages consumption, tourism, and immigrant labor. In Egypt, whose population includes the "largest cohort of adolescents (10–19 years of age) in its history,"[2] narratives of youth superficiality are tempered by recognition of the economic, employment, and aspirational barriers they face, especially to prepare for marriage. Typically, youth problems in both countries are understood to be caused by inattentive parenting, weak religious and moral education, consumerism, and other economic, cultural, and political factors. Young people, themselves socioeconomically and ideologically diverse, do not necessarily agree with the causal attributions that come from parents, intellectuals, religious authorities, or state elites. Complaints about youth are part of a larger discourse of family crisis in each country that is concerned with the causes, consequences, and solutions to higher rates of singlehood, rise in age of first marriage, exogamy, higher divorce rates (in the UAE), secret marriage, and other forms of sexual nonnormativity that evoke great social discussion and anxiety. Many women's expectations with respect to gender relations and marriage have changed as indicated by their increasing rates of singlehood, rising age of first marriage, and willingness to divorce. By contrast, most men remain conservative in their expectations of how wives should behave, if not in their own sexual desires and marital behaviors.

Singlehood and Delayed Marriage: Changing Practices, Expectations, and Desires

Marriage and fertility rates have declined among women in many parts of the world and average age of marriage has increased for a variety of reasons, although gender inequality in law, policy, and corporate culture, as well as changing gender expectations among working and educated women, are important cross-national explanations.[3] Similarly, celibacy (in its original meaning of being unmarried) and age of first marriage for both men and women have risen in many parts of the Middle East and North Africa region,[4] and attitudes toward marriage have changed. For the Lebanese single women studied by Barbara Drieskens, marriage has come to have various meanings, with some entering the institution as a "try-out."[5] Female celibacy is much more dramatic in the UAE than in Egypt. Even in the early 1980s, Malcolm Peck noticed that the "phenomenon of the [Emirati] woman who is single by choice beyond the usual age for marriage, something unheard of in this society in the past, is no longer a curiosity," with the emirates of Dubai and Shariqa particularly indicative of this trend.[6]

For imperfect comparison, in 1995, 98.5 percent of Egyptian women and 99.2 percent of Emirati women between the ages of forty and forty-nine were "ever married."[7] Between 1992 and 1997, 3.9 percent of Egyptian women and 6 percent of Emirati women between the ages of thirty and thirty-nine were "never married," a dramatic rise of the singlehood rate in comparison to women about ten years older during the same period.[8] According to 1999 data from the UAE Central Administration for Statistics and 2000 data from the UAE Planning Ministry, 12.9 percent of thirty-to–thirty-four-year-old women, and 6.2 percent of thirty-five-to–thirty-nine-year-old women were "never married."[9] The UAE in 2004 had one of the lowest fertility rates in the MENA region, at 2.5 children per national woman, probably given the percentage of native women of childbearing age who are unmarried.[10] In comparison, the 2004 fertility rate in Egypt was 3.2 children.[11] A survey reported in the *United Arab Emirates Yearbook* 2003 that included 4,760 married, divorced, or widowed Emirati women in Dubai indicates that this group's fertility rate was 4.04 per woman,[12] much higher than the fertility rate among Egyptian married women.

In the Arabian Peninsula, female singlehood is of singular concern to national and regional authorities. Indigenous female singlehood is important to the UAE state because it threatens its ethnically exclusive political demographic. While the slogan of the annual Dubai Shopping Festival is "One World, One Family, One Festival,"[13] mixed families and unregulated sex are seen to imperil national-religious ethos and demography.[14] UAE rulers depend on and nativist discourse encourages indigenous Emiratis, who comprise less than 20 percent of the population, to procreate with each other and not the country's permanent or migrant noncitizen workers, foreign tourists, and shoppers. Because of the large proportion of male expatriate workers, men have outnumbered women in the UAE by more than 2:1 for at least three decades;[15] in the twenty–forty-nine age group, the ratio of men to women is almost 3:1.[16] Strictly from a demographic perspective, then, UAE women should have little trouble marrying and indigenous men should have significant limitations. Social and legal gendered double standards, however, assure that indigenous men have no difficulty finding sexual and marital partners in comparison to women. Since marriage is the only legitimate avenue for women's sexual gratification, single-hood is also understood to pose challenges to gender and sexual norms and lead to social instability. The assumption among some is that "well-mannered" girls who remain unmarried will be "seized by depression," while those lacking in self-control "will deviate to fulfill [their] suppressed desires."[17]

Significant increases in age of first marriage have also occurred in the past twenty-five or so years in both countries, although they are more radical for women than men and more marked for Emirati women. Between 1992 and 1997, 41.4 percent of Egyptian women (compared to 64.8 percent twenty-five years before) and 33.3 percent of Emirati women (compared to 88.3 percent twenty-five years before) between twenty and twenty-four years reported being married by age twenty.[18] An internal report by the Egyptian Statistics Bureau indicates that the average age of first marriage for Egyptian women rose from twenty-one and a half years in 1981 to twenty-six years in 1999; for men in the same time span, age of first marriage rose from twenty-seven and a half years to twenty-nine years.[19] Overall, 13.8 percent of married Egyptian women between fifteen and forty-nine reported in a demographic health survey that they married before turning sixteen, whereas 23 percent of rural women in the same age group reported the same.[20] Data from 2006 Egypt indicates that 25 percent of Egyptians aged twenty-seven or older were unmarried; this group was generally "urban and educated" and "anxiously struggling to save money for marriage and find an appropriate partner amenable to their parents."[21]

The rising cost of marriage, increased poverty, decreased employment opportunities, reduced state commitment toward wealth redistribution, and increased availability, cost, and desire for furnishings and appliances for the marital home are viewed to be the primary reasons for the delay of marriage in Egypt since the late 1970s.[22] In a 1997 survey, 59 percent of Egyptian parents interviewed believed that the main problem their adolescent children faced was not having money to pay for marital housing; the remainder believed that lack of money overall or lack of money to furnish a marital home was the main problem.[23] In the 1990s, Egyptians complained that higher marriage costs had led to a flourishing in the number of poor Egyptian girls who married wealthier older men who were tourists from the Gulf, or that poor or lower-middle-class Egyptian men were increasingly marrying European foreign women.[24] Magued Osman and Laila Shahd found that in 1996, 25 percent of registered marriages among Egyptians occurred between a lower-middle-class husband and an older, economically better-off wife, usually previously married, who could offer housing, although such marriages ended in divorce at higher rates; in 1986, in comparison, marriages between older woman and younger men comprised only 2 percent of registered contracts.[25] A frequent narrative recommends following the Prophet Muhammad's example of marrying off his daughter Fatima in return for "only a mattress and a pillow filled with sponge."[26] This account is consistent with an oft-shared criticism made by young people in Egypt and the UAE that parents are too picky and make unreasonable material demands when approached by the family of a male suitor.[27] In the UAE, this choosiness by the families of young women is understood to be shaped by their unwillingness to have their daughters marry "down" on the status ladder, which occurs regularly nevertheless.[28]

In Egypt, people are most likely to entreat the state to provide newly married couples with housing assistance in order to increase marriage rates. Wealthier Egyptian parents can usually provide such housing for newlywed children, and poorer parents in rural areas are likely to add a room to an existing house for the new couple.[29] The problem is more stark in cities such as Cairo and for the poor and lower-middle classes. Dr. Faysal 'Abd al-Qadir Yunis of Cairo University explained that male university graduates from such families cannot pay for marriage and often wait until their thirties, impacting women as well. He was not unusual in viewing such delays as "dangerous" in the sense that young people are caught between economic limitations on their ability to marry and "the pressure of values" that do not allow sexual relationships and "emotional and erotic [hissi] fulfillment" outside of marriage, which often leads them to take on high levels of debt in order to marry.[30]

Despite the country's vastly greater wealth, some in the UAE also attribute "spinsterhood" to economic factors, arguing that the state should make "available the necessities of marriage for the girl and boy, such as close residence to their place of work, scholarships for youth embarking on marriage," and donations from religious charity (zakat) or taxes.[31] Emiratis complain that consumerist desires, costly weddings, and the expensive demands of the parents of many Emirati brides are partly responsible for delaying or reducing the marriage rates of native women.[32] UAE elites describe many Emiratis as "extravagant," "spendthrifts," and "show-offs." Samira Gargash, a respected lawyer in the UAE who represents many clients in divorce situations, discussed some of these practices: "If they need a bag, they buy ten bags. If they need a watch, they buy—they buy 20 watches."[33] Even regular Emiratis critically understand each other to be enchanted and "overwhelmed with the products of rapid modernization," and men as less able to resist them than women.[34] Such practices are seen to threaten the economic fabric of indigenous marriages and a gendered social calculus that expects the parents of a groom to pay for the wedding and a husband to provide for his wife and children.[35] However valid, economic explanations underestimate the degree to which marriage costs are not the only or even most important reason for women's rates of celibacy.

Dr. Ebtisam al-Kitbi, a professor of political science at al-'Ain (UAE) University, accentuates concerns with singlehood among many native women students. When she asked such students in a course to state the "most important issues that face Emirati society," expecting mention of "politics, democracy, small population," the majority wrote down "spinsterhood," explaining that they dread the social stigma attached to being unmarried.[36] Similarly, when I asked seven Emirati women college students at Shariqa Arab University to discuss their main worries, they were most concerned with remaining unmarried and being defined as a spinster ('ānis), which they argue occurred for women by about twenty-three years old. They believe that Emirati women who are educated and work are most likely to be chosen as *second* wives, in various types of contracts, of men in their late thirties and early forties. However, they report that such men largely choose a "migrant woman [*wāfida*], she has a [foreign] passport, she would be—any religion, but the important thing is that she differs from the first wife, she could be employed." This student believes that such Emirati men, who may have had an arranged marriage in their late teens or early twenties, marry a second wife because they "desire to live another life . . . with a wife who would be open in terms of dress, in terms of food."[37] Like women then, men's tastes, desires, and expectations are changing, although not necessarily in gender-egalitarian directions.

Emirati women who travel for business or education, or who work in professional mixed-gender settings, make clear that they and others like them are usually stigmatized as marriage prospects as a result.[38] Maha Khatib, who undertook research that involved more than six hundred women from throughout the Emirates in the early 1990s, similarly found widespread concern that women's higher education posed a barrier to marriage because of younger men's attitudes and was especially a problem when women studied abroad, even in nearby Kuwait.[39] Local women who worked in banks and the media were especially disrespected for mixing with a wide range of people and showing themselves to men.[40] Oil wealth, the older of these Emirati women thought, had created an "un-Islamic" situation in which Emirati men saw themselves as superior to women, although they paradoxically understood women as competing with them,[41] presumably in education and the workplace. One woman professor I interviewed almost fifteen years later believes that her unmarried status was "a tax" she paid for her advanced studies outside the Emirates (in an Arab country) and her decision not to wear hijab during this period.[42] Women believe that Emirati men prefer to marry Emirati women who are "less than him educationally, and less than him in experience."[43]

Educated women, by contrast, are unwilling to marry men who are less educated than they are because such men are seen as likely to be restrictive toward a wife. As one highly educated and well-traveled Emirati woman who was happily married to a noncitizen Muslim man put it, "The more you learn, the more your choices become difficult. . . . I want to know how this person thinks. What is his point of view toward women. . . . I want a person who respects me."[44] Although systematic research on this issue has not been undertaken in the UAE or elsewhere in the region to my knowledge, it is apparent that many Emirati women remain unmarried or delay marriage because of limits on their choices and worries that a marriage will turn out unhappy. A late twenties professional single woman shares her disquiet with the troubled experiences of her married woman friends. She believes that native men have paradoxical desires and apply cultural double standards to native women:

> There is not one of my [female] friends who is married and happy—or who I am comfortable with her situation after marriage. None of them. We have many problems [wāyid mashākil]. We have . . . the problem of people who have not married. And there is the problem of people who married because they were afraid to remain unmarried. I believe that the problem among us is mostly in the young men. They are not being socially or intellectually developed like the girls. The girls are ahead of them. Even in studying, in thinking, the majority of university graduates are girls more than young men. Most girls are compelled to marry because they have to marry. They marry men who are less than them intellectually. . . . Young men may feel that they have to dominate women they marry to alleviate inequality in the levels between them and their wives. The other issue is that most young men who studied and reached high levels married from outside [non-Emirati women]. . . . When he deals with nonnational women, he considers them open, liberated, and there is no problem because they come from an environment that accepts them. But if he . . . married a national woman—or if the national woman behaved in the same way, she would

be breaking the boundaries of customs and traditions. She becomes foreign or unacceptable in relation to her own society. He does not take this chance [*mā bujāzif hal mujāzifa*]. He may even believe internally that an Emirati woman would not accept having this level [of freedom]. At the same time, he wants a woman who is open. So how will he balance these two issues? It is difficult.[45]

In the 1950s, British officials and local rulers gave the highest priority to the technical education of boys and men as a path to "development." This education included "carpentry, vehicle maintenance, electrical installation," engineering, and agricultural skills, which were understood to assure men "a good job and a good salary." Whatever the nature of their training, native men largely worked for emirate-level policing/military bodies or governments.[46] Educating girls and women was understood as crucial to development in a different way: it enhanced their capacity to make good marriages, raise "educated citizens," and work in gender-appropriate settings.[47] By the 1970s, the ruler of Dubai was explicit that married women's national cultivation responsibilities included a requirement to maintain Arab customs that support "the teachings of true Islam."[48] These strategies, however, have not turned out the expected results. While most native women want to marry and cultivate a family life, they are unhappy with the dominant terms, conditions, and choices. Even today, the potential Emirati marriage partners of Emirati women are likely to have attended military or police academies (which do not require graduation from high school),[49] since they are guaranteed employment in these public sectors, which reduces their appeal as partners for educated women.[50] The UAE Ministry of Higher Education calculates that while more than 70 percent of Emirati women participate in postsecondary higher education, only 27 percent of Emirati men do so, and they tend to be from the wealthier emirates of Dubai and Abu Dhabi.[51] Natasha Ridge found that the high attrition and poor educational performance and outcomes of Emirati boys in comparison to girls are to a large degree related to less engaging primary and secondary schools and poorer quality teachers in boys' public schools.[52] Some Emiratis believe that the cultural, knowledge, and socialization gap produced by the two forms of education in the UAE, one liberal arts-oriented and dominated by women and the other policing-oriented and dominated by men from rural areas, partly explained what many Emiratis perceive as high divorce rates among nationals.[53] Indeed, Emirati women frequently complain of native men's low social and educational "levels" in comparison to their own accomplishments.[54]

Khatib found similar results in her wide-ranging early 1990s dissertation research with Emirati women. These women "assess[ed] various matters" according to "customs" (*adāt*) that integrated "local interpretations of Islamic teachings," which they believed should be taught by "the family and community."[55] Many of these women complained that native men had adopted new "forms of conduct" that violated these customs, such as smoking, drinking alcohol, and mixing with foreigners of both genders.[56] Rather than blaming "Islam and its teachings" for social problems or "any unfairness or injustice toward women," many thought that men were not turning to Islam for guidance.[57] Moreover, the preponderance of Emirati women interviewed by Khatib accused men of being less ambitious than women and uninterested in furthering their education or status since they could work in the military or elsewhere and receive high salaries without effort. This situation was perceived as "harmful to the Emirates," local customs, men themselves, and relations between men and women.[58]

When single Emirati women were asked in 1999 and 2000 state-sponsored surveys their most important condition in deciding on a fiancé, 50.4 percent listed "religious commitment." The second and third most important conditions were "good moral character" (22.5 percent) and "recognition of the value of married life and ability to be responsible" (9.4 percent).[59] Emirati women, then, are generally not radical in their gender expectations and demands. For example, most educated young women I spoke with stated that gender mixing among natives would be difficult for both genders given dominant child-rearing patterns that strongly reinforce gender segregation in the subjectivities of boys and girls.[60] Nevertheless, these same women seemed less inclined to marry young Emirati men schooled in hyper-patriarchal conceptualizations of family and marriage. They worried about their male peers' "irresponsibility" and were unwilling to have marriage limit their professional aspirations.[61] A woman student at Shariqa Arab University explained that while in high school, she "had a different picture of marriage," thinking it was "required and necessary." After entering university, she "changed" and began to worry about whether it was possible to balance her "want for marriage" and her "want for a degree," especially given the level of marital problems she saw "around us." She shared the story of a twenty-seven–year-old girlfriend who had married a university-educated engineer two years older in early September 2003 and divorced him by the end of the month because she learned he was taking medication for a psychological illness that was well hidden from her during their brief engagement. In addition, he was "very suspicious every time [the wife] came in or left."[62]

Egyptian women go on to university at significantly lower rates in comparison to Emirati women. The single biggest barrier to marriage that Egyptian men and women university students report is economic, especially the ability of the man to accumulate the resources needed to establish a home and "a dignified life for the girl."[63] Women make clear that their parents are the arbiters of the degree to which a suitor is appropriate in economic or other terms. However, like Emirati women, Egyptian and other Arab women also affirm that their education leads them to have higher social and cultural expectations of the men they marry, their needs and desires change: an educated girl "does not want any uneducated man." As their education and age rises, women's "choices become more difficult," since "marriage offers are reduced" as men and their families usually prefer women who are younger. This will often lead to "compromise on her desires" either to exit the stigmatization of being unmarried or to assuage the "instinct" to have children. Egyptian women interviewed believe that it is less socially ostracizing to be called a "divorced woman" than a "spinster."[64]

Divorce and Its Causes

The UAE and Egypt continue to allow men to unilaterally divorce their wives, although women also initiate a significant proportion of divorces. Divorce is popularly viewed to be a source of social instability. Didactic material produced by state officials, religious authorities, and pundits is often preoccupied with the causes of divorce, how couples can avoid divorce, procedurally restricting divorce, and the social, cultural, and economic impact of divorce. These states are fundamentally concerned with reducing the costs of divorce to their courts and budgets. It may be counterintuitive that divorce rates in Egypt have dramatically lowered over the course of the twentieth century, although information on more recent trends is mixed. Kenneth Cuno finds that the crude divorce rate in Egypt (number of divorces per thousand) and the average number of divorces in relation to number of married women in census years have regularly fallen in Egypt from the mid-1940s until 2002, primarily because of the diffusion of the bourgeois companionate marriage as the ideal.[65] Cuno argues that greater marriage stability in Egypt may also be the result of more "carefully negotiated marriages, kin endogamy [whose rate has increased over time in Egypt], and residence with or close to one's kin," thus combining practices that have historically been present with a more consensual, nucleated understanding of marriage.[66] According to an unpublished report prepared by Dr. Buthaina al-Deeb, head of Central Administration in the Population Research Center at the Egyptian Central Agency

for Mobilization and Statistics, divorce rates for Egyptian women rose from
3.9 percent in 1990 to 6 percent in 1999, with 34.5 percent of divorces in 1999
occurring during the first year of marriage.[67] Egyptian lawyer Mona Elkorashy
reports that judicial divorce cases (by definition initiated by women) in contemporary Egypt disproportionately include couples married one year or less and
women over forty years old who may have accepted problems in their married
lives, waiting until children were older or married before initiating a split. Such
women-initiated late divorces are also impacted by men losing state salaries at
an earlier age in Egypt, which means they can support wives less while women
cannot apply for state support when they are married.[68] The Deeb report indicates that 69 percent of divorced women were illiterate or had low levels of
literacy, while 5.4 percent were college educated.[69]

Using 1999 data from Dubai, the *United Arab Emirates Yearbook 2003* shows
divorce rates were 31.6 percent when national men married expatriate women,
and 21 percent among native couples;[70] this information is presented to encourage national men to marry national women. According to statistical data from
the Cooperation Council for the Arab States of the Gulf Secretariat General
(GCC), the ratio of divorces to marriages among UAE citizens was 26.1 percent
in 1999, 28.2 percent in 2000, 29.7 percent in 2001, 30 percent in 2002, 26.4 percent in 2003, and 28 percent in 2004.[71] A table that comes from 1999 survey data
of "national families" from the UAE Central Administration of Statistics shows
that the largest proportion of divorced Emirati women were either illiterate or
with basic reading and writing skills (30.8 percent); 20.9 percent had completed
only primary school; 20 percent had completed preparatory school; 18.3 percent had completed secondary school; and 10 percent had completed university
or above.[72] It is unclear whether the low representation of university-educated
native women among the divorced is indicative of their better marital success
or that fewer such women marry. Other national survey data of divorced Emirati women from 1999 indicates that the largest group (20 percent) is between
thirty and thirty-four years old, although divorced women are well represented
among all five-year age groups between twenty and forty-nine years old.[73]

Some counterintuitive information regarding divorced Emirati women
comes from a working research paper written by Dr. Muhammad Ibrahim Mansur and presented at a December 2003 UAE conference in Ajman on "Youth in
the Face of a More Challenging World." Despite the relative ease with which
native men can divorce women, more than 50 percent of the 230 native women
Dr. Mansur interviewed initiated their divorce, and more than 25 percent of the

remaining divorces were initiated by husbands. About one-fifth of the women-initiated divorces occurred because the husband had taken a second wife. The other reasons, listed in descending order, were "lack of equal social status" between the husband and wife, a husband's alcohol drinking, a husband's temper, interference from the husband's family, weakness of the husband's personality, and age difference between the husband and wife. Indicating the degree to which parental involvement remains crucial even after married life, the remaining divorces were initiated by the parents of the husband or the wife.[74] Divorced Emirati women in Mansur's study complained that their former husbands followed their "instinctive leanings" and "psychological desires," rather than "responding to the calls of their minds and moral conscience." Husbands were also accused of being immoderate and in-laws of being selfish, greedy, and violent toward daughters-in-law.[75]

Women in Khatib's early 1990s study believed Emirati men to be increasingly disinterested in being heads of households and absent as fathers, with sons suffering special neglect as a result.[76] One positive consequence of this disinterest in family life is that divorced women are often able to keep custody of their children even if they remarry, despite customs and laws that privilege former husbands in this regard.[77] Remarried women in the Khatib study perceived second marriages to be superior to first marriages given their experience and improved ability to communicate what they want in the marriage.[78] Some of the Emirati men I interviewed blame divorce and marital problems on mothers-in-law who are overly interfering in the household of the son and daughter-in-law or on wives who insist on working after marriage and thus do not fulfill their duties to the husband.[79] Emirati women and men also attribute divorce to arranged marriages in which the bride or groom feel "forced" to marry, especially if they are related, or to marriages in which either person "hides" information from the other including, for example, educational level, illness, social and cultural attitudes, previous sexual relations, or a secret marriage, leading to a "bomb" after the marriage occurs.[80]

Gendered Laws, Customs, and Tensions Regarding Exogamy

Laws and rulings in the UAE and Egypt make it difficult for Muslim women citizens to marry noncitizen Muslim men, prohibit marriage between Muslim women citizens and non-Muslim men, and allow national and religious exogamy for citizen men. State restrictions on marriage that extend beyond Islamic guidelines (such as limiting polygamy by Muslim men or restricting Muslim women's ability to marry noncitizen Muslim men) are defended and largely accepted on the grounds that they protect the "public interest" (al-maṣlaḥa al-ʿāmma).[81] "Public interest" is a long-held principle within Islamic legal theory that allows state rulers leeway to supersede aspects of shariʿa considered of lesser importance.[82] In contemporary times, public interest is seen to require conserving and fostering national material resources and social order. Here government and governed are assumed to be disposed toward the same goals, although these subjectivities must be actively cultivated in the governed.

The 1972 federal "nationality and passports" law of the UAE defined a citizen of the Emirates to be "anyone usually resident in one of the emirates from 1925," the children of an Emirati father born anywhere, the "nonnative" wives of Emirati men, or anyone granted citizenship, which can be for "noteworthy service to the state" or based on residency and other rules that differ by the national origin of those seeking naturalization.[83] Shaykh Rashid of Dubai and Shaykh Zayed of Abu Dhabi had competing views on nationality at the formative moments of the federation: Rashid implied that citizenship should be linked to "shared experience," while Zayed attached citizenship to nasab, or genealogy traced through the father. Nevertheless, a number of residents of Omani, Najdi (Saudi Arabia), and Iranian background, the latter from trading families, were granted citizenship by the ruler of Abu Dhabi and have "married their daughters to established Abu Dhabi families."[84] By 1975, federal law limited citizenship to "Arabs" and for the first time mentioned citizenship "through a national mother" if a child's attachment to a father "was not confirmed by law," the father is "unknown," or the father has "no nationality."[85] Whatever the laws, citizenship and nationality in the UAE are at the "absolute discretion" of rulers as sovereign authorities and "cannot be put into judicial question."[86]

Restrictions on UAE citizen women's ability to marry noncitizens have increased over time. The first order found on this topic is dated from December 1996 and was issued by the presidential "court" to the Ministry of Justice: it forbade women citizens from marrying foreigners and affirmed that native women would lose their citizenship if they did so. A second order followed about a month later, issued from the Ministry of Justice to judges, clarifying that "foreigners" did not include citizens from Gulf Cooperation Council (GCC) countries. Paul Dresch believes that neither ruling was published officially.[87] Given the great sovereign latitude of UAE rulers at the federal and emirate levels, their actual practices matter as much if not more than formal law. That is, these rulings are flexible, ignored, or followed depending on context, which includes the degree to which such a marriage is supported by the woman's family.[88] Muhammad Darwish of the Dubai courts affirmed in a December 2003 interview that native Emirati women are not allowed to marry non-Emirati Muslim men unless they are citizens of other GCC countries and only with the agreement of an emirate ruler's diwān, or court.[89] The male marriage candidate is reported to be researched by the state, "Is he the son of a family? Does he want to marry or does he want to take advantage? Is he considering it a trade transaction? If they find him trustworthy, they give permission."[90] In practice, such permission is increasingly difficult to acquire. While most married men and women I interviewed believe that this restriction protects women from men who simply want access to the resources attached to being a UAE citizen, single women and women married to nonnationals are more likely to consider it part of a national package of gendered double standards regarding sexuality and marriage. Young unmarried Emirati women interviewed by Jane Bristol-Rhys similarly "expressed both anxiety and anger over the laws and social conventions that bar them from marrying a non-Emirati."[91]

When I asked Dr. Ahmed al-Kubaysi whether the draft UAE personal status code allowed Emirati women to marry nonnational men, he responded in the negative but noted that relationships such as *misyār* were potential solutions for native women. Al-Kubaysi thought that allowing Emirati women to marry outside the national group was a "political" rather than "legal" issue and explained that Emirati rulers had banned such marriages because "there was terrible exploitation—an Egyptian man would come and marry a national woman, four or five years, he would take money and then leave her."[92] Concerns regarding the economic factors that lead many foreign women to marry Emirati men have not yet produced significant barriers to exogamy by national men, however, indicating the extent to which biopolitical control and national authenticity are disproportionately attached to controlling women's sexual, marital, and reproductive practices.

Emirati women who marry noncitizen Muslim men despite barriers are likely to be socially ostracized and legally penalized, and their husbands and children have great difficulty being granted citizenship and its associated resources, including health care, schooling at all levels, and jobs for the adults. If children and spouses in such families do not have citizenship or passports from another state, they are unable to travel outside the UAE for any reason. Native UAE women who marry a national or nonnational man without permission of their male guardian will sometimes do so abroad, for example in family courts in Egypt, although the apparatuses of the state can be mobilized by the woman's family to break up such marriages.[93] In May 2006, about forty Emirati women who were married to or widows of non-citizen men were part of a demonstration at the UAE Human Rights Association in Dubai demanding citizenship rights for their children and husbands, many of whom had no other citizenship or (for husbands) had waived such citizenship in the hope of being granted UAE citizenship. The demonstration was initiated after some of the women and their husbands were summoned by naturalization offices in a number of emirates. As an Emirati mother of six put it, "We want equal rights like men who marry and get national status for foreigners [foreign wives]."[94] Clearly, the UAE state's concern with national women's rates of singlehood does not extend to expanding their marital options.

The Egyptian state similarly makes it very difficult for non-Egyptian men who marry Egyptian women to gain citizenship. Also crucial is the status of children from such married relationships. Until a recent legal change, Article 2 of the Nationality Law No. 26 of 1975 limited Egyptian nationality to persons "born to an Egyptian father, or; born in Egypt to an Egyptian mother and a father of unknown nationality or has no nationality at all; or born in Egypt to an Egyptian mother where paternity cannot be proven, or; born in Egypt to unknown parents [foundling]."[95] As Fawziya Abdul Sattar, a law professor at Cairo University and formerly affiliated with the National Council of Women legislative committee, disapprovingly makes clear, this law means that

> a person who is born to an Egyptian mother and a foreign father shall not be considered an Egyptian, a situation which discriminated between women and men in passing their nationality to their children, giving this right to men but not to women in derogation of Article 40 of the Egyptian constitution which states all people are equal in public rights and duties without discrimination based on gender, etc. [This situation is particularly problematic where foreign fathers have died, divorced the Egyptian mother, or deserted her] and she lives permanently in Egypt.[96]

These laws and policies violate the Convention on the Elimination of All Forms of Discrimination Against Women and are thus often highlighted to state officials by foreign organizations and national lawyers and activists. In Egypt, thousands of children born to Egyptian mothers and growing up in the country are denied a range of rights and resources. According to the Egyptian National

Council of Women, "Many non-governmental organizations have joined with the mothers of these children and have been vocal in calling for an end to this situation."[97] As is the case in the UAE, the children of such couples are treated as "foreigners," starkly demonstrating the legal erasure of their mothers, who cannot easily transfer their citizenship to husbands or biological children. State officials in Egypt will occasionally grant citizenship to such children by decree, as indicated in the following newspaper clip from December 2003, titled "315 Foreigners Granted Egyptian Citizenship": "Egypt's Minister of Interior, Habib Al Adli, yesterday issued a decree granting the Egyptian citizenship to 315 foreigners. . . . The beneficiaries are bearing nationalities of 11 Arab and Foreign countries and who are of Egyptian mothers, according to the provision of Article 4 of the law number 26 of 1975. They include 100 Sudanese, 46 Syrians, 42 Jordanians, 14 each Iraqis and Libyans, three each Saudis, Greek and British, two Cypriots and 15 Pakistanis."[98]

Easy regional migration of native men, masculinism, patriarchal laws, and the UAE's active importation of men and women laborers in a tariff and tax-free, investment and tourist-friendly economy facilitates national exogamy by Emirati men; such relationships reportedly comprised 28 percent of all registered marriages in 1998.[99] Another analysis almost ten years earlier of eight hundred marriage contracts recorded in the Abu Dhabi courts indicates that 36 percent of the marriages were between national men and foreign women, although some of these women may have been relatives.[100] Today, Emirati men take non-Emirati sexual partners using various modalities (regular marriage, *misyār*, *'urfī*, concubinage, and so on). Compared to other Gulf countries (such as Oman, Kuwait, Qatar, Saudi Arabia), UAE law does not limit the age difference between spouses or ban citizen men (except those in the armed forces) from marrying noncitizen women.[101] Given Qur'anic principles that allow Muslim men to marry plurally and marry non-Muslim women, state officials in the UAE worry about but have largely not restricted male national exogamy, not least because Muslim men have a range of ways to marry without resorting to the state. Rulers have considered but not followed through on regulating citizen men's marriages to foreign women at a number of points in the past couple of decades; they have also considered not granting foreign wives citizenship until they have been married to natives and lived in the Emirates for ten years.[102]

Not surprisingly, male exogamy is problematic from the perspective of many native women. The 1995 annual report of the UAE Women's Federation includes a passage noting that the organization "campaign[ed] actively to discourage the practice of older male citizens taking young wives, often second wives, from abroad, generally women who are of a relatively low level of education." The report notes that suggestions for establishing "a formal legal prohibition" on native men marrying foreign women "have been stoutly resisted."[103] Dresch notes that literature produced by federal entities disapproves of polygamy, treating it as "a cause of disruption" in national families, which in their ideal forms are represented in nuclear, companionate terms: "native" mother and father with two children.[104] Emirati men who marry non-Emirati women are seen to introduce a cascade of problems that develop over time and extend beyond limiting the pool of native Emirati men available for marriage to native women. Ms. Saliha Ghabish, of the Shariqa Girls Clubs, explained her perspective on some of the immediate cultural problems introduced and long-term consequences that occur when native men marry migrant women:

> Each society has its own . . . particular characteristics. So when he marries from another society, he needs to take that into account. He has to—he either makes her like us, of course, the first thing is to make her wear the abaya [the flowing black robe most Emirati women wear in public]—she might refuse—this is on the superficial level. . . . There are many of these [non-Emirati] wives who have succeeded. . . . But most of them were destroyed and the children were fragmented in the end between here and there, between the country of the husband and the country of the wife. . . . This operation is wrong. Even though . . . our Islamic religion does not ban us from—that the man marry from another—he can marry from any other *milla* [millet], but in reality long ago the question was possibly simpler than it is now. . . . Today there are issues of borders, nationalities, passports, laws. Of course, these laws—each country has its laws—these laws may sometimes contradict [each other]. . . . Let us say that I am an English woman. Maybe I do not want to walk with the law of the Emirates, but I should follow this law because my husband is from here. This is a question that young men should pay attention to.[105]

Mr. Darwish of the Dubai courts agreed that the exogamous marriage practices of native Emirati men were a source of "major problems":

> We now have 26 nationalities of women who are married to Emirati men—even Singaporean women, Chinese women. So there is no—most of the divorces are among this sector. Here is an example: [he picks up a paper from his desk]: the husband is Emirati and the wife is Czech. It will become a divorce—immediately,

okay? Most of these situations will end with failure. . . . [W]here does the problem occur? After marriage—the first days are nice as with any marriage. Then there is pregnancy. She is divorced by him. That is it. This woman remains for the rest of her life in the Emirates because she has a child who is Emirati. And this is a problem. The problem is not the presence of the woman. The problem is that the sequence will continue. This woman is sitting in the country. And she has no work. She has permanent residency. . . . This woman marries again. And if she gets married her custody of children is lost. And these children—it is a problem if she does not marry—[F.H.: If she wants, can she leave?] She does not leave. [F.H.: It is not allowed?] No, it is not disallowed. [F.H.: She stays because of the child.] She wants to remain here. Unfortunately, many of these women—[F.H.: They want to stay.] They want to stay. [F.H.: But they want to work, yes?] They came to work but our law—we require the husband to pay an amount to the divorced woman because she has a child to raise. So she is sitting—she is taking money—some of them do work, of course. But even so, he has to provide housing and food. . . . So in the end it is a financial burden on this husband. Number two, this woman remains sitting in the country. Even if she undertakes any crime, we will not remove her. . . . For us, if [any other] foreign woman undertakes a crime, she gets a ruling and then is sent to her country. This woman cannot be sent away. . . . She has a child who is a citizen, an Emirati, who will stay. This has created major problems.[106]

Embedded in this passage is the assumption that most foreign women marry Emirati men for economic reasons, although Jane Bristol-Rhys found that native women are much more likely to suspect opportunism of non-European women.[107] As Denise Brennan has argued for the Sosúa community in the Dominican Republic, "love" can mean many things and marriage in a tourist economy is often a "get ahead" strategy for poor women.[108] It is reasonable to conclude this to be the case as well for many foreign women in the UAE migrant labor economy. One Emirati official angrily complained to Dresch that the practice of foreign women marrying Emirati men has "become a business," with "Indians and Sri Lankans" trying to have children "as fast as they can."[109] As a homesick researcher visiting the UAE, I was slow to realize that many men and women from around the world want to live and work in the UAE (especially Dubai) and would do many things to remain. For noncitizen women in the UAE, marriage to UAE men allows them to have an avenue to live, work, and gain other resources. If documented as legitimate, such marriages allow nonnational women and their children from Emirati men to housing, health-care, public schooling, and university access.[110] As Dr. Ahmed al-Kubaysi, who is originally from Iraq, put it, "This is an outstanding [*marmūk*] country. People love it, they want to be in it. . . . The Western, the Eastern, the Arab and the Muslim."[111]

From Darwish's account and others, a number of tensions are associated with marriages between Emirati men and foreign women. Foreign women divorced from Emirati men are viewed to be a drain on the national economy and *native family economies* and to create resource and emotional tensions in native-native marriages. If such divorced women remarry, their citizen children may not be wanted by the new husband *or* their biological father and his wife and children. Divorced or widowed mothers who had been married to male citizens are eligible for "social security" if they remain in the Emirates, but have "no automatic right of residence." They typically need a sponsor, who is often their own child, sometimes an infant.[112] Despite widespread ethnic miscegenation, legal Emirati progeny born of foreign women have lower social status among natives in comparison to "nonmixed" children.[113] Children of foreign women, moreover, are increasingly understood as less likely to be socialized in religiously and culturally appropriate ways, especially when their mothers are from South or East Asia. Last but not least, divorced foreign women who are the mothers of Emirati citizens are perceived as troubling the gender, sexual, and national order because they are sexually available, culturally more difficult to constrain than native women, and yet cannot be forced to leave because they are the mothers of citizens.

Ms. Ghabish believes that high dowries and other marital expenses largely explain the phenomenon of native men marrying foreign women. By contrast, the young Emirati women interviewed by Bristol-Rhys did not believe expenses are the primary reason Emirati men marry foreign women. While Emirati young men often blame Emirati women for costly weddings, interfering parents, and being too demanding, many native women believe that the main reason they marry foreign women is because such women are more easily dominated by Emirati husbands given their distance from family support and thus their dependence on the husband in every way. Emirati women believe that as natives, they are less "docile" and "subservient" than wives from Indonesia, Malaysia, the Philippines, and India, arguing that Emirati men too often want maids and sex, not wives with rights or families.[114]

State officials in the UAE were so concerned with exogamy among Emirati men and marriage delays for native women that in 1992, pursuant to Federal

Law No. 47, Shaykh Zayed bin Sultan al-Nahyan established the "Marriage Fund" (*sandūq al-zawāj*), which according to its Arabic brochures works to "develop the society and advance it in light of Islamic values and Arab traditions; establish the stability of the family, and provide care for children and guidance to youth; [and] undertake necessary research and studies to learn the social problems that face the society and the family." State officials want Emiratis to marry Emiratis and worry about demographic and citizenship boundaries, termed "red lines" that cannot be crossed by the Marriage Fund's Assistant Undersecretary Jamal Bin Obaid al-Bah: "This [Marriage Fund] is aimed at bolstering the [native] population. The number of immigrants is three times more than citizens. In the long-term, the demographic policy is in danger. There are red lines. Red lines related to these matters. . . . [I]f we do not make a residency policy and provide family education, our culture, language, customs, and traditions will weaken [*taḥtawī*]."[115]

Especially since the turn of the century, the UAE Marriage Fund has expanded educational and other projects focused on biopolitical concerns, aiming to "aid [*turfid*] the society with . . . counseling, medical tests before marriage, family education [courses], television programs, [and] educational programs."[116] Marriage Fund brochures in Arabic describe a campaign to arrange marriages between never married, widowed, or divorced nationals and appeal to Emirati men to marry Emirati women since such marriages are superior in their ability to produce socially meaningful, engaged, and culturally appropriate national families, as well as socially, intellectually, and psychologically well-adjusted national children.[117] Over time, the Marriage Fund has come to coordinate and finance state-sponsored group wedding ceremonies and parties, and to provide large grants for Emirati-Emirati weddings and housing support for such couples, although the fund has experienced financial problems that have affected the provision of these grants.[118] There are state programs for en masse weddings, on a much lower scale, in Egypt.[119]

Bypassing State and Family Through *'Urfī* Marriage

It is still common in most MENA states, including those with relatively secular governments such as Tunisia (whose state laws ban polygyny) or Syria, for Sunni Muslims to marry with the knowledge of their family and friends but without informing state institutions, including courts, for a variety of reasons.[120] The phenomenon of (re)marrying without registering with the state has since the late 1960s been used in Egypt by widowed military wives and more recently widows generally in order not to lose state-provisioned pensions and privileges, since a woman is expected to be maintained by a husband.[121] Customary or common law marriages of these varieties are commonly called *'urfi* because they avoid registration with state authorities. Although such marriages are deemed illegal by most MENA states, penalties against religious authorities who supervise them are rarely applied and have little prophylactic effect.[122] Moreover, such marriages can easily be eventually registered unless they violate a state law. These contracts are considered Islamically licit if they follow the requirements of regular marriage (which differ in various schools), but they are typically not recognized by state law until they are registered.

The customary marriages discussed in this book are relatively recent practices and violate not only state registration but often witness, maintenance, housing, and other long-standing expectations, such as agreement of the woman's male guardian according to the rules understood by some of the Islamic doctrinal schools. A precursor to such marital innovations produced great controversy when it became public in 1970s Egypt. One of the more radical and violent Islamist organizations to emerge in the country was Takfir wal-Hijra, which posited customary marital solutions for urban poor and working-class men who always had more difficulty accumulating the resources necessary for marriage. To the outrage of popular opinion captured in the Egyptian press, Takfir's leader Shukri Mustafa (killed in 1978) contended that dominant Muslim marriage practices produced suffering for young people who are forced to delay this rite of passage and licit sexual outlet. As a mobilization tactic, Mustafa arranged "Muslim marriages" between young people, usually without parental involvement or approval, in the presence of witnesses. Such marriages simply required the consent of the bride and groom, although it seems that girls and women were sometimes kidnapped. Married couples lived communally in furnished apartments rented by the organization.[123] Dr. Faysal al-Yunis explains that the "extremist groups" "exploited this question [of marriage difficulty] in order to attract young men. It would marry them with its acquaintances. By simplifying and easing marriage, by completely cancelling the traditions existing in marriage, marriage again returns to request, acceptance, witnesses, and we are done. . . . The amir [leader] of the group marries the brother and the sister [men and women members of the organization], and that is it. And the question of having a home is not relevant— they were closer to the hippies of the 1960s, some of them."[124]

Customary relationships in the contemporary period are often interchangeably referred to as "secret" marriages to stress their perceived violation of "shariʿa" and state law. Couples do not always use documents to declare these relationships. They may speak marriage vows onto a cassette tape in lieu of a written document, called "cassette marriage,"[125] or engage in "blood marriage," where two individuals mix their blood from pricked fingers. Other relationship forms include "gift marriage," in which two people state that they give themselves to each other, and "friend marriage," which was legitimated by a religious edict from a Yemeni shaykh and allowed a husband and wife in a secret marriage to avoid housing costs by sleeping separately in their respective parents' home.[126]

The most important difference between customary marriages that are not registered with the state and the customary marriages discussed in this study is that the latter are also kept secret from parents and other family members. Instead, as one Emirati man told me, "the girl [in the relationship] tells seven to eight of her trusted friends and the guy tells seven to eight of his trusted friends," which some consider to fulfill *shurūṭ al-ishhār* (conditions of announcement) in the Sunni doctrinal schools.[127] When there are witnesses to the secret marriage, they can also include "rented friends" and lawyers paid a fee to oversee and sometimes hold onto the contract. Witnesses are often sworn to secrecy.[128] The written contract, which may or may not be overseen by a lawyer, middle man, or religious functionary, often remains with the husband, facilitating lack of proof for the woman if he denies the marriage. By their nature, *ʿurfī* marriages are difficult to estimate with great accuracy. Many men will deny they have ever known the mother of a legally fatherless child, let alone had sex with her as part of a customary marriage contract.[129] A large-scale nonrandom study on customary marriages in Egypt found that the most common ways to end such marriages is to "shred the document," avoid the wife, agree to end the relationship, or say, "I divorce you."[130]

A customary marriage in Egypt and the UAE usually only comes to family or state attention when legal problems arise: a woman is pregnant, wants a divorce, or demands maintenance for a child after a husband has disappeared with the marriage contract and/or denies that they were married. States are also drawn into such cases when inheritance claims are made by a secret *ʿurfī* wife or her children; or people need birth certificates, travel documents, to register children in schools, state health care, or other welfare services, all of which are restricted to citizens (with citizenship linked to paternity) with a national number. Unless a father recognizes a child from an unregistered relationship and registers paternity with the state, the child is not issued a birth certificate, which is required for access to all public resources. There are about twelve to eighteen thousand ongoing paternity suits in Egyptian courts, more than two-thirds resulting from unregistered marriages, which are estimated at about three million.[131] Not all men deny their customary marriages. In some cases, 'urfī contracts are undertaken when a couple "falls into wrong," or engages in a sexual relationship outside an Islamically licit framework, a "non-shar'ī pregnancy occurs," and a customary marriage covers the time delay before a regular marriage can be completed given legal and social restrictions against heterosex outside of marriage.[132]

Court officials in the UAE have struggled with how to confirm in 'urfī cases whether a marriage occurred that fulfilled Islamic conditions or was simply a cover for an illicit sexual relationship, an oppositional distinction that is not perceived in this manner in social practice. The state in such situations is left with a range of related and interesting questions and problems including:

> The paper remained with the husband. And the witnesses were only from the husband's side and the wife does not know them. This has occurred often. . . . There is, of course, DNA testing . . . [but] it remains a big problem. Courts [must be involved], and so on. If no pregnancy occurred but specific rights [of the wife] are violated, this creates other problems . . . , [including] inheritance. The husband dies, the wife has two children from him, and he has a first wife in a marriage that occurred the right way. The first wife comes and says, "I am his heir. I am his only wife." The second wife comes and says, "No, I am also his wife." The problems begin. How can we confirm the second marriage? . . . [The state] will not confirm [a male citizen's] progeny from a 'urfī marriage. They will say, "go bring a shar'ī contract." In the end the father often does not register the children. I have had an example of 'urfī marriage in which the children are 4 and 5 years old. They are not registered in a passport. No one knows that this person is his wife. He had them living in an apartment. The problems begin to emerge when the children reach the stage of studying in elementary schools. [F.H.: Meaning the schools do not allow the children to be registered.] Of course not. . . . We have problems in the courts regarding inheritance that have continued for years with us trying to confirm whether these are children of the man or not. Especially if the woman is foreign, has no family here, and no one can say they witnessed her marriage.[133]

Customary marriages are undertaken in a range of situations in the UAE. Customary marriages by Emirati men are most likely to occur with foreign women, especially non-Emirati Arabs.[134] In some cases, native men marry foreign women in such contracts because the UAE requires permission from

the woman's embassy before registering a marriage, which is sometimes difficult to acquire;[135] or because they are embarrassed to inform their families
they married a foreign woman. Citizen men in the UAE military will use such
contracts to bypass restrictions on marrying noncitizen women. Participants
in customary marriage in the UAE also include non-Emirati Arab men who
live or work in the UAE, are legally banned from marrying foreign women or
women significantly younger than they are in their own countries (for example,
Oman, Saudi Arabia), and they cannot by law have marriages registered in UAE
courts.[136] Also using such unregistered contracts are men whose families have
lived in the Emirates for generations but have no citizenship or nationality in
any country (*bidūn*).[137] Most Emirati women involved in *'urfī* marriages are
divorcées, according to Mr. Darwish of the Dubai courts: "Especially because
we know in a study of the Gulf that of every seven divorced women, [only] one
remarries. So in the end, the divorced woman becomes *'ānis* [a spinster]. . . .
So she is compelled—if a man comes and tells her, 'you are the fourth wife'—
she wants to live."[138] The most important reason never-married UAE women
choose *'urfī* is to circumvent the state requirement for a male guardian when
such a person does not agree to her suitor, is temporarily absent and needs to
be tracked down for permission, or is permanently absent and this situation
must be proved to the satisfaction of the court.[139] While Sunni Muslim women
over twenty-one years (divorced or previously unmarried) in Gulf Cooperation
Council countries may request that a personal status court judge become her
male guardian (*walī*) for marriage in case unreasonable obstacles are placed
before her, most women will not take this route against a father, and if they do,
judges are reluctant to intervene.[140] The most frequent reason parents do not
acquiesce to a marriage in the UAE is the perceived lower status of the potential
spouse's family.[141]

Customary marriages in Egypt involve a variety of people and occur in all
socioeconomic classes.[142] Although women sixteen years or older do not need
parental permission to marry according to Egyptian law, parents are highly
involved for the majority of couples and male guardians are expected to be
present in a regular marriage. As in the UAE, socioeconomic status differences
between the families or a man's perceived lack of sufficient resources for marriage are the main reasons parents do not agree for offspring marry each other.
Most men involved in customary relationships do not necessarily intend to
have a long-term or public marriage and thus do not desire parental knowledge
or involvement. These types of customary relationships are most likely to occur

on Egyptian college campuses and most often involve young people fifteen to twenty-four years old. The vast majority never come to public light given social stigma, their typically short duration of less than one to two years, and the availability of contraception and hymen-repair procedures.[143] Some analyses indicate that 4–6 percent of university students between eighteen and twenty-five years in Egypt may be involved in 'urfī relationships,[144] although accurate numbers are impossible to ascertain given the limited opportunities to conduct randomized research.[145] These relationships are not restricted to urban areas or universities as they also occur in the Egyptian countryside and among young people in high school.[146]

Customary marriages are not unusual among Egyptian entertainers and the phenomenon is usually introduced to high-school-aged children in Egyptian cinema and drama, where it is commonplace as part of a plot line to the great consternation of parents, intellectuals, state officials, and religious elites.[147] These Egyptian plot lines are seen by some to function similarly "to the foreign media, especially in . . . stimulating the instincts of the younger age groups in society" and normalizing such relationships.[148] Customary marriages also occur among wealthy Egyptian businessmen who want to legitimate sexual relationships with lower-status women workers, such as secretaries.[149] For married men in classes with "money and power" secret marriages allow "distance . . . from commitments and routine family interactions" without disrupting the original family, according to an Egyptian woman intellectual affiliated with the state. Women in such relationships, she believes, agree to them for economic reasons or to fulfill sexual or companionship needs.[150]

Customary marriage is also used in more exploitative and less consensual situations that are often transnational. Many impoverished Egyptian girls and women agree to secretly marry (unmarried and already married) wealthy men from other countries, especially the Gulf, "who will give them a dowry and keep their marriage from their families."[151] For Gulf men involved in such relationships, they often consider the amounts paid to be "pocket money," according to an interview with a young man in Dubai. In other cases, poor Egyptian parents facilitate such relationships between Gulf men and their daughters because they find them "lucrative," he added.[152] Indeed, many customary marriages involve Egyptian adolescent girls from neighborhoods such as the Hamawdiya area in Giza or the League of Arab States Street in Muhandisin who are pimped by their parents through middlemen to wealthy men on vacation from the Arab Gulf countries. In the past, these were regular marriages but have been replaced with *'urfī* as states began to require that citizen men seek permission. These relationships are intended to be short-term sexual liaisons, lasting a few weeks to a few months, and they usually occur in furnished apartments (some doormen play an important role in how men find apartments), in return for a fee functioning as "dowry" that is paid to the parents of the bride.[153]

Customary marriages are hegemonically presented as "a negative solution" used by young men and women "to satisfy their psychological, physiological and social desires, instead of . . . forming a family through legal channels," as an Egyptian researcher explained on a satellite television program.[154] Religious and state elites view them as based on deception and leading to loss of a wife's rights. Customary marriages are usually condemned as "essentially fornication" and illicit, with women more than men viewing them as unjust for women.[155] Young men are often seen to use such relationships to get sexual satisfaction without "payment."[156] Egyptian women students interviewed at Cairo University report that customary marriages fulfill the short-term sexual needs of "boys" and "girls" in search of a "true love" that turns out to be fleeting. Another Egyptian student stressed that "almost everything about *'urfī* marriage works to the benefit of the boy."[157] An essay in Cairo University's Department of English student magazine, *Potpourri*, indicates the regularity of women students in *'urfī* marriages becoming pregnant and male partners "quickly disappear[ing] as if he were running away from a monster" upon hearing of pregnancy, especially if the woman refuses to abort.[158] Emirati women, like Egyptian women, generally believe that the negative consequences outweigh the benefits of such relationships for women.[159] As the fiancé of an Emirati man (who she met on the Internet) explained to me, "I am against it [*'urfī*] because it does not protect women's rights. Husbands in these situations are not committed to *mahr* or living costs. And people will always think it was done for pleasure and not take such a marriage seriously."[160]

Based on his experience in the Dubai courts, Darwish thought that the goal of most *'urfī* marriages was pleasure, "a fleeting desire [*shahwa 'ābira*] and it ends. And for this reason, the majority of *'urfī* marriages we have end with *'urfī* divorce." Dubai court officials have unsuccessfully requested the establishment of laws to punish participants in such relationships in order to deter the practice. Practitioners know they are engaged in an illicit behavior and thus are afraid to publicize or confirm the marriage in the courts with a registrar. Many women, he believes, "regret such marriage. She is pulled by a particular emotion—I loved him, he loved me, the love of one or two days, through the Internet, through getting to know each other, and then it ends after six months in failure."[161] Dr. Al-'Olama of the United Arab Emirates University contends that given their short duration, customary marriages have come "to look like *mut'a* [intentionally short-term] marriage [of Shi'i Islam] which essentially are not allowed in the Sunni schools."[162] Al-'Olama thought the customary contracts simply facilitate short-term sexual licentiousness (*da'āra*) and have a range of negative long-term consequences that "unaware" and "imprudent" partners do not fully consider in advance since they are driven by the immediate "desire of the I [*ānīya*]." One of these consequences is that the girl's parents are unaware of the marriage and when a "groom comes to engage her, the parents might agree but the fiancé does not know that she has been previously married." When pregnancy occurs in denied marriages, "the rights of the woman, man, and child they had are lost." He reiterated that "the goal of marriage in Islam is not . . . merely the satisfaction of desire. This is present, the satisfaction of desire, no argument here, because this is a natural instinct [*gharīza*] and Islam does not ignore reality. . . . But in addition to this, the larger goal of it is bringing progeny. This progeny has rights. And the door for protecting its rights is the documentation of marriage."[163]

Some customary marriages reportedly end in divorce the first night, after the husband decides that the new wife is not a virgin because she had been in a previous secret marriage.[164] Girls and women previously involved in such relationships may attempt to "remove any signs" of such a marriage by having hymen "repair" surgery.[165] The link between customary marriage and hymen surgeries was made explicit by the mufti of Egypt, Nasr Farid Wasil, who in the same April 2000 ruling condemned *'urfī* marriage among university students and declared that hymen restoration surgery was "only valid in case of rape."[166] Others in Egypt and the UAE explained to me that women can easily remain "technical virgins" and be sexually active.

A study undertaken by Cairo University researchers of a nonrandom selection of thirty-five men and women involved in customary marriages found that slightly over half of the sample were relatively middle-income; university students; and had at least one parent who had completed a university education.[167] More than half reported sexual activity prior to their customary marriage, largely masturbation, followed by intercourse, "surface sex," and oral sex; about three-quarters had not been formally married before the customary marriage.[168] These participants reported their primary motive for such a relationship as: economic (15); "social and family problems" (7); "fulfilling sexual desire" (4); "love" (4); "whimsy" (*nazwatun*) (3); "loneliness and boredom" (3); "protecting a salary" (2); "parental refusal of a regular marriage" (2); "making illicit relations Islamically licit" (2); "other" (2); and "fooling the law" (1).[169] Slightly more than half (18) reported that the marriage was witnessed by friends, six reported a lawyer as the witness, and the remainder presumably had no witnesses.[170] While most (25) did not agree to a time-limited marriage, six did and four were unclear in their responses.[171] Most couples had sex in the man's apartment or family home (8), a woman's apartment or family home (5), or the home of a relative (5).[172] Less than half reported that both partners kept a copy of the contract (14), the next largest group reported that only the husband had the contract (10), and in four cases the wife kept the contract.[173]

Mona Abaza writes that in recent years Egyptian media and state officials have cleverly used language to connect the rise of informal, unregistered housing developments (*'ashwā'iyyat*, a word that denotes these districts as "spontaneous") established by poorer Cairenes with the rise of "informal" sexual and marital relationships: "*'ashwā'iyyat* became the equivalent of chaotic and 'uncivilized' relations," such as customary marriage.[174] In this manner, a number of adjectives related to material and sexual economies become interchangeable: substandard, informal, illicit, underground, and risky. Of these two economies, sexual informality is far more likely to be condemned as the result of personal, familial, and moral failure.

"Secret" Polygyny, No Housing Needed—*Misyār* Marriage

Misyār is originally an Arabic word from the Arabian Peninsula that refers to Sunni Muslim marriages in which the husband visits ("marches to" or "travels to") a wife who lives in her own or her parents' home rather than a home provided by the husband.[175] In English, *misyār* is sometimes referred to as "ambulant" marriage. Historically, such marriages were supposedly not kept secret from an original wife or wives. According to al-Shaykh Mohammad 'Abdul Rahim Sultan Al-'Olama, a member of the Faculty of Shari'a and Law at the United Arab Emirates University, traditional *misyār* "was closer to shari'a" in comparison to "how people are now using it," since *misyār* wives may not have needed money or a house, or might be older but want to be "under the care of a husband." In turn, this type of relationship was seen to licitly fulfill the needs of traveling men who wanted to be sexually and emotionally gratified by a wife. Typically, women in such marriages were and are second or third wives of men who live most of the time with another wife.[176]

While *misyār* marriages today are uncommon in the UAE and Egypt, they are more widely used since the 1990s and have spread beyond Saudi Arabia.[177] In Saudi Arabia of the 1990s, the men practitioners of *misyār* have tended to be of the middle or lower-middle classes.[178] There are a few widely publicized and discussed cases in which *misyār* is a mutually agreed upon arrangement between professional men and women in monogamous relationships who choose to live in separate homes and not have children.[179] Most seem to be polygynous relationships, however, involving women who are widowed or divorced, possibly with children; or older (thirties and forties) never-married women who desire male companionship, sex, and sometimes a child.[180] Contemporary *misyār* marriages are usually agreed to on the same standard marriage forms and contracted in state courts in the UAE, "with formal marriage recorders, witnesses, papers, documents, and everything."[181] Depending on the requirements of the Islamic doctrinal school, *misyār* contracts may require the consent of the male guardian of a woman.[182] Wives in such marriages and their children have the same inheritance rights as other wives in Sunni marriages.[183]

Despite the similarity of the completed paper contract to a regular marriage, contemporary *misyār* contracts are based on unwritten or written clauses between the potential wife and husband in which the wife "concedes" (*tatnāzal 'an*) her rights to visitation, housing, maintenance, and in rare cases, bearing a child, depending on what is allowed in different Islamic schools;[184] these are radical differences from the hegemonic form of Sunni marriage. Darwish of the Dubai courts described the typical *misyār* marriage contract in the UAE, discussed why some written conditions and concessions can be licit, and explained why a woman may compromise on the requirement that a husband provision her with housing. Such a relationship, he shared, usually

> occurs between the two people outside the framework of the writing of the contract. The contract is written regularly, it is normal. It is a 100 percent marriage contract, just like this one. Nothing is written on it at all. It includes the names of wife and husband, dowry, and so on. . . . There is a clause [*band*] called the "conditions clause." Some people in *misyār* marriages do not write conditions. It is between him and the wife that, [for example], "I will not spend every night with you. I have a first wife. I will stop by your house once a week or so. You work, your home is in your parents' home—I will not provide maintenance for you and we will not have children for two or three years." This is not confirmed in the contract. Such a contract is 100 percent correct. But if, as a marriage

registrar, someone came and told me to register the following condition: "She cannot force me to spend every night with her." Is this a disallowed condition for us? No, it is not banned. The wife has the right to compromise [on her rights]. [F.H.: Each person can put any condition they want?] It has to be *shar'ī* (religiously licit), *shar'ī*. It cannot violate the shari'a. Meaning the wife cannot come and say, "I want him not to ban me from drinking alcohol. . . ." She can say: "He cannot ban me from working. He cannot ban me from driving a car. He cannot ban me from finishing my studies. He cannot make me live in another emirate. He has to let me live in Dubai." All of this is provided and he is required to follow through. [F.H.: But she cannot say, "He is not allowed to marry another woman?"] Eeh, we would not confirm this contract. We would not confirm it because this is an issue—but some of our schools of law would confirm the contract. Some of the registrars would confirm it—that she has the right to request divorce or be divorced if he marries another woman. We [the state] will not change [or challenge] this registration. It is an agreement between the husband and wife. But we do not register anything that violates the shari'a. [In terms of] the compromise of the woman on her right to have housing: Is it her right or not? It is her right [to have housing]. . . . So what compelled her to accept this [compromise]? That is a different question. She is older, divorced, widowed, a spinster—she is 35 and unmarried. She is compelled to accept, with respect to you, to accept anything. But it is a marriage, honestly, that has no stability.[185]

As in its previous articulations, a husband in a contemporary *misyār* relationship does not usually live with his *misyār* wife, who remains in her parents' household or, if divorced, widowed, or well-off, in her own home, arranging for sexual liaisons at home, in hotels, or in other locations.[186] Darwish explained the housing aspect of these marriages:

We have people who work in Abu Dhabi. His first wife is with him in Abu Dhabi and he is originally from the emirate of Fujayra. So he has to go down to Fujayra every week or two to see his parents. So he takes a wife over there using *misyār*. He comes to her once every two weeks. This is acceptable. As in Saudi Arabia, the man is from the people of Riyadh and he has a wife in Mecca. Instead of going to Mecca for *'umra* or *haj* and living in a hotel, he can stay with his wife there. . . . [F.H.: Has this been acceptable for a long time?] It has been acceptable for a long time in Saudi Arabia. [F.H.: What about here?] Here, it was acceptable, but . . . there were very few cases and most of them were a situation of a second wife.[187]

Al-'Olama of UAE University believed that contemporary practitioners of *misyār* engage in it either to lessen the economic requirements of regular marriage or because a man "does not have the courage to announce a second marriage."[188] This brings us to a key aspect of *misyār* contracts that explains their instability: in the UAE they almost always include a clause (written or not) requiring the relationship to be kept secret beyond the contractual parties, witnesses, woman's male guardian, and religious and state functionaries. Indeed, the "major goal of *misyār* marriage is for the second marriage to be secret so that the first wife does not know."[189] While legally considered a regular marriage by some religious leaders and states, *misyār* marriage is socially controversial because of this secrecy. Moreover, it is religiously unacceptable to many because men often do not provide wives with housing, resources, or sexual access that is equal with other wives if the husband is polygynous. In Al-'Olama's words:

> We know in Islamic shari'a that if one marries two or three wives, he must, no matter what, evenly divide between them with equality and justice. In *misyār*, it was like the woman herself compromised her right in such a division and accepts [this situation] for a particular period. . . . It was widespread among individuals who always moved around as a result of employment. . . . Today, [however,] people living in the same town have begun to undertake these relationships. Even in Saudi Arabia when it first began it did not occur in the same town—the same town. There was no necessity for such secrecy since it was a formal and announced marriage.[190]

In defense of *misyār* marriages, an Emirati man in his late twenties argued that it served the interests of women "because they get the status of being married and satisfy their sexual instincts."[191] Women further benefited, he claimed, because they could work outside the home and had "total freedom within the marriage. The child is registered by the state under the man, but she has child-rearing power."[192] Since women's obedience and sexual access to husbands has usually been premised on provision of economic maintenance and housing, Oussama Arabi has in fact asked whether these "unusual economic and cohabitation arrangements" increase the power and independence of the wife, especially in the "micro-politics of the household."[193] Many women and men, in contrast, assume these relationships to be degrading to the dignity of the women involved.[194]

Misyār marriages have produced conflicting rulings from Islamic religious authorities. A (legally nonbinding) fatwa in 1996 by Shaykh 'Abdel Aziz Ibn Baz, the grand mufti of Saudi Arabia, declared such contracts licit if the following conditions are met: presence of the woman's male guardian, consent of both parties to the marriage, two witnesses, lack of physical disability in the woman to prevent consummation, and not keeping the relationship "secret." Nonprovision of housing and maintenance were indirectly addressed in the ruling by articulating that "mutual stipulations" of the parties to the contract are allowed.[195] Oussama Arabi notes regarding this ruling that only the Maliki doctrinal school traditionally had a binding requirement of publicizing marriage, while the other three Sunni schools only "recommended" such publicity. Dr. Al-'Olama of UAE University also made the point that publicizing a polygynous marriage to the first wife was "not a condition" in "shari'a."[196] The mufti of Egypt, Nasr Farid Wasil, ruled *misyār* licit in 1998, arguing that it might be a practical solution to the "scarcity of [Egyptian] men, resulting from immigration to the Gulf countries."[197] By contrast, the former "rector of Al-Azhar, Shaykh Sayyid Mas'ud, considered *misyār* improper since housing and alimony were dispensed with."[198] The most important figure to place an Islamic imprimatur on *misyār* contracts was Shaykh Yusuf al-Qaradawi, a professor in Qatar, often associated with the Egyptian Brotherhood, who regularly appears on the Arabic satellite al-Jazeera program, "The Shari'a and Life" (*al-sharī'a wal-hayat*). He declared such contracts licit because "women themselves desire such unions" and may not need economic support from a husband.[199]

Additional Family "Crisis" Accounts and Explanations

In Egypt, marital, sexual, and family values and practices, and sociality more generally, are seen to be negatively impacted by tremendous economic insecurities and the wide gaps between the few rich, the many poor, and a precariously situated small middle-class. These insecurities and widening socioeconomic gaps accelerated with the 1970s Open Door (*infitāḥ*) Policy to foreign capitalist investment and privatization and the related enfeeblement of the post-Nasserist state as a source of wealth redistribution, price controls, infrastructure maintenance, transportation, healthcare, housing, education, and employment opportunities. Nicolas Kosmatopoulos stresses the urgency of a prevailing reality that requires the vast majority of Egyptians to "manage precariousness" given the instability of "working conditions and the labor market," which creates a situation "where social trust and future security are open to daily negotiation and constant reevaluation."[200]

A major aspect of the Egyptian economic opening that impacted marriage directly is decreased affordability of housing for newly married couples in

Egypt, since providing such housing is a crucial prerequisite for any man seek-ing to marry.[201] Dr. Riad Hamzawi, a migrant professor working in the UAE, explained that a small, two-room apartment in Cairo will cost the equivalent of US$10,000 in "key money," or a down payment, whereas the highest salary most college-educated young men can hope to earn in Egypt, whether in the private or public sphere, is $200 to $250 per month. As a result, for young people, "their dreams for the future require a very long period to be realized. . . . [Y]ou cannot disconnect at all the [sexual issues] of young people in Egypt from the political, economic, or social problems."[202] Dr. Hamzawi's compared this economically insecure situation to his own after graduating from university in Egypt:

> I was appointed in the university, and my salary was 17 Egyptian guineas. . . . But I married and opened a home. I was able to rent the apartment and I would buy meat, bread, and groceries. I lived well and was happy. And also—and pay attention to this important comment—[I had] a dream of the future. Meaning when I was in my appointment as a reader in the university, I knew that one of these days, I will be a dean [he became a dean]. . . . I knew my work plan exactly. I knew that I would take an MA, then a PhD. . . . [T]he society has changed.[203]

To illustrate the contrast, Hamzawi reported that his twenty-one–year-old son, who wants to leave Egypt, asks him, "Why are you boiling your blood to educate me? Why are you very tired? . . . After I am educated, what will I get? . . . Do you think I will turn out like you? I will struggle and . . . I will improve myself step-by-step? No, no, no. I do not have time for this." Dr. Hamzawi be-lieved that neoliberal globalization has taught people like his son that "success has to be quick."[204]

Accounts of an economically driven crisis of social relations and moral erosion are particularly prevalent among members of the educated Egyptian urban middle class who came of age under Nasserist nationalism. According to Dr. Awatef Abd El Rahman of Cairo University, "All has been privatized in the Egyptian economy. This had a very . . . negative impact on . . . social relation-ships generally. On relations between classes, within the family, and between individuals: neighborliness, collegiality, friendships. In the end, of course, all social values were impacted by globalization. . . . There is no more security, sincerity, or commitment to the nation."[205]

At the risk of stating the obvious, the Egyptian state does not constitute itself as in any way responsible for barriers to marriage. State accounts typically blame secret marriage on naive women participants, irresponsible men, "familial disintegration," and parenting failures, especially by fathers.[206] These familial deteriorations are understood to be partly caused by economic problems that have led many middle-class parents to migrate for work in wealthier countries and adult family members of all classes to work if they can. As a consequence, parental influence and monitoring of children are seen to be reduced in comparison to the influence of peers, television, and consumer values.[207] Some in Egypt contend, by contrast, that changes in family and sexual practices and values reflect resistance to the restrictions posed by families, hegemonic customs and values, and an authoritarian state that does little to provide for social needs. Mona Abaza argues that customary marriages on Egyptian university campuses are a way that young people resolve "the growing sexual tensions in a society that idolizes marriage and is rigid in conventions regarding the financial requirements of the institution. One may even speculate over the spread of *'urfi* marriages as a hidden protest of second-generation post-Islamist youths." In a context where "subversive ideologies" are lacking, Abaza argues that these relationships are "half-way solutions" that avoid direct confrontation with the "most powerful institution in Egypt: the eternal and omnipotent family."[208]

Young people I interviewed at Cairo University in 2003 and 2008 had a range of opinions regarding secret marriage and changes in marital and sexual practices more generally that were sometimes similar but usually stood in stark contrast to the opinions of most parents, professors, religious authorities, and state elites. Indeed, for the most part, they resented and distrusted formulaic ways of thinking and instruction about how to behave and what to feel from such adults.[209] Some linked sexual repression in the society with political, expressive, and intellectual repression (*kabt*), viewing these to be part of a package that young people face.[210] These students viewed Egyptian society to be morally and aspirationally deteriorating and directionless, were uncertain about their economic futures, and feared a social implosion. Students interviewed in 2008 illustrated such moral deterioration by discussing a late October 2006 mass sexual assault and harassment of women by young men who were unable to get into a sold-out showing of a recently released film starring the actress and dancer Dina in downtown Cairo.[211]

Some of the student participants in the May 2008 interview insisted that Egypt requires indigenously crafted "new social modes and new social habits," according to Ahmed, that rely on the country's intellectual and civilization traditions and "horizontally" integrates what is useful from other traditions rather than assuming any culture's practices to be superior or inferior. Among these new social modes is an easing of marriage customs.[212] A male student, Amin, shares that while dramatic cultural changes are occurring in Egypt, they appear to be unnatural and without an internal dynamism, "cutting and pasting." Rana contends that the opportunity for a uniquely Egyptian middle path—neither wholesale Western cultural importation in which one "adopts open sexual relationships" nor "holding on tight to customs and traditions and being judgmental toward people who make the other choice"—has disappeared. She believes this problem to be the result of the unwillingness of parents and elders to provide young people with social standards, to teach them to think, and to allow them to make choices on the basis of experience. Siba articulated her feelings in the following manner: "There is no social movement in our country. The place is tight and our dreams are being constricted in it."[213]

Although most were disapproving of customary marriages, one of the Egyptian woman students interviewed in 2003 hoped that such relationships will in the future be "considered a natural occurrence. [It challenges] the ideas of parents . . . that marriage needs *shabka*, dowry, an apartment, and the apartment has to have specific things. Participants in these relationships do it to be liberated from the traditional ideas of the family."[214] Most students interviewed in 2008 offered a positive gloss on secret relationships, viewing them as productive defiance of the family and part of what might be termed a "third way" that follows neither hegemonically "Western" nor "Egyptian" patterns. While ideologically diverse, including socially conservative, liberal, and radical students, these students seek more choices and opportunities to make decisions, including marital and sexual ones, and explore new possibilities for their futures rather than have imposed on them the dreams, values, and ideological frameworks of previous generations, although Habiba worries whether Egyptian society is ready for such freedom. The students actively debated the meaning of love in the interview and made clear that some of them and many of their friends are dating and sexually active, although not without ambivalence, since they are subject to the judgmental social gaze, which Rana termed *mabsūslahum*, a colloquialism implying being spied on or cast with the evil eye.[215]

The situation in the United Arab Emirates, where most natives are significantly wealthier than most Egyptians, should give pause to solely economic explanations for marital changes. In the UAE, family crisis is perceived to be caused by poor cultural schooling and deteriorated parent-child relationships, among other factors. Alienation among family members is attributed to material wealth, busyness and work outside the home by both parents, and the technological aspects of globalization, which have transformed a "conservative and private society" into one where with the click of a mouse any person in a household can connect with any idea or person in the world in the privacy of their bedrooms.[216] As Mawadi al-Rasheed contends about Arab Gulf societies more generally, "foreign domestic workers, who are placed at the heart of Gulf society, the family," are also understood as quintessential sources of family crisis and "cultural invasion."[217] From a "human resources" perspective, UAE elites prefer women citizens to remain in the labor market, to bolster the "Emirati-ness" of economy and government, rather than raise children full time. "National families" comprised of Emirati mothers and fathers who are actively involved in cultivating their children at the same time are seen as crucial sources of inoculation against social, cultural, and religious disintegration.

In December 2003, I attended parts of a two-day conference focused on Emirati youth that was sponsored by the Ajman women's association under the patronage of the emirate's ruler, Shaykh Humaid bin Rashid al-Nu'ami. Muhammad Darwish of the Dubai courts presented a paper arguing that the educational system in the UAE fulfills the economic needs of major corporations while ignoring cultural rearing, thus not preparing Emiratis for social life based on Islamic values.[218] His and other presentations at the conference illustrated the extent to which the schooling of appropriate national subjects is the focus of significant attention and resources. Dr. 'Abd al-Rahman Dhakir Hamid's paper stressed the importance of training young people to make "free" and yet responsible choices informed by Islamic moral and ethical foundations—so that religion is the primary source of knowledge and its fundamentals structure day-to-day life, producing modern and culturally authentic subjects. He criticized parents who have failed in this regard, allowing "an opportunity for [Islam's] alternatives ['the swamp of materialistic culture'] to take its place in this world." He admonished parents and teachers:

> We see youth, men and women who do not know how to practice their freedoms or choose from such freedoms because they have not been used to doing so since their childhood. There is no freedom in what they wear nor in their food and drink. . . . Nor is there freedom in their schools or universities. They do not even have freedom [to choose] their partners in life. We are then surprised after all of this and wonder: Where does this weakness in our generation come from?[219]

At the same conference, Dr. Muhammad Mahmud al-Shaykh presented a paper arguing that Arab youth have low self-esteem because of their "inability to express [their] opinions and problems," their "need to release the sexual instinct and suffering from having it pent up," lack of employment opportunities, not completing schooling or higher education, and "dictatorial" parenting.[220] Other parenting problems, apparently specific to the Emirates, include "extra pampering," absent father figures, familial disintegration,[221] and too much leisure time that leads to "misuse of free time, car racing and reckless driving, and possessing expensive things in an attempt of self-glorification. Add to that the flight from reality through drug use, provocative movies, and . . . excessive consumption, specifically by females." Al-Shaykh's paper recommends "meaningful media and entertainment programs focused on youth" to inculcate self-esteem and "love of work"; school curriculums that encourage students to "master learning" rather than receive it; university educations that focus on "economic and social development"; and freedom of expression.[222] The freedom of expression being advanced in these papers and in some interviews is carefully delimited to the parent-child relationship and schooling and silent on the larger context of state bans on free political expression, criticism of rulers and state elites, free political association, and independent political organizing.

Ms. Hisa al-Diqqi, a parent and executive committee member of the Women's Renaissance Association in Dubai, contends that parents today are more concerned with providing "everything for the child" to the detriment of "warm relationships." She attributes this to "busyness": "Everyone is running. We are in the age of speed. . . . The person is exhausted, tired, to be honest."[223] When asked about the major problems facing "women, girls, the family," "family disintegration" was similarly the concern shared by Saliha Obaid Ghabish of the Shariqa Girls Clubs, who attributes this disintegration to a range of factors:

> The busyness of the father away from the home for long hours. There was a period when women did not work and so the family was more tied together. . . . The other external influences are what the media broadcast in terms of values that are inappropriate for us and inappropriate to strong family ties. . . . [C]hildren are currently affected by [bad] friends. . . . [In addition,] there are opportunities for interconnection [*tawāṣul*]. . . . [I]n each home, each room, you will find the Internet. The girl is sitting on her Internet and the boy is sitting on his Internet. . . . [T]he homes have become larger, villas, and [this] has created real isolation [among family members]. . . . Rather than having one television in the salon in

which everyone meets, now each person [has their own television]. . . . [T]he girl
does not tell her mother her problems. She tells it to her friend. . . . On the level
of girls, there are unfortunate things that are alien [*dakhīl*] to our society. Our
society is small but as a result of the entry of different nationalities from Asia and
from—and from many other countries—I say Asia because of the servants—this
has affected some of our social values. . . . A distance has occurred—a chasm
between the mother and the daughter. . . . [Y]ou will find very few mothers
walking with their daughters in the markets together. Currently you will find the
mother with her friends and the girl with her friends.[224]

.   .   .

Family life, sexual relations, and "private" or intimate experiences more broadly
are shaped and defined to different degrees by social factors whose impact cannot be compartmentalized. These factors include prevailing inequalities based
on gender, citizenship, wealth, ethnic, educational, age, and other differences;
hegemonic ideologies and discourses that naturalize and normalize such inequalities; and the regulations and requirements of markets and states. It should
be no surprise, then, that "family crisis" discourses in these societies reflect tensions, competing agendas, and conflicting desires. The crisis discourses include
concern that the UAE and Egypt are being "invaded" by values, ideas, and
products that threaten indigenous cultural systems, particularly with regard to
gender, family, and sexual relations. What are the perceived and real impacts
of consumerism and transnational circulations on sexual, family, and gender
practices and values?

3 Transnational "Invasions" and Emerging Selves and Desires

> *The markets and shopping malls of Abu Dhabi, Dubai and Sharjah, some of them marvels of modern architecture that also reflect a happy blend of Arab and Islamic traditions, offer visitors and residents alike a tax-free shoppers' paradise.*
>
> **Women in the UAE (1995)**

DESPITE THE CAREFREE AND INVITING MESSAGE in this passage from an annual report produced by the United Arab Emirates (UAE) government on the status of native women,[1] there is great cultural anxiety among elites about how the transnational flows of people, ideas, and products influence native sexual and marital practices, family life, and gender ideologies. These flows are understood by many to be Western invasions that have negative social and cultural consequences. Foreigners are a source of demographic and cultural unease given the large proportion of migrant workers who live among a small minority of native citizens. Many Emiratis are also concerned with the cultural impact of new communication technologies and media such as mobile phones, the Internet, and satellite television, which have facilitated consumerism and reconstituted desires and appetites. Surprising given the demographic, historical, and wealth differences between the two countries, concern about the invasion of values, products, and practices perceived to be foreign and their impact on family, sexuality, and gender are also widely apparent in Egypt.

Instead of focusing on the punitive power and direct control of modern states, the governmentality perspective considers rule to be largely accomplished through methods and techniques that shape individual values and desires, with the "teaching" undertaken by a variety of social entities. But states, families, schools, and religious authorities are not the only ones concerned with creating particular desires or shaping and directing individual conduct. The profit motive, for example, drives small business owners, corporations, and others to cultivate specific desires and influence daily practices.[2] These forces are national and transnational and their projects for human well-being are particularly effective if they can be linked with pleasure, power, and freedom. Not surprisingly, the conduct agendas of state and nonstate apparatuses and their experts often differ or even clash.[3]

But what of the people in the UAE and Egypt targeted for such cultivation projects by states, corporations, families, religious institutions, cultural or political networks, and so on? As one would expect, they respond in various and sometimes unintended ways. Although states and other forces hope to foster particular values and behaviors that serve their purposes, individuals also "cultivate 'their own' selves and identities" through a range of negotiations.[4] Thus, while governance techniques encourage the development of subjects who self-manage and regulate in directions sought by dominant institutions, Foucault addresses in later work the possibility of human agencies not premised on liberal humanism in which individuals actively constitute their selves similar to how one would fashion a "work of art."[5] Nikolas Rose takes these ideas of self-oriented cultivation in political and collective directions, arguing for attention to "counter-acts,"[6] which are never formed independently of dominant discourse and institutions and yet can be claims to forms of freedom.[7]

Among the problems for social conservatives in Egypt and the United Arab Emirates is that the technologies and mass culture sites of the neoliberal age, such as cell phones, Internet chatting, cafés, and malls, have provided spaces and circuits of privacy and freedom that undermine overly restrictive gender and sexual norms. That is, consumerism and individualism—the freedom to buy things, imitate practices, and be "oneself"—have helped to reconstitute indigenous desires in a manner that is threatening for some. This chapter presents evidence of emerging subjectivities, desires, and aesthetics of pleasure among people that challenge hegemonic sexual and gender norms and undermine family and state control. While women's desires and expectations are liberalizing, men and boys are understood to be changing in somewhat different ways. Social elites and many women believe that men have lost a sense of social and religious responsibility and balance in their relations with girls and women. Men and boys are also seen to be more easily enticed than women and girls by the technological, sensual, sexual, and consumer distractions of contemporary life.

These emerging desires and sensibilities with respect to marriage, sexuality, and gender are often attributed to the impact of outside forces in both countries. But these changes, I argue, are structured by both transnational and indigenous values and repertoires of practice.[8] That is, the discourse of invasion, often totalizing, underrates the complexity of the national or "domestic" sphere. This domestic context includes status hierarchies based on family, ethnicity, religion, and wealth; gender, citizenship, and class inequalities; and multiple traditions with respect to marriage and sexuality. These factors interact dynamically with transnational processes, including consumer capitalism, the explosion of entertainment and news through satellite television, and the surge of Islam as a basis for modern identity and personal fulfillment. While their mechanisms for constituting and fulfilling desire differ, global consumerist and transnational Islamic projects are similar in their encouragement of individuated (or individualistic) desiring subjects who often challenge the corporatist interests of traditional families and undemocratic states in the region.

The prominent responses in the region typically understand such transformations in people's values and desires in disintegration terms and often call for a "return" to the authentic and indigenous. This authenticist discourse is problematic and the chapter draws attention to the complex workings of agency and the potential openings offered by consumerism and individualism to restrictive understandings of sexuality and family life. The fact that consumerism and individualism offer the potential of certain freedoms and agencies does not, however, efface what Michael Watts terms "the terrible realities of unprecedented global economic inequality," "the crude violence of twenty-first century empire,"[9] or the erasure of local values and forms of life by cultural imperialism. Globalization, after all, describes the expansionist, exploitative, opportunistic, and privatizing impulses of capitalism as a form of economic organization.[10] That is, the hybridities and freedoms made possible by contemporary transnational consumerism should be recognized as attached to a "Marxian leg of capitalist exploitation and the Weberian (and Habermasian) leg of the colonisation of the lifeworld by monetisation, rationalisation, calculation and bureaucratisation."[11] Rather than understanding these changes as wholly exploitative/subordinating or liberating, they should be recognized as having paradoxical effects on variously situated individuals and groups and examined in their impact on a case-by-case basis.

Circuits and Spaces of Consumption and Freedom in Neoliberal Globalization

> *Consumption technologies, together with other narrative forms [such as soap operas, music, and so on] . . . establish a plurality of pedagogies for living a life that is both pleasurable and respectable, both personally unique and socially normal. They offer new ways for individuals to narrativize their lives, new ethics and techniques for living which do not set self-gratification and civility in opposition—as in the ethical codes of the puritan sects that Weber considered so important in the early moments of capitalism—but align them in a virtuous liaison of happiness and profit.[12]*

Mobile phones and other informational technologies have increased opportunities to communicate privately and dramatically expanded access to ideas, information, and potential friends and sexual partners in the Middle East and North Africa, as they have in many other parts of the world.[13] Similarly, the mass culture spaces of late neoliberal globalization, such as modern cafés and malls, have created new opportunities for private socializing, unsupervised gender mixing outside of family circles, and virtual and nonvirtual romantic or lustful trysts. As indicated in the passage by Nikolas Rose, these ever-proliferating novel forms allow people to live their lives in ways that make them happy while at the same time leading to profits for merchants and entrepreneurs. These products, mediums, and spaces are also the instruments through which people are further inserted—differently, based on class, gender, race-ethnicity, and so on—into the circuits of capitalist consumption.

Mobile telephones are integrated into the daily habits of city residents in the UAE and Egypt and are important instruments of communication that are difficult for parents and others to control. As a rare mobile phone user who does not text message in the United States, it was impossible to function with only land lines, and I purchased a cell phone upon arrival in 2003, using prepaid plans in each country. People of all ages expect to finalize the time and location details of a meeting in transit using a mobile phone rather than in advance, and most used mobile phones to text message rather than communicate by voice (it is cheaper). During a field visit to Cairo in 2008, cell phones were even more ubiquitous, and I learned to send elaborate text messages. This technology is crucial as an unregulated medium of communication in the lives of millions of Egyptians, where personal computer use and Internet access are not as widespread as they are in the UAE. This lesson was reinforced when despite the fact that I lived on the campus of Cairo University during a 2008 fieldtrip, I had to daily plan how to gain wireless access for my laptop somewhere else.

Mona Abaza contends that in Egypt the "relatively reasonable price of the device means that 'everybody' can carry a mobile. . . . Those who resist it are today stigmatized as 'odd.'"[14]

In one of my earliest field interviews in the UAE, I met Muhammad 'Abdel Rahim of Dubai, who quickly taught me the extent to which technological circuits matter in any discussion of sexuality and marriage. This religiously conservative man, in his late twenties, met his fiancé from another emirate on the Internet. He listed the most important Web sites that young people use to hook up;[15] taught me the text messaging symbols used for Arabic letters that do not transliterate well into English; and explained the *tarqīm* method of acquiring a "girl's phone number" in a sex-segregated society: exchanging the numbers on papers tossed through the windows of moving vehicles (almost always driven by foreigners), a trick "guys learn when they are fourteen." He said that most Emirati women receive a cell phone as a gift by the time they begin university and are actively involved in Internet forums.[16] He assured me that parents have little control over the unauthorized ways their children use this technology,[17] and faculty members at women's universities report that they ambivalently implement regulations, the result of parental pressure, that ban student use of cell phones on campus. Even before the development and proliferation of mobile phones, the two "most visible problems" reported by Emirati women interviewed by Maha Khatib in the early 1990s were the influence of "maids and servants" on children's knowledge of Arabic and Islamic identity and the "telephone problem." The latter phenomenon described Emiratis who spent long periods talking to a member of the other gender, usually not someone they knew in another way. On gender-segregated university campuses, where telephones were not allowed in women's dormitory rooms, students were regularly observed spending "hours using the few public phones on campus," which always had long "queues" because some used them daily in this manner.[18]

Sa'id Harib captures the recognition and concern among many in the UAE and Egypt that imported technologies are not discrete in their impact but constitute subjectivities, or, in his words, bring with them "methods for a total life":

> Many state that we can import technology without importing the cultural and intellectual values that the societies producing these technologies believe in. But is this really possible in practical terms? It seems to me that it is difficult to a large extent to disconnect between the two sides, to take one of them and leave the other completely. Cars, cell phones, tourist trips to other parts of the world,

and videocassettes are not only technological steps forward, they also include
with them their specific culture, values, and even particular philosophy. So
these advanced technologies are not only devices or materials for consumption,
but methods for a total life. And from here it was inevitable that these methods
would have their impact on us, and it becomes difficult to determine the line between the results of the technology and the values of the society that exports it.[19]

While supporters of neoliberal globalization typically highlight increased
transnational interdependence and cultural sharing, they often ignore its destructive outcomes, including exploitation of people and nature, and extermi-
nation of cultural products that cannot resist powerful onslaughts.[20] Frederic
Jameson argues that the "communicational" aspects of globalization include
a "message" that culturally endorses capitalist consumerism (rather than citizenship or class politics) as a global identity with attendant practices;[21] thus,
the communication and cultural sharing enabled by globalization rarely occurs unmediated by corporate power. Nevertheless, these less regulated and
multiple circuits have also permitted the much less fettered movement of information and ideas, facilitating direct and private communication and social
connections that bypass or subvert the controls of states and families. Similarly,
Mayfair Mei-hui Yang found that in late twentieth-century Shanghai, privatized
media forms challenge state control and secrecy and decentralize information
sources.[22] Yang recognizes, however, that such freedoms are "always a prelude
to a new insertion into another mode of power."[23]

Abaza takes an optimistic view of neoliberal mass culture in Egypt, arguing
that it increases choice among classes and groups that have had limited options
and facilitates the "flowering of a new hybrid culture." Given these changes, she
cautions against viewing leftist intellectuals and activists who argue for more
globally just economic relations as necessarily "anti-globalizers."[24] But Abaza
also chides Arab leftist intellectuals as yearning for a "golden past" of class inequality when they criticize "conspicuous consumption" and poor taste among
new Egyptian consumers, viewing these as fearful elite responses to "social
mobility and class transformation due to *infitāh* policies and [rural to urban]
migration."[25] She contends that among the "paradox[es]" of these liberalizing
policies "is that for the first time in history peasants acquired passports and
traveled," presumably as migrant laborers, which loosened feudal labor relations.[26] While accepting that neoliberalism has "increase[d] class cleavages,"
Abaza believes that the "mass culture" encouraged by neoliberalism "simulates

a semblance of democratizing tastes that can blur the effects of class and economic disparities."[27]

Abaza contrasts "an older notion of cosmopolitanism" that was limited to a small elite against the more widely available fruits of globalization, including the bowling lanes, discotheques, "cinemas, atriums and passages" in Egyptian shopping malls that have been particularly attractive spaces for women and young people to "flaneur," browse, flirt, make out, and socialize.[28] Similarly, she demonstrates how the clean public spaces provided by mixed-gender coffee shops serving lattes, cappuccinos, sandwiches, and desserts but not alcohol (such as Cilantro, Tabasco, Beano's, and so on) have become "magnets for youth."[29] Anouk de Konig also found that these "up-market coffee shops," which have been established in affluent sections of Cairo since the late 1990s, have become essential to the daily routines of "upper-middle-class friends and acquaintances."[30] These leisure spaces deliberately evoke "global connections and aspirations" not only in the wireless access they provide to customers, but also in their "jazzy" ambiance, the prominence of English on their walls and menus, and their non-Egyptian drink and food items.[31]

In an argument that is unconvincing in its universalist emancipatory claims, Abaza contends that working-class youth can use consumerism to "express protest" or simply be "elevated" in opportunities to stroll "in clean, modern and air-conditioned spaces."[32] While it is true that artificially cooled spaces are heavenly on hot days in Cairo, purchasing anything in them is expensive if one is poor. This point was underlined by the working-class men employed at one of the modern coffee shops with wireless access who advised me where to go a few blocks away to buy a hot Egyptian lunch or dinner at less than one-sixth of the price paid in their place of employment for a salad, sandwich, or specialty coffee. When I asked for such an eatery in another Cairo neighborhood, I was directed by men Egyptian police officers, workers, and small business owners to a well-known place they said was in a modern shopping mall (a landmark), but upon arriving, the security guards in the mall directed me to a small to-go restaurant that was outside the mall about a block away. Such restaurants and eateries do a brisk business with Egyptians of all class backgrounds, but their customers are more reflective of the poorer and working-class sectors of society than are the modern coffee shops and mall spaces.

One can see both the limits and usefulness of Abaza's statement that poor and working-class young men and women "in these walled off, exclusive spaces . . . are offered a simulation and an elevation (through dress), a feeling that they can participate in a better world, even if it is merely window shopping."[33] While elevation through window shopping is possible, it is also conceivable that endemic class inequality can produce anger and frustration among those who can only afford to window shop. It is also true, however, that clientele in the more popular (sha'bī) eating spaces are more likely to be in family groups or men, limiting their appeal to young people who socialize in mixed-gender groups and girls and women unaccompanied by relatives.[34] Konig found that contemporary coffee shops are the sole spaces where upper-middle-class Egyptian women (and, I would add, teenage girls of more modest means) can have "a social life outside of the family." On Thursday nights, "some coffee shops become as crowded as popular bars in Western cities on Saturday night. *Shilal* [friend groups or posses] of young people meet, show off the latest fashions, and engage in a low-key flirting. Within upper-middle-class circles, coffee shops have by and large succeeded in introducing a First-World feel, while avoiding more damning associations with immoral Western night-time leisure."[35]

Communication technologies have certainly facilitated less family control over sociality. Similarly, mass culture spaces such as modern cafés and malls have provided avenues to transgress status hierarchies and gender restrictions. These choices and freedoms are for the most part only available in substantive and material terms to those with the disposable income to enjoy them. Moreover, they encourage and depend on *individual* consumer subjectivities that are consistent with capitalist logic.

"Invasions" of Individualism, Consumerism, Love, and the "Perverse"

In Egypt and the UAE, cell phones, satellite television, and the Internet have provided circuits for the influx and circulation of ideas and values often perceived to be foreign and invasive. Such mediums and the mass culture encouraged by capitalism more generally are understood to encourage practices and values that often challenge not only precepts advanced by state officials, but those esteemed by most intellectuals, parents, and religious authorities, including commitment to family corporatism, communal orientations, and modest dress and sexual behavior in public. Concern with the disintegrative and "contaminating" impact of transnational media entertainment on the "less [powerful] culture" is widespread.[36] How does one participate in economic and scientific globalization while rejecting "cultural globalization," which is seen to "abolish" "individual traits [of nations, cultures, religions] and attributes," in the words of Yusef al-Qaradhawi, the influential Egyptian Sunni cleric and scholar who lives in the Gulf?[37] Especially feared are values and practices associated with the "West," such as out-of-wedlock childbirth, cohabitation without marriage, and sexual "deviation" or "perversion" (*inḥirāf* or *shudhūdh*), which might become normalized as "free choice" and "unconventionality," according to Dr. 'Abd al-Rahman Dhakir Hamid.[38] In the caricatured understanding held by some about Western societies, parentless children, abortions, unwed pregnant teens, prostitution, rape, murder, theft, pornography, suicide, and lesbian marriages are widespread and threaten the Arab-Muslim nation that does not take steps to reinforce the boundaries of what is culturally acceptable.

One of the values seen to undermine family life is individualism. According to the UAE Women's Federation annual report: "In [a] world where the progress of communication has created an ever-shrinking 'global village,' the Government and the Women's Federation feel the need to introduce the young to their own national cultures in such a way that they can resist the influence of other, greatly differing, cultures seen on television." The affiliated Girl Guides Society focuses on this sort of schooling.[39] Ms. Saliha 'Obayd Ghabish, the cultural affairs manager of the Shariqa Girls Clubs in the UAE, sees increased "selfishness" and "individualism" (*tafarrud*) among family members.[40] This is remarkably similar to the language used by the Egyptian Dr. Layla 'Abd al-Jawad on a widely watched December 2004 segment of an al-Jazeera program: "Individual values have become dominant and people seek their own personal gain and well-being."[41] Media invasions, according to 'Abd al-Jawad and Maha al-Kurdi, have led to "exposure to several Western cultures most of which are characterized by degeneracy, an individualistic spirit, and lack of interest in the family." In turn, this has made it difficult for Egyptian culture "to impose effective restraints on individual behavior," leading to "religious and moral value" decline among young people, illustrated by those who engage in secret marriage.[42]

Mr. Darwish of the Dubai courts points out the challenges he perceives television, the Internet, and other transnational media sources pose to the Emirati marriage relationship:

> Whoever watches the television serials, or the Mexican films especially, will find that the marital relationship is based on love, betrayal [*ghadr*], and treachery. So we have begun to notice a generation that considers that this is how marital life is. Before, we had a religious authority for family culture, we have a curriculum, we have a Qur'an, we have the sunna of the Prophet [pbuh]. . . . [Now] we have

the problem I call family illiteracy, ignorance. . . . At the first problem, the girl leaves to her family to resolve them. Where did she learn this? She learned it from Egyptian films. Really. Are these correct methods? . . . Some of the wrong actions include hitting. "Who told you to hit her?" . . . He'll say, "By God, this is what I've seen." Media sources have a big impact. One of our magazines wrote an article targeted at women, titled "18 Ways for You to Infuriate Your Husband." . . . Thirty years ago, the young man took his culture from his father, mother, neighbors, a clean environment, it was still Bedouin. It had clarity. Today, where does he take his culture from? Today, he is sitting in his bedroom, opens the biggest sex Web sites . . . and he knows everything. . . . [M]ost young people do not open positive sites on the Internet, unfortunately. . . . [They open] either sex or violence.[43]

Ms. Ghabish of Shariqa emphasizes the particularly negative impact of television on girls. This medium, she argues, provides girls with gendered images and practices to imitate and products to purchase:

Issues that are foreign to our society have been introduced, especially [from] broadcast media. . . . I feel when I watch television . . . that it is really targeting girls more than any other sector, whether in terms of clothing, movement, anything. So you will find that the girl, for example, likes to wear— . . . for us [things that] we feel are not normal. . . . [T]here are some girls who take from the television what we can call the peel, not the depth. . . . When they see the woman announcer who looks like I do not know what, and wearing whatever, girls immediately want to go to the market to dress like her—they want to imitate her . . . without awareness.[44]

Consumerism elicits concern in both countries, especially in its impact on family life. In an interview, Jamal al-Bah of the UAE Marriage Fund complains of the intrusion of foreign laborers, foreign values of consumerism, and a new willingness to be indebted: "Just as Asian, European laborers have invaded us from all over the world, their traditions have also invaded us. . . . Our society did not know these patterns of consumption. . . . Our homes and family desires were very modest. Today, our desires are big. There is a lot of work. The person builds a building and wishes for other buildings. . . . He remains indebted for everything. He builds two buildings, five buildings, and he remains indebted"[45]

The projection of hyper-consumption to outsiders is fascinating given that consumption practices are mediated by cultural milieu, access to wealth and credit, education, individual beliefs, and state policies. Native Emiratis have what could be termed precapitalist status systems related to familial and ethnic background that have combined with modern consumerism. Moreover, the signification of hyper-consumption as high status for many indigenous Emiratis can partly be explained by the investment policies and consumption practices of ruling elites. UAE development plans depend to a large degree on attracting foreigners to invest, shop, work, and vacation in the country, which requires the state to sink significant wealth into grand infrastructural, real estate, and architectural dreams. Underestimated in al-Bah's formulation then is the degree to which the desires and practices of citizens are impacted by such state-led consumption and development pursuits. Alternatively, Emirati elites may understand the consequences of such practices and policies and widely fear the degree and ease with which regular Emiratis are seduced by them.

Egyptian cultural anxieties about consumerism in late modernity differ, but only in some ways. For one thing, consumption is hegemonically (in the Gramscian sense) understood within a discursive framework that posits the values and practices of the educated middle-class to be under threat from and caught between the backwardness projected onto rural, poor, or very religious people, and the dissolution attributed to the wealthy and famous, who are seen to be hyper-consuming, Western-oriented, greedy, and leading licentious lives. A male student in the Faculty of Economics and Political Science at Cairo University captures this understanding: "We found that in Egypt, the middle class has begun to diminish—it is being annihilated. It is known that this class—people in political science know that this class is the pillar or foundation of any democratic system. This class is balanced in its behaviors and actions. Members defend each other and protect social stability." He contrasted such putatively middle-class values with those of "the oligarchy or elite group," who behave provocatively and exploitatively, and "the riffraff and common people—the people who are poor, who do not have—who have a particular value system." The middle class, he contended, are the majority, "caught puzzled in the middle. . . . They are trying to protect the balance between this and that but they cannot."[46]

Lila Abu-Lughod has richly demonstrated the dominance of urban intellectual representations that situate rural and poor people as ignorant and backward national subjects.[47] She finds that Egypt's largely secular nationalist television writers, artists, and producers have sought to "undermine . . . , on the one hand, the postnational identities of a cosmopolitan business elite who work within the framework of economic liberalization and, on the other, Islamists," who are seen as undermining the secular nation-state in their support for a transnational Islamic *umma*.[48] The challenge faced by these media intellectuals, like the one shared by many of the professionals I interviewed in Egypt, is how to sustain "traditions and customs" by avoiding both the "excesses of Islamism in the popular classes and the rootlessness of the westernized cosmopolitan upper classes."[49] Abu-Lughod alternatively frames this middle-class dilemma in neoliberal Egypt as how to "become modern without losing one's values and traditions."[50] The television channels she studied present contradictory messages, heavily promoting "capitalist marketing and mass commodity consumption" in commercials and demonstrating the beautiful things money can buy, even as programming carries messages that insist on "the immorality of money" and the "dangerous seductiveness of consumption."[51]

As in the UAE, Mona Abaza contends that whether they are leftists, Islamists, or nationalists, Egyptians assume that "consumerism is mainly imposed by an outside force" and condemn it as destructive.[52] For many Arab intellectuals, consumer culture is associated with Americanization and "the destruction of indigenous values and modes of living."[53] Some of these issues are illustrated in the gendered account for customary marriage offered by Riad Hamzawi, who attributes such relationships to changes in the "very constitution [*tarkibat*] [of young people] . . . their thinking, views, values." A young Egyptian man who sees "young women wearing clothing that is a little bit overboard," previously seen mostly in films, may wonder, "Why am I denying this to myself?" Hamzawi contends that "young men are being excessively provoked and cannot endure governed by their values, upbringing, and culture." He blames this "misfortune" on Egyptians taking from Americans the "values of consumerism"— wearing, like his young female relatives, "tight pants" and blouses that show the belly, absorbing U.S. cinematic imaginaries, drinking "7-Up," and eating hamburgers—rather than "the values of production." He sees these practices to be the result of "the system" in Egypt rather than a cultural predisposition toward imitation and against work.[54]

New cultural formations and subjectivities are indeed being appealed to and constituted in the region. I spent significant time in Cairo cafés, including Cilantro, Costa, and Beano's in mid-2008. The values and messages expressed in their decor, designed to appeal to foreign tourists as well as the largely young and middle-class Egyptian clientele, are cosmopolitan notions of culture, romantic love, expression, and personhood that are made available to those who can afford the food and drink items. The cafés also provide wireless access and pleasant air-conditioned settings decorated in earth and desert colors to schedule casual meetings. Consumption is explicitly linked with life, selfhood, romance, and friendship. The jazzy wallpaper on Cilantro café walls is patterned with drawn flowers in a 1960s peace-and-love style and printed with handwritten English words commanding customers to "express" and "be" themselves. The prints include phrases such as "appetite for life" and dedicated and signed passages of love and friendship. The messages are appealing, pervasively emotional, and interpellate customers as desiring individual subjects.

Regional pundits often allege that marriage is being destabilized by Western notions of love and romance, which are ubiquitous not only on the walls of Cairo cafés but also in Arabic music videos and other entertainment programming throughout the region. In a satellite television program broadcast on al-Jazeera in December 2004, Najat al-Qawas, a guest from Yemen, attributed secret marriages to "satellite dishes" and the Internet portraying "the image of prince charming. The girl grows up, eighth grade, high school, or university age, with weird ideas. As soon as a man from abroad comes and gives her money or furnishes an apartment, she agrees to marry him in a customary marriage."[55] Such explanations trivialize women's changing concerns, motivations, and desires with respect to marriage and sexuality, whether or not they engage in secret relationships. Moreover, such accounts do not address a hegemonic gender structure that conceives of women as always dependent on men and privileges men in most social realms. Dreams of "prince charming" in such a sociocultural context, I contend, make perfect sense.

A recorded lecture by the Saudi Shaykh Ibrahim Ibn-'Abd-illah al-Duwaysh, titled "The Sea of Love," is distributed to every couple who registers their marriage in the Dubai Courts Department. The lecture instructs Muslims to aim for "affection" and "mercy" rather than love and romance. The desire for romance is seen by him and other conservative elites as a foreign import that cannot sustain a marriage over time. Nevertheless, on the same tape, Shaykh al-Duwaysh ultimately advises that loving, erotic, romantic, caring, and companionate relations between a husband and wife are crucial for avoiding divorce.[56] While the desire for love and romance is usually attributed to girls and women, an Emirati woman I interviewed believed that some native men marry non-Emirati women because they too desire emotional connections, romance, to "fall in love." She continued, "Maybe we [in the Emirates] do not speak too much about this topic on the consideration that each person must place the general interests over his personal interests. However, I consider all of these things to be destiny, fated."[57]

Music videos produce exceptional pleasure and anxiety as mediums of sex culture and sources of provocation. While the most alarming for the guardians of sexual propriety are videos produced in the region, 'Abd al-Jawad and al-Kurdi of Egypt criticize a "cultural invasion" that has brought in a "sex culture broadcast through satellite television, videotapes, or the Internet" that "stimulat[es] the sensual instincts" of young people.[58] At least in Egypt, such judgments predate the 1990s and earlier condemned the messages of Western-produced television soap operas and movies and worried about their impact on youth.[59] Complaints of religious and moral laxity and imitation of foreign sexual practices are regularly lodged against Arab actresses and other female entertainers.[60] A friend jokingly shared with me the anecdote that the Lebanese satellite channel LBC is referred to by some Sudanese as "*ilbasī*," which conflates "LBC" with the Arabic command "get dressed" (feminine), a sentiment similar to that shared with me by a maternal aunt a few years ago while we were watching the television she had turned on in her modest home in a Jordanian village. For my aunt, the bare shoulders, neck, and cleavage of the young woman performer in the music video was the same as her being "naked." Many Arabic music videos today are more risqué, with Lebanese productions earning a special position in this regard. Said Sadek writes that in the video-clip industry, "Lebanese female singers are the most provocative, stylish, and innovative. Feeling the heat of the competition, the moralistic Egyptian press launched a campaign against video clips accusing them of exploiting the sexuality of female singers and the chorus." Egyptian journalists call these videos "porno-clips," and the state at one point banned the Tunisian singer Najla "from entering Egypt to shoot a video clip in which she was to appear in her underwear trying to excite a horse."[61] Young Egyptians, who are significant consumers of these media products, entered the fray as critics as well. Sadek, citing a newspaper article by Usama Muhammad, writes of a March 2005 demonstration in which "almost three thousand students at Alexandria University of all political stripes . . . demonstrated against nudity in video clips." The leaflet circulated to mobilize the students stated that "students had 'had enough.' They condemned the music channels and described the video-clip singers as waging a war against youth. Their banners carried slogans like 'No to stimulating the desires of the youth,' and '*Kifāya* [enough] to Rotana and Melody,'" two music and entertainment television channels.[62] The students distributed alternative chaste video clips, performed a drama "reflecting the suffering of young men who are excited and frustrated by watching these video clips," and issued a newsletter condemning the stations that promoted the clips.[63]

As indicated by this fracas, while the West is often claimed to be the source of invasion, it appears that the more insidious exporters in their effective impact on the lifestyles and subjectivities of Emiratis and Egyptians include Mexico, Lebanon, India, Tunisia, Egypt (for Emiratis), the Philippines, and Gulf countries (for Egyptians). This brings to mind Farha Ghannam's very important point that in working-class neighborhoods in Egypt, "social imagination is not only, or primarily, shaped by American movies . . . and TV programs. It is also and perhaps more strongly shaped by Indian films, Lebanese singers, Brazilian soccer players, and Algerian *rai* music. . . . [O]il-producing countries in particular have a major role in stimulating desires and fulfilling dreams." Ghannam is especially interested in the thousands of working-class Egyptian men whose desires, including for consumer goods, have been impacted by their often years-long migrant work experiences in wealthier Gulf countries.[64] I argue that references to "foreign" or "Western" influences allow acceptable ways to discuss uncomfortable changes that challenge hegemonic cultural practices and values in both societies and the region more generally. The dominant interpretations of consumerism and changes in sexual and other values as the results of invasion reinforces a static understanding of culture in Egypt and the United Arab Emirates and misrecognizes the degree to which transnational processes interact with local values and hierarchies. While certain sexual behaviors, for example the purported widespread viewing of pornography on the Internet, are attributed to mimicry of Western values, sexual polymorphousness has its own histories in the region and men have widely benefitted from sexual and gender double standards, socially, culturally, and legally. Understanding contemporary practices to be the result of foreign incursion also elides the degree to which so many Egyptians and Emiratis actively participate in, produce, and consume these formations.

Appetites and Individual Sensibilities

Narratives of heightened sexual need and uncontrollable sensual "instincts" (*gharā'iz ḥassīyya*) are pervasive in explanations of nonmarital sexual activity and secret or polygamous marriages and are often attributed to increased stimulations and provocations. Capitalist expansion plainly requires the ongoing production of appetites, depends on notions of individuality and choice, and helps to constitute such subjectivities. But individualism and choice are also crucial to modern Islamic formations and identities rather than oppositional to them. In addition, both trends—global neoliberal capitalism and transnational Islamism—produce desires that often challenge family, state, and religious corporatist logic.

Many Egyptians and Emiratis express a belief that barriers to regular marriage require creativity—within perceived Islamic limits that are widely contested—in fulfilling sexual desire. Despite disagreement on what is morally acceptable behavior, there is widespread agreement that being unable to satisfy such needs and desires is a source of frustration and social crisis. Men and women often evoke "Islamic" conceptualizations of sexual desire and satisfaction as natural and good. They contend that fulfillment of such physical needs is imperative but often delayed or not occurring within the acceptable framework of heterosexual marriage. Concern with the anarchic potential of especially male sexual urges and desires that are not assuaged, constructed as powerful and easily tempted, are enduring in Islamic cultures. This concern may help explain Islamic legal acceptance of polygyny and the extensive regulation of male-female contact that developed over time in Muslim societies.[65] Oussama Arabi highlights a competing Muslim sexual ethic to "lawful male sexual indulgence" that expects men to sublimate "the libidinal impulse in moral achievement and an ascetic life."[66] As indicated in Arabi's discussion, male scholars of Islam often simply ignore women's sexual subjectivities when analyzing Muslim sexualities, thus regularly reconstituting the centrality of men's embodied desires. In such formulations, women's sexual and gendered behaviors are either invisible or relevant only in relation to their potential impact on men and boys. An Emirati marriage counselor shared a dominant gendered perspective on sexuality in her explanation of why women must avoid tempting men: "The man is like a dog, if you will excuse me. If you give him some water, he will lick it." Such an essentialist framework views men as unable to control their sexual urges and helps to explain the hyper-gender segregation that exists in parts of the Arabian Peninsula. Less recognized is the degree to which these understandings and gender segregation, whether articulated through social norms or state law, *constitute* rather than simply reflect gender relations and desire by heightening the sexualization of a variety of spaces so that the presence and sartorial practices of sexed and gendered body are always relevant.

I began to consider that sexual desire and bodily awareness might be rising rather than assuming the narratives of sexual instinct to be indicative of Muslim openness to sexuality during an interview with an Egyptian physician of middle-class background who is also a feminist activist. Dr. Nadia al-ʿAfify mentioned that some young people, even in high schools in rural areas, were having sexual relations in customary marriage contracts. Reflecting on some of her hospital experiences with patients, al-ʿAfify believed that bodily and sexual self-awareness had heightened among Egyptian young people in response to a range of factors:

> The boys and girls . . . are exposed early to the idea of knowing their bodies; it possibly differs from my generation. We were not—this is different. They feel [sexual] need and the exit for this is ʿurfi marriage. . . . They get married and mutually realize their needs. . . . Today, young people at a very young age are feeling these physical desires and there is nothing distracting or correcting them. Meaning, there are no trips or open relationships, no—in our time, we were students, we were political and had many interests. We had dreams for the future. Today, there is no future. There are no dreams and there is no joyous present. . . . Among higher-class children, even playing has become about attainment [of some goal] . . . about competition, grades, and scores. . . . And for the lower classes, of course, there are no opportunities for work, there is no dream, and schooling is very bad. . . . You open the Internet and bring up sites to show you erotic things; or you see it on television or the [satellite] dish. All of this together has made people focus on physical need. They are discovering it early and have found a solution for it. Outside [of Egypt] of course this occurred in a way that is not hidden; sexual relations are allowed from an early age. But we made it a double standard, in our way. . . . We do what we want in secret and we say to the world what pleases the society.[67]

Al-ʿAfify cautioned against uniformly constructing customary marriages as prostitution, since money is not usually exchanged. Such a commercial understanding of the sexual exchange, she argues, ignores that women and girls have also "discovered that they have their bodies and desires. . . . So I think one can say that something has changed. And that thing is positive, this awareness of the body. But the phenomenon as a whole is negative because it is not occurring openly or accepted socially. . . . The women involved want the relationship. They want intimacy and sexual relations, all the aspects of a relationship, not only one thing."[68]

The idea that instincts and desires are being stimulated also came up during research in the UAE in response to questions about divorce rates, exogamy among national men, and new forms of sexual contracts. Dr. Al-ʿOlama, a professor of shari'a and law at UAE University, thought that secret relationships could partly be explained by the exposure of youth to sexually enticing images and people, and their developmental difficulty with considering long-term consequences: "He sees attractions in life, exciting things. He sees television and he has something normal, desire and such. The other side is that there is not the closure that existed before, you did not find the excitements [*muthīrāt*] you find today. And the girl also sees television, the world, and magazines . . . and she also is excited. She does not think about the obstacles. People in moments such as these [of sexual excitement] underestimate the difficulty of these questions."[69]

Some believe that the two-directional migration of Emirati men and the immigration and importation of non-Emirati men and women for work, as well as television programming from places such as Egypt and Lebanon, have produced local male appetites for more expressive feminine sexualities than has been considered appropriate. Ms. Hisa al-Diqqi, active in an Emirati women's association, thought that divorce rates are higher because of what is available to men on the "satellites" and the Internet and the increased inattentiveness of spouses to each other:

> The husband used to see no one but his wife. Mostly he focused on his wife, he would see her, and he would be amazed by her. Now he sees all types [of women] passing by him on the satellites. This has created temptation for the man and he is fragmented with the Internet, chatting. These things unfortunately opened arenas for other relationships. These relationships have also produced a situation in which husbands and wives no longer have the same major alliance that existed before. . . . [T]hey say that in this era the distances have decreased and people have become one village. But between the two spouses, unfortunately, the distances have become farther because they no longer care about each other as they did before. Their concerns have become very fragmented and focused toward the outside.[70]

An Emirati woman professor believed that young Emirati men prefer "Russians, Filipinas, Lebanese women" because the media portray Emirati women as "traditional, materially expensive," and troublesome to men, while other women are presented as "beautiful, graceful . . . and maybe [sexual] enjoyment with her will be better."[71] The same professor shared an interaction between male students in a classroom in which one student told another that foreign and citizen "girls" could not be compared since "the foreign girl is like a car with full options."[72] Dr. Ahmed al-Kubaysi, an Iraqi religious scholar and resident of the UAE, provides further evidence of these desires. He explains how wealth, migration, consumption, and "displays" on television in "globalization" have exposed men in the region to novel sexual possibilities and created new wants:

That's globalization. There is a new display, an amazing display. Algerian, Iraqi, Egyptian, Tunisian, English, and American women . . . covetous to be here. So in the end, Emirati women—it is true they have personality—[F.H.: And they are very beautiful.] They are very beautiful, elegant, and have strong personalities, like the Bedouin. . . . Among the Bedouin, the women are strong. . . . But more beautiful women have come, and, without embarrassment, they are more creative in [sexual] relations. The old Arab Gulf woman is shy—when she married, she hid herself from shyness. Today there are arts of sex advertised on television that say, "We have developed our clothing, our homes, and how we eat, [now] we have to develop sex." In honesty, we need a sexual culture—the Qur'an is full of sexual culture. How to deal with women and even how to have sexual intercourse. This creates desire. Why do you [women] let your husband find someone else? You should develop yourself. Is it just like your mother's age? "Sleep, come, enter, and go." God said in the Qur'an, "*wa qadimū ila nafūsikum—nisā'ukum harthun lakum*,"[73] . . . and "present yourselves." This means do not have sex as if you are donkeys. Frolic—frolic for one hour, two hours, frolic, and then complete the necessity. But to finish within two minutes and get up? That is animalistic. The country has become greatly wealthy. He who used to eat only a small piece of fish now eats 50 types. He had his old wife and was happy with her. Then the Algerian, Iraqi, Egyptian, and Syrian woman came—and he saw strange new types and this created a want [*nafs*].[74]

Emirati women stress the hypocrisy of local men and dominant cultural norms on issues of sexual expression, dress, and beauty. Emirati men often accept giving non-Emirati women "all their rights" and do not feel "ashamed," for example, to have their non-Emirati wives seen with them wearing makeup and faces uncovered in public, but often deem sexually expressive sartorial or bodily practices unacceptable if coming from national women.[75] Many Emirati women believe that challenging such norms would lead to their social exclusion.[76] I shared this idea with al-Kubaysi:

[F.H.: But women are afraid . . . —the price for them is high if they exit from any aspect of their culture. The young men would not accept that they . . . what they would accept, maybe, from an Egyptian or Algerian woman—]

Yes, yes, yes! I understand. Absolutely, absolutely. The entire Gulf has found it easy with the Egyptian or Algerian wife, but with the citizen woman, there will be the highest discipline because they consider her to be their honor, glory, and prestige and men would be criticized if they behaved otherwise.[77]

Al-Kubaysi thought women as much as men were impacted by the multiple sexual provocations of the modern world and were compelled to assuage their sexual desires. For example, in response to my question about why women engage in secret marriages if the relationships appear to primarily benefit men, he responded:

If marriage does not come to a woman, what does she do? How can you demand of a woman in this society, [given the] sexual films, newspapers, magazines—and it is a human necessity—sex is like food and drink—is it possible for one to live without food and drink? It is not possible. He must eat. It is the same thing here—a woman's sexual desire [*shahwat al-fajr*] and the stomach's appetite—the erotic appetite. This is why in Islam, before the establishment of [postcolonial state] laws, marriage was very easy—with anything the marriage could be licit . . . in the past it was very inexpensive.[78]

An Emirati woman professor, Ebtisam al-Kitbi, discusses sexual needs and secret marriage, but in starkly different terms; she points to a larger context that assumes women must be attached to and dependent on men, restricts women's sexual expression outside of marriage, and reduces women to their bodies in marriage:

If we are talking about why . . . women accept this kind of marriage—*al-misyār* is not hidden, but there are no rights for women, no maintenance, I analogize it to a man whose role is like that of a male bull (or stud) [*faḥl al-thawr*] who regularly visits to fertilize the female. . . . The problem, of course, [is that] Arab societies are not like Western societies. The woman does not have the unrestraint and openness in terms of bodily issues that men do. And in the end, she suffers more—I mean, there have to be limits on her—it is codified how she can enter into a bodily relationship—it has to be according to certain codes. So she is forced—there is also a view that if a woman is not married, she has no value. There is an Egyptian saying that [better for a woman to have]: "the shadow of a man and not the shadow of a wall" [*zillat rāgil wa lā zillat ḥayṭa*].[79] This shows how women are viewed to be inferior. [And when] a woman reaches the highest levels—marriage—the problem is that this is not seen as also about the thoughts of two people coming together. . . . The bodily aspect is of course part of marriage. . . . But marriage is reduced to the bodily issues.[80]

That embodied appetites have intensified, proliferated, or changed reminds us that capitalism depends on the ongoing manufacture of "desires . . . generated within the nonhuman machinery of consumption industries or even the psychological and biochemical mechanisms of addiction," in the words of Timothy Mitchell.[81] The production of consumer desires, argues Kamran Ali from his research on reproductive policies in Egypt, requires "new notions of individuality and selves" to develop among people in the world's potential markets.[82] Subjectivation projects accordingly "introduce or foster notions of individual choice and responsibility, risk aversion, and personal independence," orientations that can challenge family control but do not aim to develop "full-fledged, right-bearing citizens";[83] rather, the goal is to produce an "individualized sensibility that would diligently follow the advice of a benevolent state."[84] While Egyptian women are undeniably manipulated by state, population control, and medical authorities through management and regulation projects,[85] human agency assures that the outcomes will not always be those intended by experts and managers.[86]

Although notions of choice and individual desire often challenge the corporatist logic of family, national, and religious institutions, they are nevertheless consistent with prevailing forms of Muslim selfhood and identity that encourage individual ethical discernment. Thus the emerging Muslim subjectivities promoted by transnational Islamic political and cultural formations are paradoxically complementary to the consumerism advanced by global capitalism because they both highlight individual choice and agency and encourage striving for different forms of freedom. For example, the marital and sexual changes analyzed in this study are facilitated by, among other things, novel applications of Islamic practices in a new media context where interpretations of the licit are outnumbered only by the circuits (blogs, Web sites, satellite programs, and so forth) that examine, discuss, and distribute them. Standard academic, media, state, and religious explanations of changes in sexual subjectivities, desires, and practices, by contrast, often attribute them to *degraded* Islamic sensibilities produced by the effects of globalization and cultural "invasion."

Dale Eickelmann and James Piscatori have demonstrated that Muslim religious interpretation is increasingly unfettered by hierarchies of epistemological authority and is extraordinarily plural,[87] with many individuals and groups producing Islamic thought outside the hegemonic system of mutually recognized competing orthodoxies. States and religious authorities have found it impossible to "monopolize the tools of literate culture" given the expansion of mass education and the accessibility of new media and technologies.[88] As Gregory Starrett has written for Egypt, the fragmentation of religious author-ity has placed "the professional religious class" in a bind since "the thinner the tradition spreads itself over social, political and economic problems—the more useful the tradition is—the more control over it [religious elites] have to con-cede to others."[89] Indeed, Starrett contends that in Egypt, "one of the results of mass religious instruction [by the state] is . . . to prepare students just enough to question the authority of the keepers of the Muslim tradition, and to ques-tion their own exclusion from its manipulation."[90] Moreover, "each new attempt to correct mistaken ideas by furthering the penetration of Islamic discourse in public space creates an intensification of the conflict between parties seek-ing to control the discourse." This hegemony of Islamic discourse in cultural and ideological battles and its strategic deployments lead to confusion at lay levels, Starrett contends: "Not knowing what is true, everything becomes true, every possibility becomes a fact."[91] In addition to challenging the control of the "professional religious class," this phenomenon undermines state and familial authority. While she was not addressing sexual behavior or subjectivity, Andrea Rugh found that activists pursuing an "Islamic society" in late 1980s and early 1990s Egypt drew upon "a tendency already present . . . in which individuals operate more independently of their families than has been the custom in the past" given widespread economic, social, and political discontent, the failings of the state, and the financial inability of many parents to reward compliant children with "marriage, money, and employment."[92] She contends that Egyp-tians were increasingly looking for personal meaning, "authenticity," "cultural self-assertion," and even "political participation" within relationships that su-perseded kinship, and that Islamist movements of various kinds were able to offer "potential solutions to the ills that affect individual lives."[93] Islamic activ-ists directed "individuals toward loyalty to the . . . community of Muslim believ-ers," led by them of course,[94] and asked people "to exhibit a sense of individual conscience—shaped by the values and norms of the movement."[95]

In the current stage of global modernity, competing claims of Muslim reli-gious propriety and ethics additionally come from outside national communi-ties and from virtual rather than geographically anchored sources. While these virtual and transnational sources further multiply understandings of ethical Muslim life, by definition they are more porous in their influence over lives in comparison to the physically proximate sway of families, friends, neighbors, the workplace, local Islamist organizations, or the legal and police powers of the state. This lack of proximity facilitates hybrid, contradictory, and syncretic frameworks constituted by individuals and cohorts, rather than unified gestalts. Fragmentation and reconfiguration of discursive formations are hallmarks of cultural postmodernity, of course. The explosions of the Internet and satellite television have intensified these processes and assured that novel articulations are transmitted more quickly than ever before. Rather than neoliberal globalization posing a challenge to Muslim transnationalism or vice versa, these are mutually reinforcing phenomena, I contend, that require and are bolstered by individuation. In this sense, I disagree with Jameson's contention that thus far, the only seemingly viable challenge to consumerist ideology is religious fundamentalism, "which offers an alternative way of life."[96] While the goals of some religious fundamentalist ideologies may differ on their face from the consumerist orientations of late neoliberal capitalism, both fundamentalist and consumerist ideologies depend on the circuits and technologies of the information age, the production of desire, the promise to assuage them, and an understanding of individuals as willful, desiring selves who make choices.

Gendered Subjectivities, Desires, Tensions, and "Intrusions"

Men are more conservative than their countrywomen in their attitudes and desires regarding marriage and gender egalitarianism in most parts of the world, according to various waves of the World Values Survey, although the differences between men and women are greatest in most Middle East and sub-Saharan African countries.[97] Women in the MENA region are more liberal than men on a number of measures related to family life and gender relations, and I suspect a gender gap has increased in this regard, although my research does not systematically measure this phenomenon.[98] Critics frequently associate such changes with external or nonindigenous forces. Women and many men complain that boys and men are increasingly immature, unable to handle marital responsibilities, lacking in self-control, and easily distracted by a range of pleasures and stimulations, indicating that male subjectivities are shifting.

Especially in the UAE, men are blamed for many social ills related to marriage. Divorce rates, according to a male Emirati student, could probably be explained by men's "inattentiveness to religion and distraction with other things."[99] Mr. Darwish, who reviews thousands of cases as head of the Dubai

Courts Family Guidance and Reconciliation Department, offers in an interview that "we find situations of divorce that are a joke, including the man who divorces his wife because of the World Cup competitions; the one who divorces his wife [because] . . . she did not bring him a cup of tea."[100] Darwish typically sees native men who are spending most of their time and money on distractions outside the home and contends they are increasingly indifferent to sustaining a relationship, either remaining unmarried or divorcing with ease. He worries that men who do not economically maintain their families undermine the basis of male authority in the household:

> Entertainments are available that allow a man to avoid his marriage. Meaning [these young men think] . . . I have money, I can spend on myself. I have a job that occupies my time. . . . Meaning the spouse is considered like something—like a watch. Maybe I will wear it and maybe I will not. . . . If I need something [sex], I can do it by illicit available means. . . . Men address problems in the home in wrong ways: beating, cursing, and many other things have emerged and made the family relationship more tense. . . . The man has lost his guardianship over the family. For us, the man has management of the family on condition that he is capable of these responsibilities and he financially supports the home. Unfortunately, some men now do not spend on the family. The wife is the one who spends [on the household], so automatically there will be instability in the family because there will be conflict over leadership [tanāzuʿ al-qawwāma]. Meaning the woman wants to be in charge of the home because she is the one who is spending, and she has the right. And the man . . . wants to be in charge of the home but this is not possible. If you have two leaders of a ship, it will sink.[101]

While Darwish discusses a range of causal factors for divorce in the Emirates, he mostly blames husbands:

> Many of the problems we have are the result of the deviation of the husband. . . . The women somewhat, but the husband much more. He has established relations outside the framework of marital life. . . . The media encourages this. The corrupt channels encourage this. The nudity phenomena from outside the home encourage this. Some of the hotels, you have seen the situation. . . . So in the end you have [gender] mixing that is unnaturally present. They lack control in dress, in speaking. The presence of a large sector of unmarried girls who come from outside in order to work and do what they want. . . . The young man has begun to play outside, spend his money on girls.[102]

Similarly, Al-'Olama of UAE University understands native young men as pampered and not accustomed to making decisions or resolving problems in comparison to previous generations: "Before, by the time one reached fifteen years old, he could open a home, bear that responsibility. Today the boy—his father bears responsibility for him. He is unable to handle the responsibilities of a home."[103]

A late 2003 interview at Cairo University with a group of middle-class Egyptian women students, ranging between twenty-one and twenty-two years, provides a contrasting evaluation of young men focused on gendered and sexual double standards.[104] These women felt that too many of the men in their milieu were insecure in their personalities, undervalued women's worth, were untrustworthy, and applied differential standards with respect to sexual behavior. Most of the young men they knew preferred to marry women with no sexual experience, while favoring "open relations without marriage" with other women.[105] A student continued this conversational thread:

> Rima: If he goes out with a girl, it is impossible that he will marry her. . . . Meaning, he encourages her freedom in this respect, [he says]: "It is normal for us to sit together and talk to each other. . . . It is not shameful, become liberated." And when she says, "Well, let us get married," he says, "No, you should remain liberated." [peals of laughter from the students]
>
> Rania: They want to marry a girl, like Rima said, in her wrapping, who does not have experience.[106]

During group interviews with university students in Egypt in 2008, women more than men criticized gendered double standards with respect to sexual behavior and marriage. Luna castigated the young woman who quits medical training after five years in order to marry ("because she does not believe in change") as well as the "young man who twists and turns and [sexually] knew 500 girls, but when he marries, he wants the woman to be unpolished and untouched."[107] Egyptian men are divided between those desiring to marry educated or employed women who can contribute to maintaining the household and those who want to marry women who are younger or less educated than themselves, since such women are perceived to be more pliable. As in the Emirates, most men prefer women whose jobs do not require a lot of "coming and going" that may interfere with child care and household maintenance. A male graduate student at 'Ain Shams University noted that research he had been involved in found that "not to be married women" included journalists, airplane hostesses, and physicians; these were also his own preferences, which initiated a passionate exchange with women graduate students in the room, one of whom called his ideas "rigid" and indicative of "errors in the way he thinks."[108] The women also pointedly noted in the presence of three male peers that educated men's "ways of thinking" often do not "develop, do not change," whereas women moving from home to university find the latter to be a "whole other world" that is inevitably transformative in the experiences and knowledge that it provides.[109]

Many accounts construct men as increasingly cowardly in their sexual and marital practices. As Luna al-Shibil, host of the Al-Jazeera satellite television program "For Women Only," baldly put it in her introduction to a segment on secret marriage: "Can an uncertain man who is scared of announcing the marriage provide security and protection for the secret wife, or is divorce the best solution for her when the bomb explodes?"[110] To an international audience of millions watching this December 2004 program, a Yemeni woman guest similarly offered: "Some men are cowards in this arena, and I believe that a man who behaves in such a manner cannot protect the woman [he marries secretly]."[111] Such a narrative is part of a widespread belief that men marry secretly in polygamous relationships because they are afraid of the first wife.[112] Darwish of the Dubai courts believes that if a man cannot afford to marry plurally or divorce a wife, or if he fears the responses of a first wife and children, he should avoid such relationships:

> If I [as a man] have the strength, I should marry again. If I do not, I should not. . . . If I do not have the means to marry, I do not marry. If I have the means and want to, I must convince the first wife, or speak with her, and marry the second wife. The issue of secretiveness means that you are a fearful person—you are behaving like a thief. . . . And truly for the man to marry secretly while he is scared, it will end in failure. Because in the end the first wife will know. . . . We are a small society. . . . Why put myself in this situation? . . . A person marries to settle down. To open a home, to have children. . . . [T]he man who marries *misyār* [secret registered marriages, often polygamous] is usually psychologically stressed out. . . . [A]nd the second wife is also psychologically stressed. . . . Did I marry to relax or to create a police film?[113]

It is reasonable to conclude that most married Muslim men are unwilling to engage in polygamy openly because most first wives are unlikely to remain married to them. That is, secret polygamous marriages indicate that a critical mass of women believe they have social, economic, and legal options that allow them to leave a marriage when a husband marries plurally. Changes in women's subjectivities and desires with respect to gender and marriage are often underestimated in family crisis discourse. The most important worries of the middle-class Egyptian women students interviewed at Cairo University is what their job futures might hold and whether they would be able to successfully balance family and career lives. They sensed that their mothers, almost all of whom held jobs outside the home, were "suffering" under this dual burden in a context where "the man is free to focus on his work." The second most important concern the interviewed students report is whether the man they married would be oppressive. As one student states, "We feel that there is a bit of duality in male society here. In his talking he is one person, and after marriage he would be another personality. It is a scary thought." These women are especially dismissive of ideas that boys and men are more strong, smart, competent, responsible, or talented than girls and women, and that men and boys are "the backbone [ṣulb] of the home" or the protectors of girls and women. They believe their more restricted freedoms in comparison to boys, especially in mobility, are unfair and do not recognize "that the girl . . . has internal control."[114]

Ideological changes regarding gender relations are also apparent among Emirati women, impacted by their high rates of postsecondary education and the new economic possibilities that have emerged for them. Many recognize that men in their generation have yet to "become comfortable" with these changes, which they contend is the primary reason native men are marrying foreign women.[115] One late twenties professional single Emirati woman interviewed criticizes gendered double standards and describes how they limit the choices of women like her. While she has incentives to "not accept being the way the society wants me to be . . . because it would be bad for me," she believes Emirati men have little motivation to change since they have great advantages in an inequitable gender system:

> For the young man, all the laws, customs, and traditions of society benefit his rights in the end, so why should he rebel against them? He has nothing pushing him in this direction. It is easy for him to—to marry anyone from outside. But as a girl, I cannot marry anyone from outside. . . . [To give another example,] most of the young men who work in a [gender-]mixed environment do not marry a person from their work environment. They marry . . . through their family. . . .

He respects the girls he works with, he sees her as a role model, but he does not see her as a wife. . . . As a girl I cannot request that my mother engage a young man [on my behalf] like he requests of his mother. All the opportunities for me are with the people available in my society and my work environment. So if men fear this sort of thing, [if] they do not prefer to marry a person they know from the work environment, then the girls who work have lost their chances except through the pathway of parents. And if the girl thinks that she would not accept being tied to someone unless she knows him first, she has no opportunity. On the other hand, it is normal for the young man to marry someone he does not know—even if he divorces her, it is nothing.[116]

Ms. Saliha Ghabish of the Shariqa Girls Clubs notes that Emirati women are increasingly unwilling to accept unhappy marital situations or male dominance, although she is ambivalent as to whether this is a positive development and shares an essentialist, albeit typical, understanding of male-female relations:

In terms of divorce—by God, divorce among us is complicated. . . . First, [it occurs] when there is no understanding between the spouses, especially now that women work outside the home. For example, in the days of my mother, the days—the days of your mother, our grandmothers, even if the husband was strict with her, she would give in. She felt that this home is her kingdom and she had her children. . . . Women now have strong personalities. . . . There is no giving in because it is considered the same as being dominated. Of course she cannot give in with regard to her dignity, no. But she does not give in by letting some things go in order to resolve—because the man is a man and the woman is a woman. Meaning we cannot—these issues of equality and such confusions are all wrong. The increase of divorce is an indication that there is no—the woman has her essence [kiyān], characteristics, and specificities and men have their essence and specificities. The man always likes to be—that is his nature. And the woman is always more soft, emotional. But when the woman— . . . of course, this is my personal opinion—if she left her softness and specificities and became just like men [mithilha mithil al-riyāl],[117] . . . I think she is finished. Then there will be two men in the family. . . . This, of course, is when the woman is the source [of the problem in a divorce]. [At times] the man is the reason [for a divorce], when the man, for example, is neglecting his family and prefers staying up late with his male friends throughout the week rather than spending time with his wife. Sometimes the wife wishes she could go out with her husband to someplace nice, romantic, as they say, and he refuses, [saying] "no." She misses these things.[118]

Changes in women's gender ideologies and expectations have elicited bitter commentary from some men. Interestingly, such critics not only bemoan the perceived loss of male privilege but also sometimes insist that women today want to be *above* men. In a television segment on secret marriages, for example, an Emirati man notes that men involved in such relationships fear the responses of the first wife and children "who will turn against him because [polygamy] is something that eliminates understanding." He further complains, "In the past they [women] knew that it [polygamy] was sent down by God and he allowed it. The woman's rank is second to the man's because our societies are masculinist [*dhukūriyya*]. There used to be harmony in such cases because it was mandated by God. Now, it is the opposite, the woman has more power than the man and she controls him."[119]

A male caller to the same program, Ahmad Bhansi from Saudi Arabia, criticizes al-Jazeera and the media more generally from a similar perspective, arguing that they facilitate the circulation of "non-Islamic" ideas with respect to marriage: "Instead of throwing accusations around, why did you not discuss openly that one of the reasons for the frequent occurrence of this [secret] marriage is the participation of the media in firmly establishing non-Islamic ideas, culture, and beliefs with respect to the sanctity of this plural marriage? Polygamy is considered a crime and betrayal [in your representations]. . . . What is the solution if the man wants to keep his first marriage?"[120]

The narrative that follows similarly attributes changes in gender ideology among women to outsiders. The only married person among six Emirati men students interviewed as a group in December 2003 at al-'Ain University in Abu Dhabi began a conversational thread that points to a widespread belief among men that marriage problems are partly caused by Emirati women who have unreasonable ideas about gender relations and their status, often from non-indigenous sources:

> Student: Some of the external and internal women's media write—give women
> more than is their right. They make the woman feel that she should reach
> the summit of the pyramid and with this knowledge she makes herself
> superior to men. . . . A small example, Toujan Faisal [Jordanian activist and
> feminist]—
>
> F.H.: I know her, I mean I know about her—
>
> Student: At the end she said since a man marries more than one wife, why
> should not a woman—

F.H.: She is against a man marrying more than one wife. She does not want women to marry four men, but she is against men marrying more than one wife.

Male Professor: She wants equality. Why should men have this right and not women?

F.H.: But really, she is against it.

Male Professor: But really, if she goes to Tibet, she can do that. [Students laugh.]

F.H.: But she does not want to. What I want to ask you—when you say that these media give women more rights than they should have, do you mean they are trying to raise her—meaning, you are against equality.

Student: I am not against it.

Another Student: What is equality? In what respect? Give me—

F.H.: In a complicated way, meaning—equality—what it actually means must be determined between two people. But [it means] there would not be repression and there is open communication in terms of dialogue, that is equality. . . . There is deep, deep respect underneath it all. . . . It is not that each one gets half in everything.

Male Professor: It is present here. . . .

Student: Equality is present. . . . Within a family, if they were not in agreement, it would not work and the family would never be successful. On the contrary, there is understanding and such. But sometimes if the man notices that, for example, she wants to act as a man, he would ban her. At the same time, a woman sees it as something natural in this era to leave the home, drive a car, visit a female friend, go out and have supper with her female friends in a restaurant. . . .

Student: In addition, doctor, equality between a man and woman, and respect and cooperation, the work between them is essentially complementary. This one has a role and that one has a role. In the end they come up with complete results. This is the nature of the relationship. . . .

Student: I notice when we speak about this problem, [it is] . . . as if the young men are the largest problem. . . . But it is not the young men, okay? In the northern areas we notice that the problem is mostly with the girls, not the young men. There is a problem with provision of some of the things [for marriage]. In terms of the girls, there is a dominant belief, "freedom in one way or another." . . . I do not know what freedom [they want], but there must be freedom. Meaning, for example, a religious young man presents himself to a female and she refuses. Why did she refuse? Merely because he is religious and if he is religious, he will ban her from many things. He might even ban her from certain ways of dressing or going out with him. There is a point of view among the girls that is a little wrong, and I do not know where it comes from.[121]

Many men and a few women in Egypt and the UAE believe indigenous masculinities and femininities are threatened by a radically gender-egalitarian agenda, purported to be a Western export. Thus indigenous women's demands for a more equitable legal system, or practices—such as not marrying, having fewer children, divorcing, expecting fair treatment from husbands, and challenging familial control with respect to marriage and sexuality—are too often attributed to mimicry of the West, itself frequently presented in a singular and caricatured form. As one intellectual expresses his anxieties, for Western women,

"equality" has become an outdated request. [Rather,] the female . . . can do completely without men. She can achieve for herself and have her child without men's help too. As an example, Italian women started to abstain from having many children or having children at all, or even getting married. She demands that the relationship between her and the man be turned into an agreement for pleasure in which the opportunities for men and women to get pleasure should be equal. As a result, the woman prefers the biological [sexual] functions over the social roles [of being a wife and mother].[122]

This passage seeks to constitute a firm cultural division between indigenous girls and women and "Italian" women, who metonymically stand in for inauthentic and Western women. The writer is anxious that indigenous women will insist on sex, marriage, and reproduction on more equitable terms, even if this means not marrying men or having children without them. Religion, he fears, has nothing to do with this system, which is based on "new values . . . such as pleasure . . . individuality . . . independence . . . sexual freedom."[123]

Conservatives reserve special disdain for Western states and organizations that attempt to impose international norms of gender and sexuality rights on the region, campaigns that are often represented as sources of cultural destabilization. Among the perceived culprits are the United Nations International Conference on Population and Development (ICPD), held in Cairo in September 1994, and the UN Fourth World Conference on Women, held in Beijing in September 1995. Media and intellectual narratives that circulate in the region about such conferences usually highlight the focus on lesbian rights, or that "the father will not have the right to ban his daughter from going out at night, or to be someone's girlfriend; and it is the right of the wife to sleep wherever; this is Western talk."[124] A UAE male psychologist framed the focus of such conferences as: "sexual freedom . . . abortion . . . the term 'gender' (instead of the term 'sex' . . .) . . . the rights of the woman, the individual, not the member of the family . . . total equality between men and women . . . canceling the 'distinction' of roles . . . scorning motherhood." He juxtaposed this vision against perceived Western ills that include rampant property crimes, rape and sexual assault, murder, "freedom of sperm," drug addiction, pornography, divorce, abandoned senior citizens, restrictions on Muslim girls and women veiling in the West, and suicide.[125]

In this vein, a 2003 paper by Darwish of the Dubai courts rightly complains of the dominant representations in Western "films, reports, and conferences" of Muslim women as "oppressed and subjugated." His narrative, however, also reproduces the idea that international women's rights discourses, captured in conferences like Beijing 1995 and in the UN Convention on the Elimination of all Forms of Discrimination Against Women, claim for women "more than her rights." He writes:

> Why do they move in this direction? This is because they want to disconnect the woman from the society, and to produce a special law called the Women's Rights Law [CEDAW]. This law will result in alienating the woman from the society, and will disintegrate the family and scatter the children. Just as they disparage volunteer work, and consider the rearing of children a part of this unpaid work, they request that women leave home for work [outside the home] because they propagate that the increase in her salary is what will increase her participation in the society. The world orientation leans toward canceling the word "husband" and replacing it with the idiom "life partner." "Life partner" does not necessarily require a contract between you [female] and him. . . . [In the] coming 50 years, the child that results from such sinful relations will not be called a child of fornication but a "child of love."[126]

.   .   .

I found Darwish's "life partner" (*sharīk al-hayāt*) criticism particularly ironic since until I read his paper, I had only heard the term used in interviews with relatively conservative UAE women in reference to companionate loving marriages. Darwish captures a more generalized sentiment among many in the region, disproportionately men, that conflates anti-Westernism and antifeminism.

As he states succinctly, "all the world conferences that have occurred in the past 20 years have concluded [with the necessity for] human freedom in sex."[127] Within a discursive framework that views such demands as the cultural aspects of Western colonial and imperial domination, calls by indigenous women activists for more just laws are easily dismissed and trivialized. It appears, however, that women are voting with their feet in marriage, divorce, and sexuality. It is difficult to avoid the conclusion that what is really frightening for many are serious indigenous challenges to patriarchal gender relations.

4 Improving the National Family

Call on the media to limit the scenes that arouse sexual desire and to be objective in discussing the subject of customary marriage. [Call on them] to avoid exaggeration and stop showing customary marriage . . . as an easy solution.
. . . Train families to bridge the generation gap and improve communication between fathers and mothers on one side, and sons and daughters on the other. [Encourage them] to discuss these matters in an atmosphere that is free of stress, worry, tyranny, and severe punishment methods.
Mu'taz 'Abdallah and Jum'a Yusif, *Common Law Marriage*

GOVERNANCE WORKS through pastoral projects designed to optimize life by directly or indirectly shaping human conduct, in this case in the domains of marriage, family life, and sex.[1] Such cultivation projects are concerned with "the ways in which one might be urged and educated to bridle one's own passions, to control one's own instincts, to govern oneself"[2] and involve courts, counselors, health ministries, philanthropic organizations, and 12–step programs. They also involve academics, as illustrated by the above recommendations to Egyptian state authorities by Cairo University researchers at the end of a lengthy study on *'urfi* marriage.[3] In Egypt, dominant accounts of family cultivation argue that family development is the foundation of national development. They present the exemplary household as moderate in its religious temperament and corporatist in its gender relations. In the UAE, didactic accounts encourage companionate patriarchal marriages and the schooling of a family culture that produces self-regulating individuals who bolster modern authenticity and national health in response to various foreign "invasions." In both countries, the model national family rests on essentialized understandings of men and women.

Governance also works through laws that redefine and attempt to enforce appropriate norms of family conduct.[4] An abiding concern of modern states is to reduce the economically costly consequences of unruly sexual and family behavior. This concern occasionally leads to "tactical collusions" between states and families. Namely, parents of unruly children, wives of feckless husbands, and children of unreliable parents often seek the help of states in order to control and manage such conduct.[5] This chapter examines the substantial legal, administrative, and procedural transformations affecting marriage, divorce, and citizenship in Egypt since 2000, the controversies germane to these changes, and some of their social outcomes. It also considers the substance of the first federalized personal status code in the UAE, promulgated in 2005, and the suggestive debates surrounding this project. In both countries these changes expanded state authority over many aspects of marriage and normalized patriarchal family structures in revised forms, although they eventually eased a woman's ability to get a judicial divorce in Egypt. Men continue to have a unilateral right to divorce, and court divorce initiated by women now requires attempts at reconciliation with state-appointed arbiters and counselors.

Many national and transnational "civil society" actors are remarkably invested in such expansions of governmental power and surveillance even when they are democratic activists. Indeed, the scholarly literature and feminist activism on marriage and citizenship in Middle Eastern and North African (MENA) states illustrates that the basis of debate is not whether expanding governance over families benefits or hurts women, but rather in what direction states should act. Whether liberal, feminist, or neither, modernizers often justify codification of law or other expansions of state power over quotidian biopolitical domains—such as marriage, health, and sex—on the argument that they improve national well-being and increase efficiency.[6] Liberals and feminists often encourage state intervention to decrease the influence of misogynist or traditional social forces, increase women's rights, and hold husbands accountable.[7] These goals often dovetail with the economic and political agendas of states. For example, states may be compelled to provide resources to children and mothers if recalcitrant fathers, husbands, or former husbands refuse to provide such support. In the MENA region, I argue, women come to rely on undemocratic or authoritarian states for their extractive, redistributive, and policing authority over husbands and fathers.[8] Indeed, the endurance of authoritarian MENA states may uniquely depend on this calculus.

Codifying Personal Status Law in the United Arab Emirates

In 2005, the United Arab Emirates (UAE) promulgated Federal Law No. 28 of 2005 in Matters of Personal Status, a code that applies across the emirates, in an attempt to solidify rule over marriage, divorce, guardianship, maintenance, and inheritance in a situation where traditions and practices varied appreciably among different native communities. This section examines the recent law in some detail, allowing for cross-state comparisons and demonstrating that whatever the benefits and drawbacks attached to rationalization, codification in the final analysis helped (at least in the legal abstract) to consolidate the hold of an authoritarian federal state over political, cultural, and religious communities and average men and women. Despite their different gender, cultural, and political ideologies, most elites supported this systemization as necessary for improving the "well-being" of women and families and increasing efficiency.

Law No. 28 defines family (*usra*) in modern patriarchal terms: a loving reproductive unit under the husband's leadership with a wife maintaining his home and raising his children. While the code is quite conservative in its gender assumptions and vision of family life, and it legally makes divorce more difficult for women to obtain, it is less conservative in places when compared to Egyptian family law. This may reflect less penetration by modernist governmentalizing logic in family relations in the Arabian Peninsula. By contrast, the UAE code includes many requirements that facilitate state intervention and monitoring (working with private industry and other organizations) in health and reproduction, very likely reflecting the state's demographic concerns to sustain and build the health and numbers of its relatively small population of native citizens.

There is typically tension between "judicial discretion" and "legislative discretion" with respect to codifying personal status laws in Arab peninsular states, writes Lynn Welchman.[9] Those supporting legislative discretion based on a unified code contend that without such a code judges are often "whimsical," leading to many different "rulings on the same question." Ghada Jamshir, a leader of the Bahraini Committee for Women's Petition, asserts that a unified code "guarantee[s] women their rights rather than leaving them at the mercy of fate."[10] In a typical and contrasting judicial discretion position, a judge in a Shi'i court in Bahrain argues that a unified personal status law risks that "cases will not be given their full due by examining the considerations that vary from one case to another. The existence of a written law binds the *shar'ī* judge, resulting in wrongs to men and women alike."[11] Rationalization and increased governmental control encroach on the independence and discretion of such judicial authorities by reducing their ability to make case-by-case differentiations or sect-based rulings in states governed by Sunni regimes but with significant Shi'i communities.

State and religious officials and other elites in the UAE interviewed before the law was passed generally agreed that codification of family law would be a positive development. For Dr. Mohamed al-Roken, president of the Jurists Association in the UAE and a professor of Islamic law at United Arab Emirates University in al-'Ain, a standardized personal status law (PSL) that applies across different emirates would allow men and women to "know their rights and obligations" rather than depending on judges who do not necessarily have sophisticated knowledge of *fiqh* compendia.[12] Al-Roken links rationalization to efficiency, arguing that a codified PSL reduces conflicting rulings that result from the existence of Islamic traditions with varying rules in different emirates, eases the burden on courts and judges overloaded with cases, and bypasses the problem of judges who are poorly trained in Islamic jurisprudence.[13] Dr. Ahmed al-Kubaysi similarly argues that "shari'a" represents too much range and too many interpretations, even within one school of jurisprudence, as well as conflicts between the opinions of a judge and a *mukhtār* (leader of a village or neighborhood), leading to contrary rulings that create "confusion."[14] Codification that chooses and codifies what al-Kubaysi (considered a liberal on women's rights) thought were the best solutions from the Islamic schools on issues of child custody, inheritance, marriage, divorce, and maintenance would address such problems, many assumed. Moreover, a standardized law was better able to incorporate improvements every few years "for the development of the society," rather than relying on jurist decisions addressing social situations that were relevant "200 years ago."[15]

Attorney Samira al-Gargash believes that a code helps lawyers dealing with family cases, people using the courts for marriage and divorce, and "the society in general." A unified PSL would ease the situation for complainants (especially protecting women) by informing them of "their rights and obligations generally in terms of law and shari'a."[16] A PSL in the UAE would clarify rather than replace Islamic law, in al-Gargash's view, who describes a benignly patriarchal family and a woman's place in it:

> These issues of personal status—the noble Qur'an laid all these issues out for us. So the differences are only in the schools of law, okay? On the issues where

there is not clear direction in the Qur'an and sunna [of the prophet] . . . they go to the school of law [to make decisions for the code]. . . . Islamic shari'a protects women's rights in a complete manner; for example, the wife does not have to bear material obligations when she is in her parents' home. When she is in her parents' home, her father, and then her brother in case her father is not present, her brother, or before the brother the grandfather is responsible in material terms for the rights of the woman. In case of her marriage, her husband is responsible. In case of her divorce, she returns to her male guardian, and he takes her rights. . . . The law just formulates these things for us legally.[17]

Widad Naser Lutah, a high-ranking family advisor in the Dubai courts, argues that a PSL code is positive if it makes uniform the requirements of marriage and divorce across the different emirates, including how long a husband can disappear before a woman can receive a divorce and under what conditions a husband can repudiate a wife (affecting whether they are technically divorced).[18] Hisa al-Diqqi, a women's association leader in Dubai, similarly believes that a standardized code would "unify the vision."[19] More generally, women elites in the UAE were supportive of such a code as a reform for the well-being of families. Unexamined in these accounts is the manner in which such a code expands the power of UAE federal authority in an authoritarian state where shari'a courts are an area of significant plurality and autonomy.

The UAE PSL project was initiated by Shaykh Zayed bin Sultan al-Nahyan, the leader of the Abu Dhabi emirate and president of the UAE who died in late 2004. The predominantly male members of the PSL committee, who were appointed by al Nahyan, were comprised of high-ranking scholars of Islamic jurisprudence from Egypt, Jordan, Syria, Algeria, and Iraq, according to one of the members of this committee.[20] Drafts of the law were shared with and received feedback from women intellectuals, lawyers, and leaders of the government-aligned women's unions, as well as male judges and other court officials in the UAE.[21] There was some resistance to standardization following the presentation of the draft law to the Council of Shaykhs from the different emirates, reportedly because some were "uptight for a particular [Islamic] school of thought."[22]

The UAE Federal Law No. 28 of 2005 in Matters of Personal Status was passed in July after more than ten years of work, issued on November 19, and promulgated in December. The law revised Law No. 1 (1972) in ministerial jurisdictions, Law No. 6 (1978) regarding local to federal transfer of court jurisdiction, and a variety of other laws related to establishing mechanisms to centralize the legal system on the basis of a unified code, rules of evidence, and dowry and marriage expenses.[23] The law (Articles 5 and 6) specifies the jurisdiction of "State Courts" in "matters of family law."[24] Article 2 states that all of the law's provisions are informed by Islamic jurisprudence (*fiqh*) and that if no rulings existed on a matter, a determination was made according to "prevailing opinion in the Sunni schools in the following hierarchy: Maliki, Hanbali [referred to as 'Ahmad' in the legal text], Shafi'i, and Hanafi followed by 'general principles of the Islamic shari'a and social justice.'"[25] Article 1 makes the law applicable to all Muslim UAE citizens (which includes Shi'is), non-Muslim citizens who "have no special laws specific to their own sect or *milla*," and noncitizens if they do not "commit to applying their own laws."[26]

The UAE PSL (Articles 19 and 54) defines marriage as "a contract that permits the [sexual] enjoyment by the spouses of each other legally [*shar'iyyan*]." Its purpose, according to Article 19, is "strengthening and raising a stable family under the guidance [*ri'āyyat*] of the husband, on bases that guarantee for both of them the ability to fulfill its charge of affection and compassion." Article 54 stipulates legal cohabitation as a requirement. A wife is due the following rights, among others, from the husband: maintenance (food, clothing, medical treatment, and services, according to Article 63), no restrictions on completing her education, no restrictions on visiting and being visited by her relatives, to keep her personal money, not being hurt physically or morally, and to be treated fairly with other wives, if any (Article 55). A wife can request an irrevocable divorce "if her husband swears that he has not had intercourse with her for . . . four months or more" (Article 132). A husband is due the following rights, among others, from the wife: obedience "in what is known to be good," supervision and maintenance of the house and its belongings, and nursing "his children by her unless there is an impediment" (Article 56). The memorandum on Article 56 asserts that men's authority over the household is based on his ability to "reason" and "control his emotions" in comparison to women, and that "all laws . . . put men a degree over women."[27] This logic interestingly bypasses the calculus of womanly obedience in return for husbandly maintenance that is more prominent in Egyptian discourse.

According to Article 27, the state will formally document a marriage contract if there is "*shar'i* evidence" (whose nature is not specified) of its occurrence and the couple submits a report from a special committee of the Ministry of Health stating lack of specific illnesses that can be the basis of forced separation;[28] such a contract is documented by two registrars and the marriage is included in a list published by a special committee of the Minister of Justice, Islamic Affairs, and Awqaf. Divorce and customary marriage that follow the other rules of licitness are registered and "ratified" by the state in situations where individuals present "proof of marriage and divorce" (Article 106), although marriage registration also requires the couple to pass the health screening. Article 49 requires two mature, rational, and hearing Muslim male witnesses to a valid marriage contract, although people of the book are acceptable if one of the couple is of Jewish or Christian background.

Article 21 requires the husband to be suitable (*kufūʾan*) in socioeconomic terms to the wife at the point of marriage and allows a woman or her guardian to "request an annulment when suitability is lacking." This article also gives a judge the right to prohibit marriages in which the groom is "double or more" the age of the bride. Article 22 defines suitability as decisively centered on the religion of the groom in relation to the bride, with "custom . . . determining suitability in matters other than religion." Article 48 does not allow a Muslim man to marry a woman who is not "from among the people of the book [Muslims, Jews, and Christians]." The same article prohibits women from marrying non-Muslim men, although it does not include a nationality restriction. Article 39 affirms that the marriage of a woman over eighteen is "null without a [male] guardian," even if the couple has had sexual intercourse, in which case they will be separated and "parentage of a newborn must be proven."[29] Article 28 articulates the contract as *between the guardian and the groom*. The law considers "customary" marriages contracted without permission of the male guardian to be illicit.[30] Article 108 allows a woman to remarry a former husband in a new contract after the waiting period without male guardian permission on the condition that her first marriage occurred with permission from the guardian or with a court ruling.

Article 41 stipulates that the request and acceptance (*ijāb wa qubūl*) of the marriage contract cannot include or imply limitations of marriage duration or be designed to begin at a future time (the same is true in Egyptian law); both request and acceptance must be uttered verbally and heard by both parties, who acknowledge the intention of marriage.[31] Articles 49–52 state that a dowry is fully owned by and at the disposable of the wife, is legally due to her before sexual intercourse, is permitted to be postponed in part if she chooses, and is "a requisite of a true contract."

Law No. 28 allows both parties to include conditions written into the registered marital contract that can be bases for annulment or divorce except if the condition "permits what is illicit and restricts what is licit" (Article 20). A woman can stipulate her ability to work outside the home during marriage in an officially verified contract, unless something occurs to make such a condition "conflict with the interest of the family" (Article 72). Article 75 allows a bride to state in the marriage contract that she does not require to live in "the housing he prepared for her," which not incidentally facilitates *misyār* relationships. While the 2003 draft of the law required registration of *misyār* marriages and "limited publicity" to the guardian of the woman involved, the law in final form does not include such a provision.[32] Article 31 does, however, exclude "waiving the financial rights that result from marriage."[33] Welchman makes the point that a woman in a *misyār* marriage "would be unlikely to pursue her rights at court, being either personally persuaded of the benefits of the arrangement, or expecting divorce if she sought to challenge the mutually agreed conditions and bind the husband to responsibilities he explicitly sought to avoid."[34]

The law spells out the obligations of wives and husbands and the bases of paternity. A wife loses maintenance, according to Article 71, if she does not sleep with her husband, or she refuses to move to the marital home, leaves the home, prevents her husband from entering the marital home, and refuses to travel with her husband, all without legitimate excuses. Article 76 requires a woman to accept a husband's parents and children from another family in the same abode "on the condition that she is not harmed as a result." It also states that a wife cannot have children from a previous marriage live with her unless there is no other custodian, they will be harmed by separation, or the "husband agrees," although he can retract such agreement. Article 116 stipulates that women requiring but not paid their dowry before intercourse (*ghayr al-dukhūl biha*) can have the marriage judicially annulled if the husband obviously does not have the money. If they do have sex, this dowry remains a "debt of the husband," but does not necessarily lead to annulment. Articles 124 and 125 allow a wife to ask for separation if the husband refuses or is unable to maintain her. Articles 89 and 90 make proof of paternity dependent on the matrimonial bed, even if the parents are married less than the pregnancy period or only "interrupted intercourse" occurred. Paternity can also be proved "by admission, or by proof, or by scientific methods if the matrimonial bed applies." Women can be pregnant a minimum of six months and a maximum of twelve months for the purposes of determining licit paternity, according to Article 91, "unless a medical committee formed for this purpose decides otherwise."

Divorce has been made legally more complicated for women to acquire by the federal law. Article 16 and others indicate that men continue to have unilateral right to divorce without judicial intervention. Women, by contrast, must get their divorce through a court and are required by the federal law to go through "guidance" and arbitration in all the emirates before such divorce is granted. Articles 98 and 117 require the Committee of Family Guidance, followed by the judge if this committee fails, to "reconcile the dissent" before ruling to separate the spouses if harm is proven. If harm is not proven and the judge is unable to reconcile the couple, he appoints two other arbitrators who should investigate and try to resolve the conflict for no more than ninety days, although the period of arbitration "can be extended by court order," as stipulated in Articles 118 and 119. Article 120 allows a regular judicial divorce for women with all its obligations if the husband is found to be at fault by the arbitrators and a separation requiring compensation to the husband if the arbitrators determine the wife is at fault. Article 121 requires all evidence and details of the arbitrators' decision be presented to the court, which will rule if they agree and appoint a third arbitrator if the arbitrators disagree. At least in the legal abstract, then, the law places more obstacles before women seeking divorce on the basis of being harmed. Parties are not required to go through guidance before their claim can be heard by the court in cases of inheritance, wills, orders for maintenance, and registering "marriage and [male-initiated] divorce" (Article 16).[35]

The law outlines situations in which women can gain divorce without demonstrating harm. Article 100 allows a wife to divorce if her husband grants her sovereignty over herself. Article 110 allows married women to initiate a *khul'* "annulment" (*faskh*) in court, calling such a separation a "mutually agreed upon *contract* to end the marriage contract with compensation [to the husband] from the wife or someone else"; the compensation in such cases should be the dowry amount, although former husbands must continue to pay for the maintenance and care of their children. Notably unlike what is called *khul'* in Egypt's Law No. 1 of 2000, men in the UAE must agree to such dissolutions.

A wife divorced through no fault of her own (Article 140) must be compensated by one year of alimony (*mut'a*) by the husband, who can pay it in judge-determined installments; the alimony amount is determined based on the husband's financial situation, the nature of the damage the judge deems befell the woman divorced, and the expectation that it be suitable to "others like her" (her status group). In addition to a year of alimony, Article 69 requires men to provide alimony and housing to the pregnant woman and housing only to the nonpregnant woman during the period (*'idda*) a divorced wife may not remarry. This waiting period is about three months when a woman is not pregnant, according to Article 139.

Custody of children after a certain age (eleven for boys and thirteen for girls) accrues to the father in case of divorce.[36] Before passage of the personal status law, divorced women in the emirates of Shariqa and Ra's al-Khayma, following the Hanbali school, could keep custody of children until they reached sexual maturity (*bulūgh*), which differs for boys and girls. In Dubai and Abu Dhabi, by contrast, following the Maliki school, divorced women could keep custody of their children until they remarried.[37] Thus the federal personal status law decreased divorced women's child custody rights in Abu Dhabi and Dubai. The limited custody rights of divorced mothers who remarry was illustrated during my casual conversation in 2003 on an airplane with an Emirati woman lawyer who represents clients in divorce cases in the Dubai courts and who lost custody of her children upon divorcing her husband and marrying a man she loved, a nonnational Arab Muslim.[38] The most important aspect in determining which parent gets custody of Muslim children in the federal personal status law seems to be that they live in a household in which both the husband and wife are Muslim if biological parents marry another partner (Articles 143–145). A non-Muslim divorced mother should not have custody of her Muslim (determined by paternity) biological children beyond five years of age; she is not to be granted custody at all unless a judge deems it necessary "for the sake of the one being nurtured" (Article 145). Article 158 makes clear that custody and guardianship orders as well as issues related to "separating the married couple" (for example, if a woman did not gain permission from her father) will be implemented "by force, even if this leads to the use of force and entering of homes."

In sum, codification expanded federal authority into one of the few realms—marriage and divorce—that were not incorporated into the UAE federal apparatuses in a number of emirates; it also not incidentally extended the power of the state over the Shi'i community. Because the political field in the UAE is less open to opposition than in Egypt and demographic issues are a significant shared concern among Emirati nationals, little public opposition was apparent regarding these changes. Moreover, few people can argue against changes aimed to increase human "well-being," even if well-being means different things to different people. Similarly, rationalizing changes that claim to increase efficiency are compelling and fundamentally linked to modernity. Thus whatever other disagreements they may have, few social sectors will actively lobby for inefficiency. More than in Egypt, the UAE legal changes seem particularly attentive to using family law, state institutions, and private entities to monitor and intervene in the biomedical realm for the good of native Emiratis, which is likely related to the state's demographic anxieties. Divorce in the abstract has been made more difficult for women and remains relatively easy for men. Additional field research is required to assess the social consequences of and responses to these legal changes, and the degree to which they have been effective from the perspectives of elites.

Recent Shifts in Egyptian
Personal Status Law and Procedure

The most dramatic recent legal change with respect to citizenship and marriage in Egypt occurred in January 2000, with the passage of Law No. 1 for Reorganization of Certain Terms and Procedures of Litigation in Personal Status Matters, which reduced the 318 clauses of the previous procedural laws to 79.[39] Sectors and personalities in the state, religious authorities, and members of the media, professional organizations, and activists staked out varying positions motivated by different agendas, including ameliorating gender inequalities, improving court efficiency, or aligning personal status law with international gender norms.[40] The legal change followed years of strategizing by a coalition of individuals that included members of the ruling National Democratic Party, lawyers, and independent activists. Advocates thought the new law would procedurally and indirectly give women "substantive legal rights" and would reduce "the amount of time taken by litigation procedures."[41] The executive branch's stated goals were to reduce a court backlog of approximately five million divorce cases and streamline the bureaucracy in marriage-related legal cases.[42] Atef Sa'id called the legal proceedings typically associated with divorce in Egypt a "package," with each case often taking as many as fifteen interventions from a number of courts and offices.[43] The objectives of increasing efficiency by reducing cost and time in marital conflict cases came up often in the statements of lawyers, judges, legislators, and feminists.[44]

Mulki al-Sharmani argues that underlying the debate about the proposed law were anxieties regarding socioeconomic conditions that allow few men to fit the hegemonic model of a male family breadwinner in return for wifely obedience.[45] The most controversial aspects of the law related to allowing women in registered marriages who could not prove harm to a court's satisfaction to get judicial "no-fault" divorces (termed *al-khul'*) against a husband's wishes more easily by forfeiting all legal material claims against the husband, including post-divorce alimony, returning the marriage gift (*sadāq*), and submitting to reconciliation efforts with court-appointed arbitrators that last no more than three months (Articles 20, 19, 18);[46] allowing women in marriages not registered with the state and denied by the husband (if a woman is at least sixteen and a man is at least eighteen at the time of the lawsuit) to raise a court claim for judicial annulment (if the marriage is deemed incorrect because it was secret or did not have two reliable witnesses) or divorce (if the marriage is deemed correct), "if the marriage was confirmed by any form of writing" (Article 17), although such women cannot receive alimony or child support rights;[47] and allowing women the right to travel without a husband's permission, a piece of the proposed law that was excised before its passage in response to widespread male outrage that it violated the principle of a husband's guardianship over his wife.[48]

Demonstrating the complicated entity that is the Egyptian state, men parliamentary members allied with the ruling party and men opposition party members from a range of ideologies resisted Article 20, fearing "that the new law was going to be abused by women because of their assumed lack of moral values and rational thinking."[49] Huda Zakareya, an Egyptian sociologist, writes, "As the parliamentarians described us, we women are hypocritical, fascinated by men other than our husbands, easily seduced, impatient, disobedient, violent, prone to infidelity, offensive, [and] prone to betraying our families and damaging our children." By contrast, a husband was represented as "generous and gracious, loving his home, caring for his family, yet tragically betrayed by an evil wife who would rob him of all his savings . . . , obtain a *khul'* divorce, and take his children before proceeding to marry another man." Women legislators were generally silent in the parliamentary debates, writes Zakareya, while the "pro-status quo" group included judges, religious authorities, intellectuals, and pundits who "blocked victories round by round."[50]

Islamic elites and institutions were divided over the proposed changes and whether they violated "shari'a."[51] The presidentially appointed Shaykh of al-Azhar supported the law's passage as "in accordance with religious injunctions."[52] Atef Sa'id argues that President Husni Mubarak's government effectively used leaders of state-affiliated Islamic institutions, such as the chief mufti in Dar al-Ifta' and the Shaykh of al-Azhar, to legitimate the law and assure its passage.[53] Nevertheless, editorials published in a range of newspapers and other evidence suggest that many religious scholars, including some affiliated with al-Azhar University, strongly opposed easing women's ability to gain a judicial divorce and "published a letter of opposition" to the president that argued the law threatened male leadership power within Egyptian married households.[54] While these Islamic scholars believed that such divorces were sanctioned by the Qur'an and hadith, they did not agree on the legal interpretation and application of *khul'*. The dissenters argued that husbands should have to consent before such divorces are granted and should be able to revoke them during the waiting period.[55] In advance of the law's passage, Al-Azhar scholars contended that "hatred and dislike were not objective grounds that could serve a *shar'ī* ruling, and using them as grounds for divorce against the will of the husband was a serious matter that would throw a time-bomb into the Muslim household which the wife could detonate at any moment," while other jurists argued for the more women-friendly aspects of the law that passed.[56]

In a regularly used strategy, Egyptian state officials referenced the Qur'an, sunna, and hadiths and bypassed the Islamic schools of *fiqh* to make the case for the religious legitimacy of "no-fault" divorce initiated by women. Indeed, actors on all sides of the debate used religious discourse, including feminists who argued that Law No. 1 was more economically punitive of women seeking "no-fault" divorce than were the traditions of the Prophet on this question.[57] Mariz Tadrous contends that the government encouraged the media to focus on the Islamic legitimacy of the law and this "discourse was used sometimes to camouflage political programmes that opposed *khul'* for social or cultural reasons." Simply using such language encouraged Islamist opposition members "to put forward contrary interpretations of the same religious text." Such framing, she argues, bypasses the language of citizenship rights, "women's rights, equality, or emancipation. They always spoke in terms of the family."[58] Feminist activists and scholars such as Zakareya stress that their use of religious terminology was a conscious strategy, a way to challenge "the fundamentalists [who] had always presumed [this terminology] was their monopoly."[59]

State power is particularly useful to women when it can be used to extract resources from men or police them. The legislative committee of the National Council for Women (NCW) originally included an article that would have imprisoned men who did not pay court-ordered maintenance, although it was removed by the male-dominated People's Assembly before passage. Law No. 1 instead repealed a regulation (Law Decree no. 78 of 1931) that had allowed thirty days imprisonment of a man who was able but unwilling to pay his court-ordered marital and child-support obligations. Given state difficulties in holding men accountable for maintenance of women and children by attaching their assets or income in the following months, in May 2000 the assembly amended Law No. 1 to allow thirty days imprisonment in such cases.[60] Thus state resource concerns trump the material interests of men, even in the People's Assembly. This example also illustrates the microbattles over "interests" and "well-being" based on gender and ideology between and within different state apparatuses even as all work within a rationality of governance.

After passage of Law No. 1, the Ministry of Justice and the National Council for Women legislative committee coordinated the drafting of related legislation that followed.[61] In August 2000, a new marriage contract form was issued that had "blank spaces in which the couple could insert stipulations,"[62] titled "special conditions" followed by "the married couple agreed on: . . ."[63] Before this section, the contract form includes language (consistent with 1985 Law No. 100) asking a husband to affirm to the registrar whether he is married to other women and three lines for the names and addresses of wives to be provided if he is plurally married.[64] Each contract is attached to "an annex" of possible stipulations that the marriage registrar is to suggest.[65] Rather than the annex, the original contract draft presented by women's groups included nine check-off stipulations that were removed because of major opposition from the religious establishment.[66] Marriage registrars are to assure that photographs and fingerprints of the bride and groom are affixed to the marriage contract, to obtain declarations of any existing diseases that may be basis for separation if they are not revealed before marriage, to clarify in the contract who gets the furniture and home in case of divorce or death, and to document the amount of money due to the wife if the husband divorces her through no fault of her own. The registrar is supposed to ask whether the husband would stipulate not to take an additional wife without the first wife's "written approval" and give "the authority to the wife to divorce herself from the husband" in the contract (*'isma*). The notary is required to document in the contract any stipulation or condition made by the bride or groom unless it "legalize[s] something [Islamically] illegal or prohibit[s] something that is legal."[67]

In March 2004, Law No. 10, which passed "with no heated debate," introduced as a procedural change a consolidated family court system with branches throughout the country whose declared aim was "a legal system that is non-adversarial, attentive to the best interests of the family, accessible, and affordable."[68] State discourse advocating consolidation stressed (1) Islamic principles of sustaining families based on "amity, compassion and stability"; (2) the importance of families as "the first cell in the fabric of the community"; and (3) that

"streamlin[ing] the litigation procedures" saves "time and money for the liti-
gants."[69] Court consolidation had been the focus of lobbying for many years by
Dr. Laila Takla, director of the Association for the Union of Egyptian Women
Lawyers, in order to resolve family disputes before they reached litigation.[70]

The new system requires women who seek a divorce to first file for mediation in a specialized section of the family courts. The mediation would occur
over fifteen days that could be extended two more weeks and be undertaken by
"specialists" with "training in law, psychology, and social work," one of whom
must be a woman. Mediation agreement is legally binding. If mediation fails,
Law No. 10 requires that all personal status lawsuits be handled in "first instance" family courts with a panel of three judges who work with information
provided by the mediation specialists. The law also (1) calls for the establishment of a public prosecutor focused on family law in each branch and requires
this prosecutor to attend "all [family] court sessions"; (2) requires consolidating information regarding a family conflict into "a single court file so that the
judges can be well informed about interconnected disputes"; and (3) stipulates
that court rulings in regular divorce "can only be appealed [by husbands] at the
Court of Appeal but not at the Court of Cassation," as was the case previously,
whereas *khul'* rulings "cannot be appealed at any level."[71]

In case of a dispute regarding a husband or former husband's income, Article 23 of Law No. 1 of 2000 requires "the office of the public prosecutor . . . to
carry out an investigation to identify the level of income."[72] Article 72 of Law
No. 1 states that a married or divorced woman (or children or parents of a
man) can go to Nasser Bank with a judicial ruling to extract maintenance
payments if the issue is not resolved amicably, and the details would be clarified by a ruling from the Ministry of Justice.[73] In 2004, Law No. 11 accordingly
"set up a government-run Family Fund to facilitate the implementation of
court orders for alimony and child maintenance through Nasser Bank."[74] The
money for this Family Fund comes from a requirement that married couples
pay "LE 50 for each marriage contract, LE 50 for each divorce to be paid by the
[person initiating the divorce], and LE 20 for each registered birth," as well as
additional funds from donations, estates, and the state.[75] Since passage of the
law, Nasser Bank has required significant paperwork from divorced women
and established rules restricting access to the money that state officials, lawyers, and feminists argue the bank has no right to since "the resources in the
Family Fund come from fees . . . that do not belong to the bank, and so it cannot choose not to pay women."[76]

On child custody issues, the NCW worked for passage of Law No. 4 of 2005, which allows divorced Muslim women, if they remain unmarried and are considered fit, to keep custody of daughters and sons with continued maintenance from the father until the children are fifteen years old. Family judges determine custody status from fifteen years until marriage for daughters and fifteen to twenty-one years for sons based on discussion with the children. Whatever the custody arrangement, legal guardianship of children remains with the father until the age of twenty-one unless he "commits a crime against the child or is negligent."[77] In addition to affirming women's negligible legal power in relation to their children, such a guardianship arrangement can be a major problem for divorced women with custody of children, since all state notices and permission forms related to schooling and health are sent to the "natural guardian" (the father) or his male relatives.[78]

Law No. 1 and the changes that followed were criticized by many feminists and women's activists who were not aligned with the state. Some argued against a procedural focus that bypasses transformation of inequitable family laws, and some believed that mediation requirements hurt women seeking divorce.[79] Azza Souleiman and Azza Salah were concerned with the level of "discretion afforded judges in applying the law."[80] The government was criticized for excluding independent women's organizations and regular women from the process of drafting the laws. It was also accused of rushing laws through without attention to gaps in legislation and mechanisms for enforcement in order to "claim credit for the reforms in the eyes of the Egyptian general public as well as international donors."[81] A number of women and men activist lawyers, including at least one involved in the National Council for Women legislative committee, challenged the usefulness of compulsory mediation and criticized the lack of law enforcement mechanism for court judgments.[82]

The new court system continues to work within a sexist legal framework that allows men unconditional right to divorce (with economic penalties) and polygyny; requires wifely obedience in return for maintenance from the husband; and makes it difficult for women to prove harm.[83] Mulki al-Sharmani, a social anthropologist affiliated with the American University in Cairo, argues for a new code based on more equitable marital relations, so that the system reflects the mutually supportive "marriages that exist in reality" and translates "women's financial contributions" to the household into "recognizable legal rights," including the possibility of being paid (past) wages for their housework in cases of unilateral divorce.[84] Most women's rights groups in Egypt are increasingly arguing for a more equitable marriage model and lobbying for "a new and comprehensive family law code that would be based on gender equality,"[85] even as activists recognize that some women would be "ambivalent about giving up their existing legal right to financial maintenance from their husbands in exchange for a model of marriage based on equal gender roles."[86] As Nawla Darwiche of the New Women's Research Center clarified in an interview, "As a member of a feminist organization, I cannot ask for *shar'ī* marriage in which the man provides. There has to be equality. . . . If I have enough courage, I should also ask for civil marriage. We still haven't entered this topic in Egypt."[87] The National Council for Women, by contrast, wants to introduce narrow changes such as raising the minimum age of marriage for girls, restricting plural marriage, and articulating more equitable standards of harm for women seeking divorce.[88]

Assessing the Impact of Legal and Administrative Changes in Egypt

Over time and despite mediation requirements, the legal and administrative transformations in the realms of personal status have made divorce easier to acquire for Egyptian women willing to forfeit male economic support. As a result, "no-fault" divorces that do not require women to demonstrate harm to a court's satisfaction have increased. The extraction of resources from men continues to be the most frequent issue fought in the courts, with women either suing husbands for economic support for themselves and their children or suing for divorce ("no-fault" or "prejudicial") because a husband fails to provide acceptable maintenance. The system continues to rely on a complementary family logic of women's obedience and reproductive work in return for male patriarchal dominance (benign) and economic maintenance. Women generally expect men to provide such support, the state to extract it from men if they fail in their obligations, and the state to provide it if women or the state fail in forcing men to do so. The authoritarian state, in turn, seems very unlikely to extricate itself from such an arrangement. Issues related to the quotidian realms of marriage and divorce are the most persistent and systematic means by which the state interpellates Egyptians. If state officials did not govern sexual and marital unruliness, moreover, they would have to contend with more resource and welfare demands from women and children. The real paradox is that advocates for women, even those who argue for a more gender-equitable marriage system, often recommend mending perceived cracks in the authoritarian state's ability, efficiency, and efficacy in compelling men to participate in mediation, extract resources from them, and police them.

A field study published in 2003 and conducted by the Center for Egyptian Women Legal Assistance (CEWLA) in the two years following the application of Law No. 1 in six large governorates found that very few women applied for or received *khul'* in comparison to regular divorces, with little difference between urban and nonurban areas. Divorce cases continued to move very slowly through the system, taking an average of eight months in sixty-two *khul'* cases that resolved during the study—most of these cases had originally been suits for divorce on the "grounds of harm" that had languished for years.[89] A 2005 comparative study of *khul'* and regular divorces in the new family courts by Nadia Halim and colleagues at CEWLA concludes that whichever type of divorce women sought, the most common reasons they cite are similar: "husband's failure to provide, husband's desertion, and spousal abuse," but women chose *khul'* because of "the lower costs and shorter period of litigation."[90] Delays were common, however, as husbands often claimed that wives owed them a higher amount of advanced dower; "some judges repeatedly postponed court sessions until investigations were conducted by the Family Prosecution Department"; and husbands avoided receiving court summons to postpone a ruling.[91]

Al-Sharmani of the AUC Social Research Center led a research study of family court branches in different parts of Egypt between January 1 and December 31, 2007, to examine the degree to which the new court system was "meeting the legal needs of female disputants and strengthening their rights."[92] The most common cases in the courts continue to be about maintenance amounts and their payment.[93] The typical scenario is that wives sue husbands for lack of maintenance and husbands respond that wives are disobedient. When maintenance issues resolve during mediation, women often have difficulty enforcing the ruling. Their biggest challenge is "providing proof of a husband's financial assets and earning capabilities" as husbands often pay bribes to inspectors or employers do not provide honest information.[94] Family court judgments in maintenance cases were much easier to enforce in comparison to mediation office judgments.[95]

Al-Sharmani found that women who filed for "no-fault" divorce in the family courts had "grounds for prejudicial divorce [on the basis of harm], but opted for . . . [no-fault] divorce because it was thought to be easier," faster, and less expensive to obtain, especially since harm remains difficult to demonstrate and requires witnesses. Lack of maintenance from the husband was the most reported cause for "no-fault" divorce, followed by physical and emotional abuse, and sexual abuse of the wife or one of the children. Women explained that being married but not receiving maintenance made it impossible for them to be eligible for welfare benefits from the government or "financial assistance provided by religious and privately owned charity organizations in their local communities."[96] Given the above factors, al-Sharmani found that women of limited means are more likely to resort to the "no-fault" divorce option,[97] which is ironic as many critics of *khul'* argued that it was designed to benefit bourgeois and wealthy women.[98] Ministry of Justice statistics indicate an increasing national trend of women suing for *khul'* divorces: 2,886 cases in 2004; 3,492 cases in 2005; and 8,045 cases in 2006.[99] Women in the al-Sharmani study who filed for prejudicial divorce cited grounds similar to women filing for no-fault divorce: lack of economic support, maltreatment, travel of the husband, sexual and other abuse, and polygyny. Unlike women who chose the "no-fault" option and forfeited compensation, however, women in this category had better financial means that allowed them to wait out the court system and were probably married to better-off men.[100]

Al-Sharmani found that while the new court system potentially provides "female litigants with quick, affordable, and accessible mechanisms of claiming legal redress," this possibility was "diminished by . . . legislative gaps, procedural shortcomings, lack of effective implementation mechanisms, and the gendered politics inherent in the legal process." Her team found that "mediation . . . does not work," and women disputants agreed, noting that mediators pressured them to reconcile with husbands and disapproved of women using the "no-fault" option. Court personnel generally consider women disputants to be irrational, "emotional and hasty," expect women to be sexually available to their husbands, and define sexual harm in narrow terms. Very few women reach a settlement during mediation since most husbands do not attend sessions. Mediation rooms were noisy and lacked privacy, telephones, copy machines, and other basic supplies.[101] Many lawyers believe mediators are incompetent and mediation is unnecessary since most troubled relationships have been through unsuccessful informal mediation;[102] lawyers who represent women complain of too many notification requirements for husbands and the gender-conservative orientations of the mediation staff.[103] Judges do not find mediation reports useful, consider it problematic that no legal text compels both disputants to attend mediation sessions, and express concern that mediation staff members do not receive guidance or monitoring.[104] Al-Sharmani's team observed mediation sessions and found that the mediators range from competent and empathetic to insecure, incompetent, and uninterested.[105]

Al-Sharmani advocates better training in law and gender awareness and "capacity building" at all levels in the family courts; more financial support for needy families; increasing the enforcement aspects of the courts, including requiring attendance at mediation sessions; and more assistance to men and women "seeking a marriage partner," including training them in communication skills, conflict resolution, legal knowledge, and "sensitivity to gender rights." She also calls for a public awareness campaign using the media and training media personnel in gender awareness and legal knowledge.[106] These recommendations indicate the manner in which the agendas of gender-equity advocates, including feminists, intentionally and unintentionally promote the expansion and proliferation of power that administers life.

When I suggested that feminists and other progressive activists facilitate governmentality in an authoritarian context when they work on such projects, al-Sharmani responded that women's rights activists strategically work within the given Egyptian political field. She stressed that state authority over marriage remains limited given legislative, training, procedural, and enforcement gaps in the new system. Moreover, the legal, procedural, and administrative changes are interpreted and applied differently by litigants, judges, and lawyers, leading to unintended consequences that the state has little control over—the process "takes on a life of its own." Relatedly, she emphasizes that women often use the family courts for their own sometimes gender-conservative purposes, such as "sending a message" to a recalcitrant husband, or they treat court requirements as bureaucratic steps for reaching a personal goal.[107]

Revisions of Citizenship Law in Egypt

Egyptian families are also constituted and regulated through citizenship discourse and apparatuses. Citizenship law has barred Egyptian women from transferring their citizenship to children or non-Egyptian husbands. Following the late 2003 public call by President Husni Mubarak, which itself followed an October 25, 2001, report prepared by the National Council for Women, the NCW legislative committee worked with the Ministries of Justice and Interior and university faculty members (such as Fawziya Abdul Sattar) to draft an amendment to the nationality law. This amendment granted citizenship to the children of Egyptian women who married non-Egyptian men on the basis of Article 11 of the Egyptian Constitution asserting that Egyptian citizens have equal rights.[108]

Per the usual discursive strategy, the NCW used Islamic idioms as well to make the case: "Although [the citizenship] problem was not addressed directly in Islamic jurisprudence, the general principles in the Islamic shari'a provide for equality between men and women in their human value in general."[109]

After much debate and earlier drafts that would have excluded the children of Palestinian men (the largest group), the Egyptian parliament passed Law No. 154 in July 2004, which amends Law No. 26 of 1975 to grant citizenship to *future* children from all married relationships between Egyptian women and foreign men. Law No. 154 also allows children born of such relationships before the date of passage to apply to the Interior Ministry for citizenship, impacting "up to one million individuals." The law, however, prohibits children from such mixed relationships from joining the military, police, and certain "governmental posts" as adults.[110] The granting of Egyptian citizenship to children whose fathers are non-Egyptian has been highly bureaucratic, expensive, and frustrating for many. In summer 2006, the Interior Ministry decided to exempt applicants from the fee of LE 1,200 (approximately US$240). Although many children of Syrian and Sudanese fathers were granted citizenship by the Interior Ministry, children of Palestinian fathers have been denied despite the inclusive legal language.[111] Resistance to granting citizenship to the children of non-Egyptian men is related both to patriarchal nationalist concerns *and* the state's unwillingness to bear the welfare burden of such children. The lawyer Ahmad 'Arafat calculates that the Egyptian state's education and health costs for each child in this situation is about LE 20,000 (about US$4,000) per year and wonders, "Why doesn't the state of the father take on this responsibility?"[112]

Lamya Lutfi is an activist with the New Woman's Research Center in Cairo and responsible for the Campaign to Establish Affinity. Although the government does not release documentation on the number of children without citizenship, Lutfi's research team understands that thousands of paternity/citizenship cases involving *Egyptian* fathers exist in the courts. The cases are divided between those in which Egyptian women had children as a result of nonmarital sexual relations, male-denied *'urfi* marriages, and male-denied rapes. All such children are treated as if they are the result of illicit extramarital sex (*zina*). Another proportion of affinity cases involves Egyptian women in troubled but formal marriage with Egyptian men who want to apply for a child's birth certificate, a right that had been limited to Egyptian fathers and other males in the father's family.[113] In 2007, the Egyptian Administrative Court ruled that Egyptian mothers in such situations can file a lawsuit for "official recognition of her child" and apply for a birth certificate at the Civil Status Organization.[114] By 2008, however, another administrative decision revoked this ruling.[115]

Improving the Family Through Instruction

Solutions to perceived youth and family crises in Egypt and the UAE often center on developing pedagogies to improve the behavior of parents, spouses, and children, as well as designing and providing stronger Islamic morality education on the hope that subjectivities could be better molded toward self-restraint and sustenance of the authentic national family. It should be noted that the hegemony of a modernist-nationalist Muslim family with the good mother—rational, scientific, pious, domestic, hygienic, and ultimately bour-geois—defined against "internal other" mothers[116] has a much longer geneal-ogy in Egypt than it does in the UAE. This is partly because of the significantly younger age of the UAE as an independent state and in some measure because Western colonization and its attendant reinforcing cultural models and raisons d'etre appear to have been much more deeply integrated into Egyptian subjec-tivities, although both peoples experienced degrees of British colonization and imperialism from the late nineteenth century. People in the UAE and Arab Peninsula states more generally demonstrate a much stronger defense of indig-enous cultural superiority in comparison to other parts of the MENA region, where "traditions" are more likely to be associated with cultural backwardness.

Notwithstanding these historical differences, both countries evidence calls for sophisticated values "reeducation" programming produced by the state and others to encourage modest weddings, marriage, and labor informed by "mod-erate" and "correct" Islamic morality. Such programming is seen as necessary to compete with existing programs that offer contradictory Islamic answers, producing "religious chaos," or moral licentiousness.[117] The value-focused peda-gogies offered by religious authorities, intellectuals, religious activists, state of-ficials, social workers, "development" apparatuses, television personalities, and women's organizations can diverge. Nevertheless, they typically reinforce the value of the state as a source of support and protection for families, women, and children and present family stability as crucial to national well-being.

Developmentalism and Family Corporatism in Egypt

In Egypt, the ideal national family is often middle-class and urban, a vision that is contrasted with perceived lower-class conservativeness and upper-class licen-tiousness. The preferred national family is a corporatist formation anchored by religious moderation, enlightened husbands who lead and economically support the household, and wifely acceptance and obedience. In these accounts, national development depends on healthy and stable families as well as the individual "development" of people perceived to be backward in their family values and behaviors, such as illiterate women, rural Egyptians, and poor people.

As Lila Abu-Lughod demonstrates in *Dramas of Nationhood*, Egyptian state-supported television and radio dramas are particularly important mediums for defining appropriate national citizenship, morality, and family life.[118] Even as many of their writers, producers, and actors are liberals and independent of the state, these television serials have helped to constitute a discourse of personal and national development dominated by the priorities of Republican Egypt's urban centers and middle-class modernist values.[119] An important linchpin of Egyptian television has been "developmental" programming concerned with transforming "cultural illiteracy," whose special targets have been rural residents and women.[120] Such projects, she argues, are part of "a powerful public national discourse of reform and uplift whose contours can be traced to colonial and anticolonial nationalist efforts to transform Egypt into a modern place and whose objectives are supported by state institutions set up especially under President Nasser in the 1950s and 1960s."[121] This developmental orientation, which can be patronizing to rural women who may not be highly educated and often have different perspectives on "selfhood and community belonging,"[122] also pervades urban-based feminist organizing in Egypt.

Egyptian television storylines and characters normalize familial and social inequality, and bolster the legitimacy of state authority.[123] For example, plot resolution in Egyptian dramas often relies on experts and state authorities who are "assumed to be enlightened, as a result of being middle class and educated," discursively justifying social hierarchy.[124] Egyptian television dramas are also significant sources of pedagogy on marriage and sexuality, particularly for women, who have lower rates of literacy than men.[125] Egyptian serials usually represent companionate marriage based on "choice, true love, mutuality," and a small number of children as the ideal and happiest for all women.[126] This ideal is biased toward urban middle-class lifestyles and is "benignly patriarchal," with the loving husband and father at work and the mother in the home.[127] A contemporary serial examined by Abu-Lughod offers "a new form of patriarch who is monogamous, involved in a marriage of mutual love and companionship, loving, caring, and concerned deeply about the lives and happiness of his children."[128] Abu-Lughod flags the active, plural, and unpredictable responses of audiences to such messages, which depend "on the experiences they have on the ground and the alternative discourses they have available to them."[129]

The family instruction offered by a set of ten women's legal education cassette tapes, titled "On the Path of Life," which focus on Egyptian personal status issues and are produced by the Egyptian National Council for Women, offer a less urbane and bourgeois vision of the good Egyptian family when compared to Egyptian dramas. The cassette tapes are similar, however, in their developmental orientation and the evidence they provide that education and empowerment are often designed to reinforce the state's relevance to and authority over individual Egyptian lives, in this case rural and illiterate women.[130] More generally, the series reinforces how the personal status system requires and encourages Egyptian women to rely on the state to protect them from men and to extract resources from men for themselves and their children, while at the same time bolstering a conservative family structure. The instructions at points also seem driven by the logic of bureaucratic rationality, aimed to train women not to waste the court's time by (1) clarifying for them the situations in which a lawsuit will definitely fail and (2) instructing them in the language and reasoning of valid bases for lawsuits.

The stated goal of the "On the Path of Life" project, according to the introductory brochure, is to ameliorate "widespread legal illiteracy among women . . . , especially [of rights] connected with personal status." The tapes are organized in question-and-answer format, read in dramatic voices, and focus on legal questions that address "the largest number of practical problems" that women ask about: maintenance and dowry, registration requirements for male-initiated divorce,[131] valid bases of divorce,[132] customary marriage, and inheritance. The substantive material in the series was produced by a special committee of legal experts, Ministry of Justice representatives, and Muslim and Christian religious leaders to assure adherence to the requirements of the "heavenly" religious laws, including Judaism.[133] The questions are usually posed by women's voices and answered by men experts (judges and lawyers), although there are times when men's voices ask questions. The answers indicate significant judicial discretion and give contradictory advice.[134]

A number of additional aspects related to this series are worth highlighting. First, although family issues are governed by civil and criminal codes and statutes within a rationalized and state-controlled legal system, the taped material largely operates from Islamic religious idioms and logic, and speakers often reference the Qur'an, hadith, and sunna material, as well as Hanafi traditions for Muslims—calling these "shariʻa"—and Christian traditions for Coptic Egyptians. This is consistent with Azza Karam's contention that Islamists, feminists, and state actors (including among them representatives of official Islam and state feminism) in Egypt negotiate gender issues within the terms set by an Islamic framework.[135] To a lesser but significant degree speakers on the cassette series also reference the domains of *qānūn* (laws of the state) and *ʻurf* (custom). Second, despite the fact that the series is produced by the National Council for Women, a secular organization that includes many women's rights advocates and is led by Suzanne Mubarak, it reinforces a conservative religious-national vision of family and its obligations. For example, the material asserts marriage as necessary to "keep the land/country full of people" and make sexual relations licit; prohibits marriage if one does not have "the financial and health abilities"; obligates marriage otherwise, since family life is the sunna of the Prophet and his companions; constitutes women as the basis of contract between others rather than one of two equal parties in a contract; and declares that the marriage contract must be licit before "God" and "the government."[136]

The conservative national-religious vision of family life articulated on the cassettes is further illustrated in the corporatist language used to instruct the objects of state education. A husband has the right to be obeyed by the wife, since "he is the driver of the vehicle of married life; he is the manager; he is responsible for the *usra*, its security and provision of maintenance for all its members. The president of any administration or interest cannot manage it well unless all the individuals obey him. This obedience does not include harming requests. If he does not provide security and maintenance, obedience is not due to him." Wives must remain in the home unless a husband gives permission otherwise in order to "reduce public talking, the involvement of the devil, and instability." Husbands have leadership rights over the household, conceptualized as "the company," and he has rights to plural marriage, which should be respected by the wife. He was given such leadership because he is ultimately "responsible before the people [*al-nās*], family, and government for this company and its preservation. This is a commandment from God [*taklīf*] rather than a power that should be used arrogantly [*tashrīf*]." Women's rights in this corporatist arrangement are to receive and keep a marriage gift and a dowry that demonstrate a husband "considers her valuable"; to be respected as a body and a person; to receive maintenance during marriage; and to be dealt with justly, including in plural marriage (if not, men will be punished on the day of judgment).[137]

Dr. Suʻad Salih, a renowned scholar and professor of jurisprudence at al-Azhar University, provides a strikingly similar corporatist vision of the good family during an interview, although she is more critical of male dominance in the household and does not emphasize the efficient male-headed family's instrumentality to state preservation. (She was firm, however, that state registration of marriage contracts was crucial to protect women.) Salih stresses that the Qur'an asserts the equality and mutuality of obligations between husband and wife. She contends that men have leadership in the household not because of superior virtue but for administrative efficiency: "Any society must have a leader. . . . Each country has one president. Each ship has one driver. Each airplane has one pilot. If there were two, this will lead to conflict and differences between them." Economically able husbands lose this guardianship authority if they depend on the wife for support or are negligent in their responsibilities. She criticizes "masculinist" interpretations that translate the Qur'anically articulated "step" men have over women as allowing men to disrespect the humanity of women or dominate them in the family.[138]

The NCW actively articulates a vision of appropriate patriarchal Egyptian family life and modern gendered citizenship in other publications, such as *Women in Egyptian Legislations*, by Fawziya Abdul Sattar. Islamic idioms and state law are deployed together in a discourse that constitutes the state as the guarantor of women's rights, assures that such rights are reconcilable with women's family duties, and deflects accusations that state policies and laws are anti-Islamic or antifamily.[139] For example, according to the NCW booklet, if a husband "fulfills his duties toward his wife, that is if he pays her dowry, prepares a suitable home for her, acts scrupulously towards her, she has to owe him obedience, live with him, and give him his matrimonial rights. If she disobeys him afterwards, she will be considered disobedient and loses her right to alimony."[140] Citing in the same paragraph both Qur'anic interpretations and Egyptian penal codes, *Women in Egyptian Legislations* explains that husbands have the right to discipline their wives if they demonstrate "ill-conduct," first by admonishing them, then refusing to share their bed, and then "beating her lightly and without degrading her." If a husband "misuses his right and transcends the limits prescribed to him," he is punishable by the Egyptian penal code and the "wife in such a case might ask for divorce on account of being inflicted by harm."[141] Another section of the booklet describes the Egyptian state as working to protect motherhood and childhood without violating "Islamic jurisprudence."[142] Similarly, the report highlights that Article 11 of the 1971 Constitution stipulates that "the state shall guarantee the proper reconciliation between the duties of woman towards the family and her work in the society, considering her equal with man in the fields of political, social, cultural and economic life without violation of the rules of Islamic Shari'a."[143]

The obligation of wifely obedience to male rule/guardianship in return for a husband's economic maintenance is made explicit in a circular, and yet familiar, corporatist account: "Obedience is a requirement necessitated by the need to maintain the entity of the family since the husband is the head of the family, and he cannot fulfill his duties unless he is obeyed. He is deemed the head of the family because he is the one assigned to look for its subsistence and provide for it, in addition to his physical constitution which makes him capable of defending and protecting it."[144] The author refers to the Qur'an, Surah 4, Verse 34 on the issue of male guardianship, although the reference to men's "physical constitution" to justify such family authority seems modern. By contrast, the document insists that such male leadership only applies to marital life and does not extend to women's "financial affairs."[145]

Customary or 'urfī marriage contracts come up a number of times in the "On the Path of Life" cassette series published by the NCW. The experts insist that for such contracts to be acceptable according to Islamic and state requirements, they must fulfill all the conditions and pillars of regular marriage, most importantly "public announcement of the marriage." Women married in unregistered contracts are warned that they are not considered married by the state and thus cannot sue for maintenance, state benefits, or state advocacy if such a marriage is denied by the man. Documentation that proves age-of-marriage requirements have been met is also necessary before the state will intervene in a case. Secrecy or concealment (kitmān) of marriage is unacceptable, and marriages under such conditions are considered "corrupt." The cassettes nevertheless affirm that women in such marriages can appeal to the state to confirm a child's paternity and can request judicial annulment.[146] Interviews with lawyers and women activists indicate that women in such relationships avoid confirming paternity because of social stigma and fear that they will not "reach a positive result" if they approach the courts.[147] The cassettes also assert that a woman who agrees to marry this way is not valued by the man, who "in the end . . . leaves her with ease after he takes what he wants from her" since he only cares about his "passions" (shahwa).[148] The language is often strident regarding customary marriages, including telling a woman she has no right to a judicial divorce because "you are the one who oppressed yourself."[149]

Instructional and reeducation discourses directed at family and sexual practices dominate the Egyptian landscape, although they differ in approach and the areas of concern they highlight. Islamic idioms are important aspects of most of these discourses, although they largely reflect socioeconomic anxieties, a sense of cultural crisis, and a developmental orientation that constitutes the good family to be at the heart of the nation-state's well-being and progress. The good family in these accounts appears to be strikingly similar to the Egyptian state: a corporatist structure ruled by a (not so) benign patriarch. The well-being and stability of this structure requires obedience in return for certain protections and resources. Consistent with the rationality of modern governmentality, education on marriage and sexuality often seems to discursively and materially expand or reinforce state influence and relevance over biopolitical domains and groups perceived to be socially marginal or resistant to such control. Women are special targets of "cultural illiteracy" discourse, partly because they seem to be viewed as the weakest link in the state's developmental logic but also because women are channels through which the state can directly or indirectly better manage men.

Soft Patriarchy and Self-Regulation in the UAE

Maybe more than in Egypt, there is strong recognition in the UAE that education, which for natives has been financed by the federal government from early in the country's history, is essential for socializing *national* (rather than local) norms and behaviors that can "perpetuate the political system."[150] State investment in "human resources" more generally was from the beginning "designed to raise the country's absorptive capacity for investment and accelerate the development process in the seven emirates."[151] The perceived crisis in sexual and family life in the UAE is often seen to require particular kinds of schooling by educational institutions, parents, women's organizations, and media designed to cultivate self-regulating subjectivities and behaviors that reinforce "family culture." UAE elites often view men more than women as in need of such moral and cultural retraining and worry that public and private schools are failing to provide such schooling to native children. These cultivation projects are undertaken by different apparatuses and actors working under the auspices of the state and take a range of forms. This section analyzes these cultivation issues as they emerged in papers written by UAE elites, interviews with a number of these officials and leaders, and didactic materials distributed by the state to native couples. Instructional narratives designed to school marriage success manage a fine line between emphasizing the importance of companionate and loving patriarchal marriages and condemning "Western" notions of romantic love. An article in a family-focused magazine produced in Shariqa illustrates well what I term "soft patriarchy." It criticizes men dominating children and wives in ways that increase conflict in the home, reduce communication, and produce distrust. Daughters compelled by fathers to marry unwanted men, or whose groom choices are rejected by parents, might turn to secret marriage, the article argues. Islamic teachings giving men governance rights within the family are not license for oppression or unreasonableness, continues the narrative. Fatherly authority should be used more wisely, even as "mistaken ideas about freedom that are controlling the minds of a lot of our daughters" are condemned as Western and whimsical desires.[152]

Independent and state-affiliated Emirati community leaders, professionals, and intellectuals, whether men or women, share a belief in maintaining native women's dignity. With the exception of the more radical visions of a handful of independent indigenous feminists, this dignity is believed to require establishing a new and improved Muslim patriarchal family in which men and women know their respective emotional and family roles. Family stability is also seen to require couples learning to communicate more effectively, share in agenda setting, and have mutual respect. More surprising was the number of Emiratis across gender who shared a "men are like dogs" analysis, as one female government official put it, who have little ability to control themselves when faced with new sexual possibilities, putting significant pressure on state, religious, and women's organizations to successfully engender new embodiments and subjectivities.

Many Emirati social institutions focus on constituting and imparting methods, knowledge, and skills to address perceived problems in family life. Dr. 'Abd al-Rahman Dhakir Hamid, a clinical psychologist employed by the Justice Department, Section for Family Counseling and Reform in the UAE, posits instruction as a solution for the generation gap between youth and their parents. He argues for instilling Islamic values that encourage freedom of opinion and expression for children and honest and open "dialogue and discussion." Hamid assumes that children are more likely to behave appropriately if they are convinced of behaviors rather than compelled or restricted, arguing that parents and educators must "be armed with the necessary knowledge," especially in Islamic fundamentals.[153] Dr. Muhammad Mahmud al-Shaykh similarly suggests in another paper that the state design "meaningful" media programming and school curriculums that increase youth self-esteem, "love of work," inquisitiveness, "ethics," and "freedom of expression."[154]

Elites, including state and religious officials, are particularly concerned to encourage education that leads to self-control and regulation, especially given difficult to control transnational circuits that challenge parental and state efforts to limit information and to police sexual practices. Darwish of the Dubai courts argues that in the "age of globalization," a "father cannot raise his children with the stick. The boy has left the control of his father. Now children hit fathers. . . . So we must raise in them intrinsic control, not extrinsic control." The state is especially concerned with the "dangerous" consequences of the private schooling of Emirati children, since such institutions do not "raise children, but [only] teach." While government schools have a degree of "supervision and follow-up" with respect to appropriate morality, culture, and family life, private schools do not. This lack is seen as an urgent problem since private schools educate half of native children, particularly "the children of decision-makers."[155]

While the UAE has legally prohibited flirting in which young men leave their phone numbers for women to call in this largely sex-segregated society, "now there is deeper and easier flirting [through the Internet] but it is not banned." Similarly, although, "sexual films" are banned,

> through the Internet one can watch such films every hour. . . . Many books are banned from entering the country. We have a book fair that opened today in Shariqa. The books are censored on all levels, this is immoral, this encourages violence. . . . But you can open the Internet and get the books you need. . . . The planet is now small. What is the alternative? To cancel it? It will not be cancelled. Some speakers discuss globalization as if it is a cup of water I can throw in the trash. [They say,] "We must ban globalization! We must ban satellite channels!" There is no way to ban the satellite channels or the Internet. . . . Parents need to be taught how to deal with these technologies with skill. Like a knife. I can teach a child to stab someone with it, or maybe I can teach him how to use it to cut a fruit. The problem is not in the Internet, but in the child who wants to use it. Why don't I teach my daughter that when a scene comes up that is not good she should change the channel?[156]

Dr. al-Shaykh Mohammad 'Abdul Rahim Sultan Al-'Olama, a professor and associate dean in the Faculty of Shari'a and Law at UAE University in Abu Dhabi, focused on similar issues when I suggested that a changed world may require new values, including an end to gender separation, and that the high degree of conspicuous consumption in the country might impact sexual desires and behaviors. Al-'Olama agreed that new values are required, although gender mixing was not among them. The focus of schooling should be to train young people in what is acceptable and unacceptable behavior in cultural and Islamic terms and to teach them to consider the long-term costs and consequences of unregulated sexual behaviors:

> We were a closed environment. When the opening came with one push, there was a shock. The failing now is in the educational curriculum [of the schools]—. . . . There must be an effort to raise awareness so that every person knows his limits. . . . —we have limits as to what is allowed and not allowed in behavior. . . . Some people lived in a period in which women were banned from learning—this was not in or from Islam. In order to have neither that situation nor the current situation requires a type of preparation so that the boy—whether—even if I called for [gender] mixing, there will be many problems for up to about twenty years at least—until the people begin to what? To get used to it and become normal. So I cannot open this [topic]—and essentially mixing is not aspired to—meaning there is no need for it. But each person must know the other side [gender], and know the limits of behavior. . . . Everything is not banned. Right now, for example, if I were to ban my daughter from picking up the telephone to answer a man who may be calling—and I say, no, no, by God, because she is a girl, she cannot raise her voice. No, I cannot do this. And neither the opposite. To allow her to take her ease at all hours in her room, for hours, to talk. . . . So we need awareness and preparation for these things, we need the rearing of responsibility in the young person. . . . The girl needs to know that she has something she must protect [her virginity]. She must not give it up with ease. She needs to take into consideration the cost and obstacles of the situation. We teach them in business that when you open a project, you have to make a business plan so that you know the proportion of profit and loss. You cannot just enter a project and then lose. Same thing. . . . But the impact of this project [sexual relations] is for good. Meaning it is a life. And because of this in Islam there are restrictions, there are questions, there is research about this person [potential mate], who is he?[157]

Another problem is that television channels sell opulence, calamities, or occasional stiff informational programming focused on young people but not appealing to them, Al-ʿOlama continued. High-quality educational programming is required to teach appropriate Islamic behavior. Young people should be reared with a sense of self-restraint (*wazaʿ*), told why something is "forbidden," encouraged to ask even difficult or "impudent" questions of parents and schools, and convinced about why a behavior is wrong rather than simply fearing punishment.[158]

Marital relations are also a significant source of pedagogical attention. Darwish, like many others in the UAE, believes that "even if the young person has a PhD, they have zero in terms of family culture."[159] As a result, a range of institutions focus on inculcating this family culture. When interviewed, Ms. Hisa al-Diqqi was director of a newly established counseling and training center for native women associated with the Dubai Women's Renaissance Association that "will directly focus on resolving the problems of marriage" and sponsor "courses specifically for providing marriage skills." These courses are designed to educate different women's sectors: "young girls, those who will soon be married, newly married women, [and] women who have been married for a while." The organization also planned to develop courses for divorced women.[160]

A major goal of family pedagogy in the UAE is to make marriage more loving and romantic, an ambition targeted at both genders, but emphasizing men more than women. The campaign is well captured by the materials in a navy-blue velvety box distributed by the Dubai courts to couples planning to marry or the newly wed.[161] The materials, Darwish explains, focus on "family culture": "How do you deal with the wife? . . . How to be with the woman, how to strengthen your relationship with her. You as a wife, how to strengthen your relationship. How to get closer to his heart. How to make him love you again." Darwish believes that such projects have "reduced the percentage of divorces among newly married couples from 16 to 6 percent a year." The material in this box is part of a larger national project focused on Emirati families that includes "173 lectures to increase awareness among university students," teaching them how to "marry correctly" and "begin a good married life."[162]

Among the materials included in the marriage box is a sea-shell-shaped and decorated card produced by the Dubai Family Guidance and Reconciliation Office with a hanging string attached and prints of two small red heart-shaped candies on the back and front covers, with the word "Family" printed on one heart and "Priorities" on the other (al-awlawiyyāt al-ʿāʾilīyya). The opened card lists on one side, in bulleted form, "What does the wife need?" and on the other, "What does the husband need?" A husband, the card instructs, needs:

> to feel that his wife trusts him and his decisions; to feel accepted by his wife completely as he is, without her wanting to change him; to feel valued in his leadership of the family, maintenance, masculinity, and care and rearing of his children; to feel admiration by his wife for his person, understandings, personality, behaviors, and manners; to feel convinced that he is truly the heroic

[*fāris*] husband, with agreement on his effort and work; [and] to receive continuous encouragement for what he does, his efforts, and his concerns.

A wife, in turn, needs "to receive care and concern for how she looks, her clothing, and her sensitivities; to feel that she is understood by listening to her without advanced or unjustified judgments; to feel that she is in her husband's heart;
to receive affirmation of her feelings, sensitivities, and desires; to regularly receive assurance that she is loved, wanted, and valued."

The blue box also includes a "Study and Analysis" by Ahmad Jasim M. al-
Mutawwaʿ, a personal status judge in Kuwait, titled "Do you Know the Priorities
of Married Life?"[163] The first section of this booklet, titled "Between the Conquests of the Companions and the Collapse of Nations," argues that the companions of the Prophet Muhammad were successful in the world "in terms of
conquests, victories, and facilitating and spreading the call to God" because
each was "settled [*mustaqir*] in his home and with himself . . . , just as social
relations in their era, which depended on clarity and honesty, were stable." Al-
Mutawwaʿ argues that while there were "incidents of unraveling of families
[*tafakuk al-usra*]" and divorce was not banned in this early period, "the proportion of these problems was minor and reasonable." He linked the "collapse of
many large states in history, Byzantine, Persian, or Arab" not only to "economic
or political" causes, but also to "the destruction, loosening, and decline of the
family," which "all agree" were "the most important reason for the collapse." As
in the Prophet's time, al-Mutawwaʿ argues, strengthening social relations and
resolving conflicts "strengthen the state and increase its authority."[164]

Another important item in the marriage box is a two-sided cassette tape
wrapped in tan and brown plastic packaging on which is printed an image of
a beach, flowers, and calligraphy that includes a heart and a pink ribbon. The
tape is titled "The Sea of Love . . . A Tour of the Dangers of the Meaning of Love
. . . and Some Tales of Affection . . . and other Recollections about Longing and
Yearning."[165] The content is a "heart-to-heart" lecture about marriage success
by Shaykh Ibrahim Ibn-ʿAbd-illah al-Duwaysh of Saudi Arabia to a live audience that is apparently comprised of bachelor men. Al-Duwaysh is concerned
with divorce rates of about 30 percent in Saudi Arabia, which he considers a
"disaster by all measures." While ultimately a happy marital home depends on
submission to God, Shaykh al-Duwaysh stresses that from a Qurʾanic perspective it also requires affection and mercy/forgiveness between spouses, which he
sees as lacking, especially after people have been married for a number of years.

Al-Duwaysh worries about the "invasion from all directions by images of longing, passion, and love [which 'equals cheating'] through the satellite channels," and complains of foreign women, television serials, songs, films, and alcohol use. Relationships cannot be solely based on passion ('*ishq*) and pleasure (*mut'a*) and should not be taken for granted; they require work. Muslim family goals are to sustain the religion, be close, and have and rear children, as illustrated by the Prophet and his companions. It is "adolescent thinking" to assume that marriage requires sexual love or chemistry and passion. Real love is built after marriage, is not time delimited, and requires understanding, companionship, cooperation, affection, a sense of responsibility, and commitment to religious morality. He warns of obsession with romantic love, which is illusory, limited to the period of youth, and dies as flowers do.

In addition to deficits in affection and mercy, al-Duwaysh views boredom and emotional and expressive incompetence to be significant causes of marital discord from his experience counseling married people. Unhappily married women complain of cold and unexpressive husbands, harsh treatment, and men's perusal of "illicit things." Unhappily married men complain of household conflicts, wives they are not attracted to, emotionally cold wives, and wives who don't care for their "beauty like women on the satellites." Al-Duwaysh ends the cassette with a lengthy list of instructions for marital success. He advises spouses to use caring, sensitive, "loving words" rather than "emotional dryness" or meanness in their communication; to demonstrate affection through physicality; to avoid anger; to care about their grooming and appearance to each other; and to respect each other. Men are warned not to compare the wife to other women and are encouraged to "demonstrate you cherish her and love her"; "cooperate regularly on important projects such as doing laundry, cooking or something related to the children," that allow "you to think and laugh together"; recognize that women feel differently during pregnancy or their menstrual cycle; and be a responsible father and husband. Boredom can be alleviated by symbolic gift exchange (a card, flower, perfume); finding time to talk together regularly without the children present; looking at each other with mindfulness, love, flirtation, and smiles, using eyes and voices; sharing warm hellos and goodbyes; complimenting and respecting each other; and taking small vacations or walks together without the children. Men can feed the wife a bite of food; take a day off from work, since "marriage is about sustaining the self and soul, not just our bodies"; and give his wife a loving nickname.

Al-Duwaysh assures listeners that having plural wives is possible if the wife a husband is with feels that she is the most important when he is with her. Spouses are told to recognize that total freedom is not possible; be optimistic in crises; avoid repressing anger, fear, or sadness, since storing up emotions "has a major impact on loss of affection"; cooperate and dialogue about problems; not ignore each other at the end of the day; leave the anger and stress of the day behind at bedtime; thank, compliment, and forgive each other; communicate need of each other; say sorry when you are wrong; don't say, "I told you so" or humiliate each other; and always remember the good things about the spouse. Women are instructed to ensure that their child-rearing responsibilities do not exclude care for the husband and his feelings, since "husbands are big children."

Elites perceive a lack of "family culture" to be a systemic problem in the UAE. Men and women are understood to have new marital expectations and aesthetic, emotional and sexual desires, although men are viewed as the main source of family crisis. Responses seem particularly attuned to teaching self-regulation and emotional competence, marital and parental loving strategies that are "Islamic," and companionate marriage based on a soft patriarchal model. The goals are to stem the impact of new technological instruments, media flows, and other aspects of cultural "invasion" that are apparently appealing to too many indigenous people in the Arabian Peninsula. More so than in Egypt, the survival of the nation-state and indigenous culture (complicated as that is) is seen to require procreation within a stable national family. At the risk of stating the obvious, while the visions of ideal Emirati family life differ in certain respects, the dominant pedagogies and visions do not advocate for democratized marital relations.

.   .   .

The UAE and Egypt evidence efforts to reshape the conduct of citizens in the realms of marriage and sexuality through legal and procedural changes, putatively for the purposes of assisting women and families, but which I argue further empower authoritarian states over people's daily lives. Recent instructional discourses in both countries are also concerned with schooling self-controlled individuals who can resist modern temptations and yet sustain benignly patriarchal happy families. While the debates and pedagogies on how to improve the national family are multifaceted, all players articulate the family as foundational to the health, well-being, and development of the nation-state.

Conclusion

I BEGAN THIS BOOK with the "family crisis" story of Hind al-Hinnawy, who defied her lover/husband and the Egyptian state when she publicly—and to many, outrageously—insisted that her customary marriage to Ahmad al-Fishawy and the child conceived in that informal, unregistered, secret marriage be formally recognized as legitimate and licit despite al-Fishawy's denials that he married or had sex with her. Like many young people, al-Hinnawy had ignored her family and the state by directly negotiating the relationship with al-Fishawy. Al-Hinnawy used different avenues and techniques to eventually compel the resistant state and al-Fishawy to acknowledge the licitness of the marriage and her daughter. "Hind" became a poster child for different social positions. For many conservatives—religious authorities, parliamentarians, parents, and other lay people—she was an irresponsible and promiscuous woman who like many young people in Egypt was willing to violate gender, family, and sexual expectations. For disapproving state officials, she was the most public and emboldened representative of thousands of poorer and less confident women in courts clamoring for the state to resolve maintenance, marriage, paternity, and citizenship claims for themselves or their children. Many feminists, liberal activists, and young women understood al-Hinnawy and her daughter Lina to be victims of usually taken-for-granted sexual and gendered double standards, as well as masculinist state laws and policies that do not allow Egyptian women to transmit citizenship to their children. Al-Fishawy was widely viewed as an opportunistic young man who like many other pundits and moralizers publicly espouses conservative sexual values for instrumentalist reasons while violating them in private. Al-Hinnawy's situation, like that of millions of others who challenge sexual norms and expectations in the UAE and Egypt, demon-strates the degree to which family and heterosexuality are paradigmatic sites of biopower for the contemporary nation-state. The years-long saga between al-Hinnawy, al-Fishawy, and Egyptian state and judicial apparatuses should be understood within a history of governmentality in family domains. At the same time, the al-Hinnawy case, like thousands of other examples of "family crisis," illustrate the uneven penetration and plural responses to governmentalizing projects. Despite the hegemony of corporatist family life, millions of people increasingly undermine these norms by remaining single, delaying marriage, divorcing, having sex outside of marriage, marrying foreigners, and participat-ing in "secret" marital and sexual liaisons that are often temporary.

Instead of focusing on the punitive and directly controlling power of states, the "governmentality" approach assumes they largely rule by schooling partic-ular values and conduct using a variety of techniques; managing populations through the cultivation of particular "mentalities." Personal status domains are crucial arenas for such cultivation in the United Arab Emirates (UAE) and Egypt. Preferred family conduct is cultivated through legal and procedural rationaliza-tion, documentation and registration requirements, policing, and more recently, marriage-counseling imperatives for women seeking judicial divorce. These practices are typically framed as intended to increase efficiency and promote development and well-being. From a governmentality approach, rules and laws related to sexual behavior and family conduct are most significant as attempts to reconstitute norms of behavior. Although these legal and procedural processes are secular in the sense that they serve the temporal needs of government, they are often referred to as "shariʿa"-derived or consistent with shariʿa given the le-gitimacy attached to Islamic idioms. Rather than using reform or modernization lenses, I view state-initiated marriage and family projects as largely function-ing to manage life, resources, and behavior for the purposes of efficient rule. Codification and other rationalizing mechanisms have increased the centrality of these undemocratic states and their opportunities for intervention in the most intimate aspects of daily life. Legal governmentality did not and does not occur on "blank slates" in social or political terms. Consolidating Egypt into a modern state required displacing Islamic legal systems as independent sources of legiti-macy and authority. In the UAE by comparison, state-led legal rationalization and expansion of federal dominion over competing "tribal" and religious sources of authority are more recent, more subject to resistance, and thus more porous. State-led projects to restrict independent Islamic jurisprudence or delimit tribal authority systems—which are fluid, contested, and socially constituted—are complicated by the fact that UAE rulers rely on tribal idioms for their "kin"-based political power at the emirate and federal levels.

Marriage in both societies is seen to facilitate social and sexual satisfaction, procreation, and child rearing and to limit the social instability and moral hazards of prolonged sexual abstinence or nonmarital sexual activity. Nevertheless, many people violate these expectations by remaining single and/or having sexual relationships outside of formal marriage. Interestingly, men are viewed to be the main source of family crisis in a variety of ways by state and religious elites as well as women. Considered more likely to be sexually and maritally unruly and immature subjects, men pose challenges to family well-being, state budgets, citizenship rules, and national demography—especially when they easily resort to divorce, behave irresponsibly toward wives and children, marry noncitizen women, or have sex with women who are not their wives. Men more than women, it appears, test the biopolitical agendas of modern states. When men are disorderly in their sexual or marriage behaviors, they also challenge the state's self-appointed role as the guardian of moral behavior, which Middle Eastern and North African (MENA) states more than others consider to be within their ambit, to some degree in lieu of political legitimacy and accountability.

Challenges to hegemonic family and sexual norms are made on unequal terrains. For example, women are more likely than men to be punished for sexual and marriage transgressions and to have less control over the terms of relationships. These challenges to dominant marriage and sexual practices are motivated by multiple and often complex desires and conditions. "Family crisis" discourse often obscures these desires and conditions. For example, dominant family crisis explanations overemphasize economic factors (such as costs of weddings and housing, and dowry amounts as explanations of female singlehood) and failures of moral cultivation (by parents, teachers), while neglecting to address the patriarchal legal and cultural contexts of marriage, divorce, and citizenship and gendered double standards with respect to sexual behavior. It is rarely acknowledged that cultural change is inevitable and potentially an improvement over the status quo, although the latter is difficult to know in advance and undoubtedly produces great apprehension. Because family crisis discourse is so pervasive, moreover, critics of their governments can discuss with impunity the "deterioration of the moral fabric"—and often call for state action and expansions of power in these domains—as proxy for issues more difficult to address, such as corruption, economic stagnation, lack of accountability, lack of opportunities, and restrictions on political organizing and the press.

The shaping of subjectivities and desires—or the cultivation of human conduct—is a matter that involves many entities with often competing agendas. While modern states aim to rule efficiently, usually framing governmental projects as concerned with improving human life and well-being, corporations make money by selling products and services advertised as advancing human happiness, choice, pleasure, and even survival. A range of other entities (human rights organizations, religious groups, feminist groups, UN apparatuses, and so on) are just as concerned to cultivate particular subjectivities and behaviors. These entities deploy terms such as "freedom," "rights," and "well-being" as they are applicable to their agendas and workable within given contexts. While the UAE and Egypt exhibit strong evidence of changing practices, desires, and norms in relation to family, sexuality, and gender, these changes are often reductively attributed to invasions of Western culture, values, and products. The fragmentation and proliferation of Islamic religious discourse, the rise in communication technologies, capitalist consumerism, and the multidirectional flows of ideas, products, and people of course have an impact on family, sexual, and gender norms. Moreover, the discourses of transnational Islam and neoliberal capitalism augment rather than conflict with each other in that both encourage individuation and personalized decision making, which often challenge the authority of families, nation-states, and religious orthodoxy. But emerging forms of subjectivity and desire also form in interaction with diverse national, indigenous, and regional factors, including popular knowledge that different "local" forms of sexual, marriage, and divorce practices are possible; plural Islamic theories on human need and licit behavior; status systems based on idioms of kin affiliation that interact with new opportunities for consumption; the laws and policies of postcolonial states as they affect every life realm, including economy, politics, citizenship, sexuality, and marriage; and cultural and institutional forms of gender and other inequality that have always produced social tension.

Since "the family" is persistently articulated as a fundamental concern of the nation-state and an important site of its health and development in the UAE and Egypt, perceived crises in this domain produce a noticeable range of legal and didactic projects concerned with schooling appropriate national family culture and sexual subjectivities and behaviors. These biopolitical projects are structured by a combination of nationalist and Islamic discourse, generally reinforce gender inequality within the family (albeit in modern forms), and rely on gender-essentialist assumptions. But they must also respond to multiple and shifting wants and "needs" with respect to marriage, sexuality, and gender. While gendered, sexual, and family subjectivities and desires are changing, state and religious elites (and most intellectuals) reinforce a conservative vision of family. This may be because family patriarchy is one arena of male authority that is useful in undemocratic states in which men are disfranchised in other domains. In this respect, family and state patriarchies can reinforce each other.

Feminists and women's rights activists in the region often advocate legal rationalization because they believe it increases women's rights by reducing individual discretion in male-dominated institutions. Similarly, expanded counseling requirements and policing are understood to produce better marital behavior and hold husbands accountable. State officials frequently advocate rationalization and increased control over biopolitical domains as saving money and time, part of which requires policing men's economic responsibilities to wives, children, and parents. Feminists, elites, and state officials usually share the belief that state control increases the ability to "positively" impact family life and increase community well-being, although they are likely to disagree on the substance of particular state policies. It is important to underscore, however, that in authoritarian contexts, changes intended to increase gender equality seem to be institutionalized only to the degree they are perceived to serve or be harmless to state interests, which should give pause to feminist or liberal gender activists. Nevertheless, MENA states support women in their family policies and politics more often than is recognized by feminist scholarship, and women may disproportionately rely on these authoritarian states for their ability to control men and extract resources from them. The most paradoxical aspect of the legal and procedural personal status changes examined in this book is not the expansion of biopower or the rearticulation of patriarchal social forms. Rather, it is that most social sectors take expansion of authoritarian state control over the family for granted and even encourage the logic of efficient management and regulation of these relationships of exchange. Such modern forms of power over everyday life are pervasive and ultimately designed to serve state interests even when they are benign or positive in their effects. For this reason it makes little sense to consider governance projects as automatically "bad" or "good," "necessary or unnecessary."[1] Given the persistent lack of democracy among modern Arab regimes of different ideological persuasions, it does make sense to wonder whether feminists and liberals should consider these states suitable allies for democratizing gender and marriage relations. Moreover, what if regime authoritarianism in the region uniquely depends on the penetration of family life made possible by personal status or family laws, as I posit?

Scholarship influenced by the writing of Michel Foucault on governmentality usually has embedded within it a critique of the ends of such projects, which are assumed to be effective social control since power works best through the production of self-regulating behaviors and identities. This critique may romanticize ungovernmentalized realms, whose subjects are understood to be freer of regulation and discipline. The reality is that governmentality projects are not developed on power-neutral and regulation-free terrains. They often compete with other systems of regulation and subjectivication, including patriarchies, racial-ethnic-religious stratifications, and so on. While "traditional" systems of power and subjectivication are often less formal, rigid, and rationalized, they are difficult to categorize as necessarily superior to all modern governmentalizing projects, which partly explains why the latter can be so compelling for people without a stake in the expansion of state power or authoritarianism. In the cases addressed in this book, for example, male-dominated religious, tribal, or ethnicity-based authority systems do not fairly represent the admittedly plural interests of women or marginalized individuals and groups within their domains. It makes sense, then, that many members of such groups would find "modern" forms of subjectivication and organization that serve state interests, such as codified family legal systems or new pedagogies, to also suit their goals of weakening, challenging, or displacing existing authority systems. In Egypt and the UAE, modern governance projects have unfortunately also normalized and helped to consolidate undemocratic states that to varying degrees absorbed and rationalized preexisting systems of inequality if they served state purposes.

I end this book with a "family improvement" story focused on Widad Lutah, an Emirati marriage counselor I interviewed who was recently the subject of a *New York Times* article, titled "Challenging Sex Taboos." Ms. Lutah was the first counselor (and remains the only woman among seven people) appointed by the ruler of Dubai to the Dubai Courts Family Guidance section, which was established in 2001 to mediate between and advise unhappy spouses. The story clearly indicates that discussing intimate details before representatives of the state for the purposes of improving and stabilizing national families has become normative. The Family Guidance office, writes Robert Worth, "has become an all-purpose therapy destination for people with marital problems." In January 2009, Ms. Lutah published *Top Secret: Sexual Guidance for Married Couples* in the UAE, which became an "instant scandal." The book provides "erotic advice" and is "packed with vivid anecdotes" from her eight years on the job. Ms. Lutah's book also discusses family problems such as infidelity (and how texting and e-mail have made it easier) and high divorce rates, highlighting the confusions wrought by social, cultural, and economic transformations in the Emirates. She teaches her clients that sexual pleasure in marriage is Islamically licit, necessary for wives as well as husbands, and crucial for marital sustenance and stability.[2]

The Lutah story illustrates not only the degree to which therapeutic talk and instruction about sex and pleasure in marriage have become normalized, even in conservative Islamic public spheres, but also the extent to which such projects are integral to biopolitical agendas that understand family stability to be imperative to the efficient working, security, and reproduction of the nation-state. Family counseling is now required by law in the UAE and Egypt for women, but not men, seeking divorce. There is evidence that many ruling regimes would like to require counseling for men and otherwise restrict their marriage and divorce options but understand this would not be tolerated by men. While MENA states are often recognized by feminists to support a patriarchal agenda, they only do so to the degree that such a system reinforces state interests. Indeed, it is men and not women who state authorities and religious elites are more likely to consider threatening to family and social stability. Allowing men patriarchal authority within their families is a useful means to assuage and manage them, given that these states are generally minimally accountable to their citizens. But male dominance in family life is being challenged by concerns that it threatens the national family, especially in contexts where women may want more mutual, emotionally and sexually fulfilling relations. The dominant solutions to perceptions of family crisis, including those posited by Lutah, rarely acknowledge the possibility of a relationship between family crisis and pervasive gender inequality and sexual control. As Lutah indicates in her discussion of women's sexual pleasure and satisfaction in marriage, however, expectations and desires in the region are dynamic. This dynamism is often reductively attributed to external factors rather than recognized to be the result of complex local-global articulations. Both the al-Hinnawy and Lutah stories indicate that sexual, gendered, and other individuations and desires are emerging that challenge corporatist forms of family and state. In the modern world these challenges, indeed the desires themselves, are always to some degree structured by the penetrating and commodifying processes of global capitalism, and yet the "crises" they produce also seem to invite further insertions into intimate life by states.

Reference Matter

Notes

Introduction

1. Sadek, "Cairo as a Global/Regional Cultural Capital?" 168.
2. Abou el-Magd, "Single Mother Shocks"; "Egyptian Court Nixes."
3. MacFarquhar, "Paternity Suit"; Abou el-Magd, "Single Mother Shocks."
4. Ibid.
5. Saleh, "Paternity Scandal Divides"; MacFarquhar, "Paternity Suit"; "New Paternity Law Stipulating."
6. MacFarquhar, "Paternity Suit."
7. Ibid.
8. "New Paternity Law Stipulating"; "Egyptian Appeals Court Rules."
9. "Egyptian Court Nixes."
10. Al-Naggar, "Egypt: Actor Is Father"; "Egyptian Appeals Court Rules."
11. Samir 'Umar reporting on Luna al-Shibil, "Secret Marriage in Our Arab World."
12. Video from "al-Bayt Baytak" program interview with Ahmad al-Fishawy.
13. MacFarquhar, "Paternity Suit."
14. 'Umar reporting in al-Shibil, "Secret Marriage in Our Arab World."
15. Saleh, "Paternity Scandal."
16. For examples, see Baron, "Making and Breaking of Marital Bonds"; Sonbol, *Women, the Family, and Divorce Laws*; Charrad, *States and Women's Rights*; Mir Hosseini, *Marriage on Trial*; Joseph, *Gender and Citizenship in the Middle East*; Molyneux, "Law, the State"; Arabi, "Itinerary of a Fatwa."
17. Singerman, *Avenues of Participation*, 74; Inhorn, *Local Babies, Global Science*, 227.
18. Mir-Hosseini, *Marriage on Trial*, 31–32.
19. I appreciate a useful conversation on this issue with Dr. Moulouk Berry. Other words exist for heterosexual intercourse, including *waṭa'* (as in *waṭi'-ha*, to have sexual intercourse with her), or more mutually, *'ilaqāt jimā'* (sexual relations).

20. El Alami, *Marriage Contract in Islamic Law*, 10–11.

21. Stowasser, *Women in the Qur'an*, 21.

22. Judith Tucker's analysis indicates that muftis of all traditions during the Ottoman period in Syria and Palestine viewed the "asymmetrical rights and obligations" of men and women in marriage as reflecting "innate biological difference," although they disapproved of "unbridled male domination" within marriage. Tucker, *House of the Law*, 70, 82–84. Also see Moors, "Debating Islamic Family Law," 145–46.

23. Mir-Hosseini, *Marriage on Trial*, 35.

24. Tucker, *House of the Law*, 75.

25. Abdal-Rehim, "Family and Gender Laws in Egypt," 104.

26. Esposito with DeLong-Bas, *Women in Muslim Family Law*, 33, 51.

27. Hanafi traditions only allowed two legitimate reasons for women to gain a judicial divorce: in cases where the husband was incapable of consummating the marriage, or in cases where he was an apostate from Islam. Arabi, "Dawning of the Third Millennium"; Hanafi traditions allowed two reasons for women to gain judicial annulment (*faskh*): male impotence or castration and the husband being missing. Hasan, "Granting Khul'," 82.

28. Tucker, *House of the Law*, 80, 95–97.

29. Sonbol, "History of Marriage Contracts," 178–79.

30. Abdal-Rehim, "Family and Gender Laws," 105–6.

31. Zakareya, "Khol': A Socio-Legal Study," 46–47.

32. Zulfiqqar, "Equality and Equal Opportunities," 56. Even if the husband initiates divorce, claiming wifely disobedience similarly has the potential to release him of economic obligations. Mir-Hosseini, *Marriage on Trial*, 34–41, 55–60.

33. Soffan, *Women of the United Arab Emirates*, 30, 43.

34. Heard-Bey, *From Trucial States*, 147.

35. Ibid., 148.

36. C. Eickelman, *Women and Community*, 110.

37. Heard-Bey, *From Trucial States*, 149.

38. Cuno, "Divorce and the Fate of the Family," 210–11.

39. Fargues, "State Policies and the Birth Rate," 121.

40. Soffan, *Women*, 44; Heard-Bey, *From Trucial States*, 147.

41. Jane Bristol-Rhys associates this high maternal morbidity rate to a discontinued practice "of inserting salt into the uterus after childbirth to staunch bleeding" and clean "out any remnant placenta. The uterine wall hardened with this treatment and would often tear under the pressure of labour." "Weddings, Marriage and Money," 31.

42. Soffan, *Women*, 43.

43. El Alami, *Marriage Contract*, 57; Tucker, *House of the Law*, 48–49. For a detailed discussion of the issue of guardianship in marriage for girls and women, see Sonbol, "Adults and Minors," esp. 246–50.

44. The Hanafi school was the most strict about the requirement of equal status, which was to be determined according to custom but was generally based on lineage, property of the groom in comparison to the bride's father, and occupation of the groom in comparison to the bride's father. Shaham, *Family and the Courts*, 44.

45. Tucker, *House of the Law*, 50–51; El Alami, *Marriage Contract*, 57, 68–69; Sonbol, "Adults and Minors," 242–48; Abdal-Rehim, "Family and Gender Laws," 97–102. I am grateful to Amira al-Azhary Sonbol for a useful e-mail discussion on guardianship issues (e-mail correspondence with author, June 28, 2007).

46. El Alami, *Marriage Contract*, 52–53; Sonbol e-mail 2007.

47. Sonbol, "Adults and Minors," 247, 249–51.

48. Ibid., 247–48, 251–52.

49. Shaham, *Family and the Courts*, 47–48.

50. Sonbol, "History of Marriage Contracts," 161.

51. Sonbol, "History of Marriage Contracts," 161; Moors, "Debating Islamic Family Law."

52. El Alami, *Marriage Contract*, 58; Sonbol e-mail 2007.

53. Sonbol e-mail 2007.

54. Interview by author with 'Abdul Salam Muhammad Darwish; Interview by author with Mohamed al Roken.

55. Heard-Bey, *From Trucial States*, 146.

56. Mir-Hosseini, *Marriage on Trial*, 32; Shaham, *Family and the Courts*, 43; Wikan, *Tomorrow, God Willing*, 244.

57. Sonbol, "History of Marriage Contracts," 169.

58. El Alami, *Marriage Contract*, 22–23, 65.

59. Ibid., 66.

60. Ibid., 108–12.

61. For example, unlike weddings in most countries in the Arab world or even coastal Oman, Christine Eickelman found that most weddings she attended in 1979–80 "in the Omani interior are unostentatious and so little remarked by nonfamily members that it is difficult for an outsider like me even to know when one is taking place." These ceremonies were intimate affairs attended by few people. C. Eickelman, *Women and Community*, 106–7. Zubaida, *Islam, the People*, 114.

62. Singerman and Ibrahim, "Cost of Marriage," 89.

63. Wikan, *Tomorrow, God Willing*, 244; Singerman, *Avenues of Participation*, 85–87.

64. Amin and Al-Bassusi, "Education, Wage Work," 1,294.

65. Singerman and Ibrahim, "Cost of Marriage," 89; Hoodfar, *Between Marriage*; Ali, *Planning the Family*, 133–34; Abdal-Rehim, "Family and Gender Laws," 97–98; Singerman, *Avenues of Participation*, 86–87.

66. Wikan, *Tomorrow, God Willing*, 244.

67. El-Kholy, *Defiance and Compliance*, 110–11; Singerman, *Avenues of Participation*, 119.

68. El-Kholy, *Defiance and Compliance*, 116, 118.

69. Singerman and Ibrahim, "Cost of Marriage," 80; Singerman, *Avenues of Participation*, 74–75.

70. Interview by author with Dr. Faysal 'Abd al-Qadir Yunis.

71. Amin and Al-Bassusi, "Education, Wage Work," 1,293–96.

72. Hoodfar, *Between Marriage*, 68; Singerman and Ibrahim, "Cost of Marriage," 97.

73. Yunis interview.

74. El-Kholy, *Defiance and Compliance*, 123–24.

75. Singerman, "Economic Imperatives," 13, figure 2–1.

76. Hoodfar, *Between Marriage*, 65.

77. Data from 1999 indicate that 39 percent of couples who had married in the previous five years lived with the family of the groom and such a strategy was much more likely to be favored by couples with less education and status. Singerman and Ibrahim, "Cost of Marriage," 103, 105.

78. About 37 percent of Egyptian couples and 65 percent of couples who married in Cairo between 1990 and 1995 included no dower in the contract. In 1999 only 27 percent of Egyptian couples reported exchanging a dower, although in such cases the bride's family expects the groom to purchase a larger share of home furnishings and gifts. Singerman and Ibrahim, "Cost of Marriage," 99–100.

79. In 2006, key money constituted about 32 percent of the costs of marriages for the average Egyptian. Singerman, "Economic Imperatives," 5. El-Kholy, *Defiance and Compliance*, 125–27; Wikan, *Tomorrow, God Willing*," 244–45; Yunis interview; Interview by author with Nawla Darwiche, Cairo, December 22, 2003; Singerman and Ibrahim, "Cost of Marriage," 105.

80. Abaza, *Changing Consumer Cultures*, 161.

81. Bristol-Rhys, "Weddings, Marriage and Money," 21, 23.

82. Hurreiz, *Folklore and Folklife*, 98.

83. Bristol-Rhys, "Weddings, Marriage and Money," 25–26.

84. Darwish interview.

85. Bristol-Rhys, "Weddings, Marriage and Money," 20–36, 24.

86. Interview by author with Ms. Widad Lutah, Dubai, 2003.

87. This ceremony was also called *milka* in nearby Oman in the late 1970s. Eickelman found that it usually took place "early in the morning . . . in order not to disrupt the day's work. . . . After coffee or sweets, the men of the two households have the tribal leader, judge, or other qualified notable read the marriage contract. . . . The groom kneels in front of the notable as the contract is read and repeats after him the words of the contract in classical Arabic. The father or guardian of the bride then comes in front of the notable. The conditions of the contract are read to him. On behalf of the bride,

he repeats the words to signal consent to the agreement." Women celebrated separately the same day with visits from family and neighbors; neither "the bride nor the groom is a central figure" in the day's events. C. Eickelman, *Women and Community*, 104–6.

88. Hurreiz, *Folklore and Folklife*, 98.

89. According to a statistical study undertaken in 1994 and 1995 that sampled more than two thousand married women in the UAE (median age of twenty-five), 50.5 percent of the women had married a relative. First-cousin marriages were the most common, at 26.2 percent of all marriages. Consanguineous marriage rates were higher in Al 'Ayn City, Abu Dhabi (54.2 percent) in comparison to Dubai City (39.9 percent). Al-Gazali et al., "Consanguineous Marriages," 29.

90. Heard-Bey, *From Trucial States*, 147–49.

91. Ibid., 148.

92. Soffan, *Women*, 33.

93. Ibid., 33–34.

94. Ibid., 34. The government of nearby Oman similarly decreed a lowering of the dowry in 1973 and ruled that the home furnishings provided by the groom were not legally required and should not be insisted upon. Wikan, *Behind the Veil in Arabia*, 193.

95. Group Interview by author with six men students at United Arab Emirates University, December 9, 2003. Interview by author with Muhammad 'Abdel Rahim, Dubai, UAE, December 1, 2003. Parents of the bride and groom violate this decree by writing the dowry amount up to the legal limit in the marital contract but verbally agreeing to a much higher dowry.

96. Singerman and Ibrahim, "Cost of Marriage," 83.

97. Hurreiz, *Folklore and Folklife*, 99–100. Unni Wikan provides ethnographic description of an Omani wedding in the mid-1970s in *Behind the Veil in Arabia*, 212–30.

98. Soffan, *Women*, 30.

99. Lutah interview.

100. Peck, *United Arab Emirates*, 85.

101. Interviews by author with Ms. Amal Bachiri and Mr. Ahmed Chahine, Dubai, UAE, 2003.

102. Lay, "Interpretations of Islamic Practices," 189.

103. Krane, "Arab Police Arrest 22."

104. Hala 'Ahed Dib, guest on al-Shibil, "For Women Only"; Darwish interview.

105. Haeri, *Law of Desire*.

106. Ibid., 4–5.

107. Ibid., 52–55, 15, 28–29, 59.

108. Informant did not want to be identified. Interviewed by author in Abu Dhabi, UAE, December 2003.

109. I use the term "discourse" in the Foucauldian sense that understands symbolic systems (such as language) as co-constituting human subjectivities and ways of

living, thinking, feeling, and doing. The discourse approach assumes words to circulate within larger histories, materialities, and symbolic frameworks that give them meaning, determine what is included and excluded, and organize oppositions. Michel Foucault was particularly interested in the institutional and social "conditions within which discourses [and selves and identities] are formed and transformed." Hunt and Wickham, *Foucault and Law*, 7–9.

110. Starrett, *Putting Islam to Work*, 161, 164, 186.

111. Some scholars argue that Islamic law, recognizing the "anarchic dimension" of the "sexual impulse" with respect to the biological reproduction of the group and the transmission of property, regulates it through a gendered legalistic approach that allows male polygamy and defines explicit criteria for licit heterosexuality within contractual relations. Arabi, "Itinerary of a Fatwa," 150.

112. 'Abd al-Jawad and al-Kurdi, "Social Change and the Customary Marriage"; Interview by author with Mr. Jamal Obaid al-Bah, UAE Marriage Fund; Davidson, *United Arab Emirates*, 262; al-Shibil satellite program.

113. Appadurai, "Disjuncture and Difference."

114. Al-Rasheed, "Introduction: Localizing the Transnational," 3.

115. Davidson, *United Arab Emirates*, 263.

116. Ibid., 78–79, and n. 88 on same pages.

117. "Dubai 'sex on beach' couple."

118. Long, "Raped by the State," 126–27.

119. Approximately four million people live in the UAE, less than 20 percent of them citizens, and about eighty million people reside in Egypt. While the legal system and certain Egyptian state policies play a role in accentuating Coptic Christian minority status, intercommunal religious tensions have frequently risen in modern Egypt as a response to the deployment of this difference by politicians seeking to reinforce their political positions, often by constituting Christians as a disloyal fifth column. David Zeidan emphasizes that Egyptian Muslims hold "multiple world views" and prioritize their Egyptian, Arab, or Muslim identity "according to context." Moreover, Muslim-Christian tensions exist within a broader history of contestation and ambiguity over what it means to be Egyptian. Zeidan, "Copts," direct quotes from 60.

120. The UAE government does not provide population numbers according to citizenship given the political sensitivity of such data. Ahmed Kanna contends that while the lower tiers of these workers are often visible in their racial and sartorial differences, they have few rights and are highly regulated and restricted, and thus their significance to the political economy is made invisible. Kanna, "Dubai in a Jagged World"; Kanna, *Not Their Fathers' Days*.

121. Kechichian, "Unity in the Arabian Peninsula," 285.

122. About seventy thousand Emirati citizens are of Iranian background and an

additional one hundred thousand nonresident workers are Iranian. Marchal, "Dubai: Global City," 96.

123. Kanna, *Not Their Fathers' Days*, 10–11. Khatib, *Beyond the Mysterious*, 174–75, 177–78. Another liminal category of residents in the UAE and other Gulf states are *bidūn*, people "without" passports, citizenship, or state nationality and limited access to state resources. Their ancestors or they came from nearby countries such as Yemen, Oman, or Iran when documentation was not required to move around or live any- where. Al Roken interview. For further discussion on policy (especially in Kuwait) to- ward this category of noncitizens and the tensions surrounding them, see Kapiszewski, *Nationals and Expatriates*, 53–57.

124. Kanna, *Not Their Fathers' Days*, 191–92.

125. Khatib, *Beyond the Mysterious*, 37–39.

126. Singerman and Amar, "Introduction: Contesting," 25.

127. Wickham, *Mobilizing Islam*, 97, 99; Davidson, *United Arab Emirates*, 78–79; Carnegie Endowment, *Arab Political Systems*.

128. Karam, *Women, Islamisms*, 23.

129. Singerman and Amar, "Introduction: Contesting," 3.

130. Ibid., 4–7.

131. Davidson, "Arab Nationalism and British Opposition."

132. Ibid., 890.

133. Davidson, *United Arab Emirates*, 274–75.

134. Soffan, *Women*, 90.

135. Ibid., 91.

136. Ibid., 90–98.

137. Ibid., 93.

138. Fakhro, "Changing Role of Women," 410, 421.

139. Ibid., 422.

140. Ibid., 410–11, 421.

141. Al-Ali, *Secularism, Gender and the State*.

142. The first state organization focused on women's rights, the National Com- mittee for Women, was established in 1993 by Suzanne Mubarak, the wife of Presi- dent Husni Mubarak, and was affiliated with the National Council for Childhood and Motherhood. The charge of this committee was to "to promote women in all spheres of life." The committee held three conferences in the 1990s, including the final one in 1998, which centered on raising "the awareness of women, especially ru- ral women, of their political and legal rights." In Abdul Sattar, *Women in Egyptian Legislations*, unnumbered pages. This special and at times patronizing attention to rural Egyptian women is in keeping with a long tradition of constructing them as in special need of modernizing education. For example, see Abu-Lughod, "Dialects of Women's Empowerment." The National Committee for Women was reconstituted

into the National Council for Women (NCW) in 2000, established by Presidential Decree No. 90, which affiliated the organization with "the President of the Republic." The NCW mandate includes proposing "public policy matters for the society and its constitutional institutions concerning the development and the empowerment of women to enable them to play their social and economic roles, and to integrate their efforts in comprehensive development programs." In Abdul Sattar, *Women in Egyptian Legislations*, 47. The NCW gave itself the power to draft laws, advise the People's Assembly on laws and policies related to women, and "organize training sessions to raise awareness of the role, rights and duties of women." The first three NCW conferences focused on "women, citizenship, and development" (2000); "gender mainstreaming" in the state's five-year plan for 2002–2007 (2001); and "women and the modernization of society" was the title of the 2002 conference held in Minya, Upper Egypt. The 2004 conference focused on "Egyptian Women and Development Goals of the Millennium" (held in Alexandria). In Abdul Sattar, *Women in Egyptian Legislations*, 48–49. Among the recent services initiated by NCW legal activists has been a Complaints Office for women to present their personal status issues and be assigned free legal representation in family courts if they cannot afford a lawyer. Interview by author with Mona Ibrahim Al-Korashy, lawyer in the High Appeals Court, Giza, Egypt, May 26, 2008.

143. The booklet notes the low representation of women in the People's Assembly and other political apparatuses and long-running attempts to address this problem with a policy of "positive discrimination." In 2000, women comprised about 2.4 percent of the People's Assembly and are reported to have low representation at other political levels. In 1979, the Sadat executive branch instituted a law of "positive discrimination" favoring women running for office, although this was reversed by the Egyptian parliament in 1986 as unconstitutional and discriminatory against men. Abdul Sattar, *Women in Egyptian Legislations*, 37, 41–42, 45.

144. Group Interview by author with seven women students at (Arab) Sharjah University, UAE, December 14, 2003; Group Interview by author with six men students at UAE University, Abu Dhabi, December 9, 2003.

145. Khatib, *Beyond the Mysterious*, 305–6.

146. In a 2002 survey that included 250 women students from nearby emirates studying at Zayed University in Dubai, 40 percent had a driver's license and 29 percent owned their own car. L. Walters and T. Walters, "Transitional Woman," 227.

147. Ibid., 222.

148. Fakhro, "Changing Role of Women," 396; Khatib, *Beyond the Mysterious*, 227.

149. Schvaneveldt et al., "Generational and Cultural Changes," 79. Poroma Rebello found that in Dubai, native women who wore these fashions do so "more as a symbolic gesture that marks them out as honourable and respectable women who wish to avoid undue attention." Rebello, "Politics of Fashion," 18.

150. In the 2003–2004 academic year, of 43,581 national children in government secondary schools, 57 percent were girls and 43 percent were boys. The balance was reversed in UAE private secondary schools during the same year: of 3,967 national children, 59.8 percent were boys and 40.2 were girls. In total, 55.6 percent of secondary students were girls and 44.4 percent boys, with another 1,511 national boys (no girls) attending technical and vocational high schools. The gender differences are even more dramatic at the university level: in 2003–2004, 68.1 percent of undergraduates were women and 31.9 percent were men. From GCC *Statistical Bulletin* 15, chap. 2, tables 11, 15, 32, 38, 2006.

151. Hasso, *Resistance, Repression, and Gender Politics*.

152. For discussion of the "political field" idea, see ibid., xvii–xxi.

153. The concept of scale is often understood and deployed in different ways by ecological, political, and feminist geographers. For example, Neumann, "Political Ecology"; Sayre, "Ecological and Geographical Scale"; Marston and Smith, "States, Scales and Households."

154. Nagar et al., "Locating Globalization," 260–62.

155. Sayre, "Ecological and Geographical Scale," 280–81.

156. Haraway, "Situated Knowledges"; Collins, "Black Feminist Epistemology"; and Visweswaran, *Fictions of Feminist Ethnography*, 41–42, 50.

Chapter 1

1. Following shari'a requires Muslims to "perform the mandatory and refrain from the prohibited." Lombardi, *State Law as Islamic Law*, 12–13. The derived adjective *shar'ī* can refer to a behavior or law being Islamically licit according to a range of orthodoxies or to the more secular understanding of "legal."

2. Kozma, "Negotiating Virginity," 63.

3. This train of thought was initiated during a 2008 interview with Dr. Su'ad Salih, when she and I discussed the two terms in response to my use of the word "*'ā'ila*" (which she preferred) rather than "*usra*" in a question. Definitions come from Baalbaki, *Al-Mawrid*, 105, 109, 787.

4. Walby, "Contributions," 552; Foucault, "Subject and Power," 792.

5. Foucault, "Subject and Power," 793.

6. Foucault, *Birth of Biopolitics*, 77.

7. Abrams, "Notes on the Difficulty," 122.

8. Derek Sayer argues for (1) recognizing the "fragility of power and the permanence of alternatives"; (2) avoiding unitary understandings of "the state" that overinvest it with cohesiveness and ideological persuasiveness; and (3) acknowledging that state efforts to consolidate rule are often both oppressive and empowering given their "polysemic, ambiguous, and contradictory quality." The state, Sayer contends, "lives in and through subjects" in quotidian "forms of state formation" that "define the

boundaries of the possible" in everyday life. Sayer, "Everyday Forms of State Formation," 369–73, 375–77. Informed by Antonio Gramsci rather than Foucault (or Marx or
Weber), William Roseberry similarly cautions that state-driven ideological projects
often do not achieve their aims—that is, they are not necessarily hegemonic. Roseberry, "Hegemony and the Language of Contention," 365.

9. Abrams, "Notes on the Difficulty," 117–19, 113–14, 122–23. As Timothy Mitchell
points out, however, even armies (and prisons and police forces) have no independent
existence apart from "individual soldiers," so constructing them as superordinate and
apart from citizens is part and parcel of mystification. Mitchell, "State, Economy," 180.
Also see Foucault, "Governmentality," 142.

10. Sharma and Gupta, "Introduction: Rethinking," 13.

11. Foucault, "Governmentality." Also see Foucault, *Birth of Biopolitics*, 78.

12. Foucault, "Subject and Power," 789–90.

13. Asad, *Formations of the Secular*, 217.

14. Foucault, "Political Technology," 161–62.

15. Dean, *Governmentality*, 34.

16. In the art of government perspective, "economy" calls for use of methods com-
mensurate with "wise" family governance, whereby "individuals, goods and wealth
within the family" are correctly managed by a "good father" in order to make "the
family fortunes prosper." Such state management should allow rule of "the bee-hive
without needing a sting," with all willing to "obey the laws, accomplish the tasks expected of them, practice the trade to which they are assigned, and respect the established order." Foucault, "Governmentality," 134, 135–37.

17. Hunt and Wickham, *Foucault and Law*, 79–80.

18. Foucault, "Governmentality," 142–43.

19. Foucault, *Birth of Biopolitics*, 187, 296–97. Abrams similarly maintains that the
state as an ideological project is produced at least as much outside its formal apparatuses as within them. Abrams, "Notes on the Difficulty," 119. Gupta argues that using
the term "civil society" reinforces the idea of a "unitary entity that stands apart from,
and in opposition to, 'the state'" in a way that is "mutually exclusive" and "jointly ex-
haustive of the social space." Gupta, "Blurred Boundaries," 230–31. Mitchell contends
that "producing and maintaining" what are often elusive distinctions between states
and the realms of society or economy "generates . . . power" in modern political orders.
Mitchell, "State, Economy," 170, 174–76.

20. Foucault, *History of Sexuality*, vol. 1, 137, 140–41; Foucault, *Birth of Biopolitics*, 21.

21. Foucault, "Subject and Power," esp. 783–90.

22. The "technologies of government" include "surveys, reports, drawings, pic-
tures, numbers, bureaucratic rules and guidelines, charts, graphs, statistics, and so
forth—that represent events and phenomena as information, data, and knowledge."
Inda, "Analytics of the Modern," 8–9.

23. Foucault, *History of Sexuality*, vol. 1, 139–40; Dean, *Governmentality*, 108.

24. Foucault, "Political Technology," 151.

25. Foucault, "Subject and Power," esp. 784.

26. Foucault, "Governmentality," 140.

27. Asad, "Ethnographic Representation," 76–77. Rhoda Kanaaneh examines the regulative and transformative goals of Zionist "political arithmetic" targeted at Palestinians in the Galilee in *Birthing the Nation*, esp. in chap. 1. For history and analysis of census-taking in Egypt, see Owen, "Population Census of 1917," 457–72; Fargues, "Family and Household," 24–25; Cuno and Reimer, "Census Registers," 193–216. The Egyptian Central Agency for Public Mobilization and Statistics was established in 1964 by state decree and is led by a staff major general in the Egyptian military. The earliest population census of the Trucial States, the previous designation of what became the UAE, occurred in March/April 1968, under the auspices of the British-coordinated Trucial States Council. Heard-Bey, *From Trucial States*, 73, 505. The first UAE national census was held in 1974–75 by the statistics section of the United Arab Emirates Ministry of Planning. UAE Census 2005. The UAE Central Statistics Department exists within the Ministry of Economy.

28. Foucault, "Governmentality," 139.

29. Inda, "Analytics of the Modern," 6; Foucault, "Subject and Power," 789.

30. Foucault, *History of Sexuality*, vol. 1, 144–45; Dean, *Governmentality*, 110.

31. Dean, *Governmentality*, 107; Foucault, "Subject and Power," 789–90.

32. Foucault, "Political Technology," 150. For a summary of the differences between the exercises of sovereignty and government in Foucauldian terms, see Dean, *Governmentality*, 105–6.

33. Foucault, "Governmentality," 141; Dean, *Governmentality*, 2–3.

34. Dean, *Governmentality*, 20.

35. Walby, "Contributions," 554. Also see Hunt and Wickham, *Foucault and Law*.

36. Walby, "Contributions," 556–57.

37. Golder and Fitzpatrick, *Foucault's Law*, 2–4.

38. Foucault refers to "clamorous legislative activity" in "normalizing society." Foucault, *History of Sexuality*, vol. 1, 144.

39. Ewald, "Norms, Discipline, and the Law," 138.

40. Ibid., 139.

41. Ibid., 138–39, 159.

42. Foucault, *History of Sexuality*, vol. 1, 144.

43. Ewald, "Norms, Discipline," 159.

44. Ibid., 159–60.

45. Dean, *Governmentality*, 187–88, 190.

46. Foucault, *Birth of Biopolitics*.

47. Ibid., 27, 29, 37, 145. Dean argues that Foucault's explication of governmentality

"responded most explicitly . . . to the changing status of liberal government and the recession of the welfare state ideal." Dean, *Governmentality*, 2.

48. Foucault was particularly interested in policing as a discipline that emerged in the second half of the eighteenth century in Europe, one of whose aspects was "devoted to the conduct of individuals, their morals, their occupational capabilities, their honesty, and how they are able to respect the law." Johann von Justi's pedagogical writing on these issues, wrote Foucault, "draws an important distinction between what he calls police (*Die Polizei*) and what he calls politics (*Die Politik*). Die Politik is basically . . . the negative task of the state. It consists in the state's fighting against its internal enemies and the army against the external ones. Von Justi explains that the police (Polizei), on the contrary, have a positive task. . . . The aim of police is the permanently increasing production of something new, which is supposed to foster the citizens' life and the state's strength. The police govern not by the law but by a specific, a permanent, and a positive intervention in the behavior of individuals." And although this "semantic distinction" has "disappeared from political discourse and . . . vocabulary, the problem of a permanent intervention of the state in social processes, even without the form of the law, is . . . characteristic of our modern politics." Foucault, "Political Technology," 158–59.

49. Foucault, *History of Sexuality*, vol. 1, 136; Dean, *Governmentality*, 138.

50. Dean, *Governmentality*, 138, 145.

51. Ibid., 131, 132–33.

52. Ibid., 132. Even when modern states wage "bloody wars" and "holocausts on their own populations," they do not wage them "in the name of a sovereign who must be defended; they are waged on behalf of the existence of everyone; entire populations are mobilized for the purpose of wholesale slaughter in the name of life necessity: massacres have become vital." In Foucault, *History of Sexuality*, 137. It is only since the twentieth century "that fostering the life of the population comes to depend on disallowing the life of those deemed unworthy of life." Dean, *Governmentality*, 148.

53. Dean, *Governmentality*, 147.

54. For interesting articles on the lack of national political engagement or public discussion among most nationals in the autocratic UAE, and the poor work conditions and invisibility/visibility of the migrant underclass of laborers from South and East Asia, see Shadid, "Towering Dream of Dubai"; Kanna, "Dubai in a Jagged World."

55. Dean, *Governmentality*, 108.

56. Donzelot, *Policing of Families*.

57. Ibid., 24–25, 92, 94.

58. Ibid., 26–29.

59. Ibid., 25.

60. Ibid., 31–32.

61. Ibid., 33–35.

62. Ibid., 36.

63. Ibid., 26–29.

64. Merry, "Governmentality and Gender Violence," 84–85.

65. Ibid., 82, 85, 93, 96, 104.

66. Ibid., 102–3.

67. Arabi, "Itinerary of a Fatwa," 152, and n. 16.

68. Zubaida, *Islam, the People and the State*, xxiii.

69. Ottoman authorities refused to allow the printing (based on use of mechanized techniques) rather than handwriting of the Qur'an, hadith (things the prophet is reported to have said or done in his daily interactions), Qur'anic exegesis, and jurisprudence because, according to a European observer, they believed that "their sacred books—would no longer be *scriptures* if they were printed." In 1727, Ottoman authorities granted formal permission only to print "dictionaries and books in such fields as medicine, astronomy, geography, and history. Permission to print the Qur'an was not obtained in the Ottoman Empire until 1874." Messick, *Calligraphic State*, 115–16. The only clear Qur'anic injunction regarding writing is one where the Prophet Muhammad encourages written documentation of purchases or debtor-debtee transactions. Ibid., 203–4. In legal documents, there is "the representation of a verbally constituted human contractual undertaking in the form of the document text, and the representation of the legitimizing act of the human notary-witness in the form of his handwriting." In this understanding, "the worth of a particular witness's handwriting is more important than the document itself," since "script, it is assumed, conveys (as precisely as a fingerprint) the person, whether just or a forger; the mark of the pen transmits the qualities of the human witness." Ibid., 215.

70. Ibid., 23–26, 28.

71. Ibid., 204–5. Like unaware individuals, texts "'loose' in the world," rather than well guarded at home, were considered to be "in trouble and troublesome," carrying within them "a separation [from their source, context, and original meaning] and a threat of falsehood." Ibid., 210–11, 213.

72. Mitchell, *Colonising Egypt*, 153.

73. In such cases, the word "innovation," *bid'a* in Arabic, would not be acceptable to Muslims (lay or religious scholars) who believe or want to argue that they are abiding by Islamic norms, presumably because the word implies "newness" rather than a change that abides by the essential criteria of religious licitness.

74. Hallaq, *Origins and Evolution of Islamic Law*, 128. The major Sunni doctrinal schools that survive are Hanafi, named after Abu Hanifa (d. 767); Maliki, following Malik Ibn Anas (d. 796); Shafi'i, following Muhammad Ibn Idris al-Shafi'i (d. 820); and Hanbali, after Ahmad Ibn Hanbal (d. 855).

75. Lombardi, *State Law as Islamic Law*, 14–15.

76. Ibid., 16, 18.

77. Ibid., 11, 16, 17, 46.

78. Al-Muhairi, "Shari'a in the Pre-Modern Period," 294–95.

79. Messick, *Calligraphic State*, 17.

80. Arabi, "Itinerary of a Fatwa," 147. Also see Tucker, *House of the Law*, 12.

81. Tucker, *House of the Law*, 10, 16.

82. Skovgaard-Petersen, *Defining Islam*, 103.

83. Lombardi, *State Law as Islamic Law*, 18–19, 49.

84. Ibid., 53.

85. Hourani, *History*, 272.

86. Mitchell, *Colonising Egypt*, 34–62; Hourani, *History*, 273.

87. Messick, *Calligraphic State*, 54, 57.

88. Asad, *Formations of the Secular*, 211.

89. Messick, *Calligraphic State*, 2–3, 57.

90. Ibid., 56.

91. Skovgaard-Petersen, *Defining Islam*, 66.

92. Lombardi, *State Law as Islamic Law*, 21.

93. Ibid., 41, 42–43.

94. These Muslim intellectuals were *salafi*s who argued for the moral, analytical, and religious superiority of the first Muslim community. Skovgaard-Petersen, *Defining Islam*, 65, 66–67.

95. Skovgaard-Petersen, *Defining Islam*, 66–68; Lombardi, *State Law as Islamic Law*, 26, 79, 84–86. Talal Asad, in contrast, argues that "there is no such thing as a 'real' *ijtihād* . . . there is only *ijtihād* practiced by particular persons who situate themselves in various ways within the tradition of *fiqh* [Islamic jurisprudence]." The premise here is that the tradition of *ijtihād* does not depend on "employing the principle of universal reason." Rather, it "provides specific material for reasoning—a theological vocabulary and a set of problems derived from the Qur'an (the divine revelation), the sunna (the Prophet's tradition), and the major jurists . . . who have commented on both—about how contemporary affairs should be configured." Salafis such as Abduh and Rida, Asad argues, viewed *ijtihād* as coming into play in situations where the consensus of scholars "has failed," making it important to return to revelation and the Prophet's traditions for further analysis. Rather than being a radical break, then, Asad argues that Abduh and Rida's disagreement with other Muslims on the issue of *ijtihād* makes their position "part of the tradition of Islamic jurisprudence." Asad, *Formations of the Secular*, 220–21.

96. Skovgaard-Petersen, *Defining Islam*, 66; Lombardi, *State Law as Islamic Law*, 74–76; El Shakry, "Schooled Mothers," 152.

97. Lombardi, *State Law as Islamic Law*, 26–27. *Ijmā'* refers to unanimous agreement by major Muslim jurists, or 'ulama', at a particular time on a particular issue to produce a ruling that abides by shari'a. The authority of this method comes from a re-

ported saying of the Prophet that "My community will never agree in error." Esposito and DeLong-Bas, *Women in Muslim Family Law,* 7. Zubaida points out changes and contradictions regarding *ijmāʿ* and other Islamic scholarly methodologies in acquiescence to political realities, a situation that solidified by the fourteenth century. Zubaida, *Islam, the People,* 5–8.

98. Skovgaard-Petersen, *Defining Islam,* 26; Asad, *Formations of the Secular,* chap. 7.

99. Al-Muhairi, "Shariʿa in the Modern Era," 42, 47.

100. Pollard, *Nurturing the Nation,* 2.

101. Ibid., 2, 11, 4–5.

102. Ibid., 5.

103. Ibid., 2–3.

104. Abu-Lughod, "Marriage of Feminism," 256–61.

105. Skovgaard-Petersen, *Defining Islam,* 62; Kholoussy, "Nationalization of Marriage," 324–25; El Alami, *Marriage Contract,* 11.

106. Sonbol, "History of the Marriage Contract," 170.

107. Asad, *Formations of the Secular,* 209, 229.

108. Lombardi, *State Law as Islamic Law,* 57–58.

109. Shaham, *Family and the Courts,* 12–13.

110. Skovgaard-Petersen, *Defining Islam,* 4; Sonbol, "Law and Gender Violence," 279, 283; Abdal-Rehim, "Family and Gender Laws," 97.

111. Asad, *Formations of the Secular,* 211.

112. Lombardi, *State Law as Islamic Law,* 66, 72.

113. Sonbol writes that from around this period, the Italian origin term "personal status" would be attached to laws and procedures related to "gender and family" in Egypt. Even supposedly indigenous areas of law were strongly inflected with the Code Napoleon and French legislative decisions, structures, and teachings. Following British occupation of Egypt in 1882, "European teachers were imported" and "foreign advisors with executive powers were placed within all parts of the Egyptian administration." Sonbol, "History of Marriage Contracts," 181–82.

114. Asad, *Formations of the Secular,* 211.

115. Shaham, *Family and the Courts,* 11–13.

116. Asad, *Formations of the Secular,* 211.

117. Al-Muhairi, "Federal Penal Code," 203.

118. Lombardi, *State Law as Islamic Law,* 64.

119. Skovgaard-Petersen, *Defining Islam,* 28. Also see Lombardi, *State Law as Islamic Law,* 74–76. Starrett points out that governmentalizing projects often had unintended consequences or failed. For example, the nineteenth-century "transfer of religious socialization" in Egypt from private to new public schools that delivered mass "modern" instruction, considered "a cost-efficient means of social control, instead helped to generate the intellectual, political, and social challenges posed by the country's broad-

based 'Islamist' movement." State education "has encouraged rather than discouraged attachment to Islamic culture, contrary to the expectations of educational theorists who encouraged schooling as a remedy to 'traditional' mentalities." The "spectacular" failures of some of these projects often led to aborting their wider application. Starrett, *Putting Islam to Work*, 6–7, 59, 63, 90, 91.

120. Lombardi, *State Law as Islamic Law*, 60–61, 63.

121. Cuno, "Divorce and the Fate," 199–200.

122. Shaham, *Family and the Courts*, 55.

123. Ibid., 155.

124. Ibid., 160.

125. Ibid.

126. Ibid., 155, 163.

127. El Alami, *Marriage Contract*, 87–88.

128. Shaham, *Family and the Courts*, 156.

129. Shaham, "State, Feminists and Islamists," 464–65.

130. Esposito and DeLong-Bas, *Women in Muslim Family Law*, 51.

131. Abdal-Rehim, "Family and Gender Laws," 105. A woman who sought a non-mutual divorce in the courts without demonstrating such harm was expected to compensate the husband. Egyptian Ottoman archives also indicate that divorce and re-marriage were frequent, both men and women were expected to remarry, and divorced and remarried women frequently kept custody of children from a previous marriage even though minors were technically required to go to the father or his family with a woman's remarriage in most Islamic schools of jurisprudence. Sonbol, "History of Marriage Contracts," 164, 166, 170; Abdal-Rehim, "Family and Gender Laws," 110–11.

132. Sonbol, "History of Marriage Contracts," 173–74, 165; Tucker, *House of the Law*, 185–86. Also see Moors, "Debating Islamic Family Law," 151, 152, 161, 162.

133. Sonbol, "History of Marriage Contracts," 185.

134. Welchman, *Women's Rights*, 33.

135. Sonbol, "History of Marriage Contracts," 180–81.

136. Ibid., 171. Two contracts referenced by Sonbol from 870 AD, written on papyrus, indicated greater freedom in constituting these documents than in the Ottoman period: the grooms agreed to provide the brides a good life or "to let [her] go in peace," gave the right to dissolve the "marriage knot" to the wife if he married plurally, gave her the right to divorce "whenever she wished," and agreed not to delimit her from visiting with her family. Ibid., 168.

137. Ibid., 182–83, 176.

138. Welchman, *Women's Rights*, 33. Also see El Alami, *Marriage Contract*, 22–25.

139. Baron, "Making and Breaking," 285; Naveh, "Tort of Injury," 20, 21–23. Arabi, "Dawning of the Third," 169–70; Sonbol, "Gender Violence," 283. Nevertheless, Naveh demonstrates that judges applied Article 6 differently when women used it to seek di-

vorce. Naveh, "Tort of Injury," 20–21, and n. 11 on same pages. Also see Hasan, "Granting Khulʿ," 83.

140. Naveh, "Tort of Injury," 23–24.

141. Welchman, *Women's Rights*, 34.

142. Kholoussy, "Nationalization of Marriage," 324–25; Cuno, "Divorce and the Fate," 205.

143. Kholoussy, "Nationalization of Marriage," 319.

144. Ibid., 335.

145. Moors, "Debating Islamic Family Law," 152, 154, 161, 167–68; Charrad, *States and Women's Rights*.

146. Kholoussy, "Nationalization of Marriage," 337.

147. Ibid., 329.

148. Ibid., 317, 319, 322–25.

149. El Shakry, *Great Social Laboratory*, 166–67.

150. I use the term "subjectifying" in the "subjectivation" sense where "individuals . . . acquire their [social] intelligibility by becoming subjects." In this understanding, subjection is both a "power *exerted on* a subject" and a "power *assumed by* the subject, an assumption that constitutes the instrument of that subject's becoming." Butler, *Psychic Life of Power*, 11.

151. Bier, "From Birth Control," 64–67.

152. The age requirements were circumvented in a variety of ways. Shaham, *Family and the Courts*, 57. The 1923 Egyptian Code of Organization and Procedure for Shariʿa Courts had earlier instructed such courts "not to hear claims" related to marriage "if the bride was under sixteen and the groom under eighteen" when married, not to marry such young brides and grooms, and not to register their marriages. These state concerns with marriage age are particularly intriguing given Beth Baron's finding that the 1907 and 1917 Egyptian censuses recorded that less than 10 percent of Egyptian females married while younger than twenty years old. Baron, "Making and Breaking," 281–82.

153. Cases in which a father denied paternity of offspring were excluded. El Alami, *Marriage Contract*, 83–84; Shaham, *Family and the Courts*, 56, 159–60.

154. Shaham, *Family and the Courts*, 56, 66, 159–60.

155. Ibid., 66–67.

156. Skovgaard-Peterson, *Defining Islam*, 104–5.

157. Naveh, "Tort of Injury," 17.

158. El Alami, *Marriage Contract*, 6; Shaham, *Family and the Courts*, 12.

159. El Alami, *Marriage Contract*, 6; Naveh, "Tort of Injury," 16–41.

160. Shaham, *Family and the Courts*, 12; Naveh, "Tort of Injury," 17–18.

161. Naveh, "Tort of Injury," 18.

162. Lombardi, *State Law*, 69–70, 72, 133. Also see Arabi, "Dawning of the Third," 173.

163. Arabi, "Dawning."

164. Singerman, *Avenues of Participation*, 283, and n. 56; Souleiman and Salah, "Legal Aspects"; Skovgaard-Petersen, *Defining Islam*, 170; Naveh, "Tort of Injury," 29–30.

165. Arabi, "Dawning," 173.

166. Arabi, "Dawning," 173–74; Skovgaard-Petersen, *Defining Islam*, 171; Naveh, "Tort of Injury," 30–31.

167. Article 18(a) of the 1985 law requires such alimony to be equivalent to "at least two years of matrimonial maintenance," with the amount determined by the courts on the basis of the "husband's economic capability, the circumstances of the divorce and the duration of the marriage." Shaham, "State, Feminists," 470.

168. Abdul Sattar, *Women in Egyptian Legislations*, 103. Karam, *Women, Islamisms*, 147; Souleiman and Salah, "Legal Aspects," 14, and n. 6; 'Abd al-Jawad and al-Kurdi, "Social Change," 30; Naveh, "Tort of Injury"; Abdul Sattar, *Women in Egyptian Legislations*, 100–103. In fact, Mulki al-Sharmani found that judges usually ordered husbands to pay very little for housing costs when they divorced a wife with children. Al-Sharmani, "Recent Reforms," 7. For further discussion of Law No. 44 of 1979 and Law No. 100 of 1985, see Welchman, *Women's Rights*, 35–39.

169. Naveh, "Tort of Injury," 24. For discussion of "khul'" in Maliki, Hanbali, and Hanafi perspectives, see Arabi, "Dawning," 169, 188. Law No. 100 of 1985 also defined *nafaqa* (maintenance) to include food, clothing, and housing for the wife, and *nafaqa shāmila* (complete maintenance) as these plus medical expenses and additional support a wife may ask for; it also stipulated that men cannot refuse to pay maintenance to a wife on the basis of disobedience because she works outside the home, unless this hurts family life, a nursing infant, or a sick child. The Arab Republic of Egypt National Council for Women, "On the Path of Life," cassette four.

170. Souleiman and Salah, "Legal Aspects," 13; Zulfiqqar, "Equality," 56.

171. Zulfiqqar, "Equality," 56.

172. Al-Sharmani, "Recent Reforms," 7.

173. Arabi, "Dawning," 174–75; Skovgaard-Petersen, *Defining Islam*, 177–94.

174. Foucault, "Technologies of the Self," 18.

175. Sonbol, "History of Marriage," 160–61.

176. Ibid., 162–63.

177. Ibid., 163, 166. The earliest Islamic contracts found in Egypt date from the ninth century AD and earlier contracts exist in hieroglyphics. Before paper, these contracts were recorded on papyrus and leather, and for the wealthier, textiles. Ibid., 167, and n. 5–6.

178. Ibid., 179–80.

179. Ibid., 164, 172.

180. Ibid., 175.

181. Ibid., 171.

182. Abdal-Rehim, "Family and Gender Laws," 97–103.

183. Ibid., 102–3.

184. Abdal-Rehim, "Family and Gender Laws," 97–103; Hanna, "Marriage Among Merchant," 147.

185. El Alami, *Marriage Contract*, 92.

186. Shaham, "State, Feminists," 463.

187. Hanna, "Marriage Among Merchant," 147.

188. Shaham, "State, Feminists," 463.

189. Hanna, "Marriage Among Merchant," 148.

190. Sonbol, "History of Marriage," 183–84.

191. This word is part of the term: *'iṣmatu-al-zawāj* or *'iṣmatu-al-nikāḥ*, referring to "the bond of marriage." In this case, *'iṣma* is a shorthand reference to maintenance of the bond of marriage being "in the wife's hands" or under her control. I thank Zeinab Abul-Magd for clarification on this issue.

192. Sonbol, "History of Marriage," 184.

193. Shaham, "State, Feminists," 464.

194. Ibid., 465.

195. Al-Sharmani, "Recent Reforms," 6; Shaham, "State, Feminists," 465.

196. Al-Sharmani, "Recent Reforms," 8, and n. 7.

197. Al-Sharmani, "Recent Reforms," 8; Welchman, *Women's Rights*, 11.

198. Al-Sharmani, "Recent Reforms," 8.

199. Al-Ali, *Secularism, Gender*, 165–66, and n. 13 on page 166.

200. Al-Sharmani, "Recent Reforms," 9.

201. Ibid.

202. Zulfiqqar, "Equality," 56.

203. Heard-Bey, *From Trucial States*, 362–70.

204. Dresch, "Debates on Marriage," 142–43.

205. Ibid., and n. 16–17 on pages 265–66.

206. Ibid., 143.

207. The Abu Dhabi emirate is the wealthiest city in the world. Gimbel, "Richest City."

208. Al Tamimi, *Practical Guide to Litigation*, 1–2.

209. Dresch, "Debates on Marriage," 150.

210. Al-Mutairi, *Impact of Federalism*, 288–89.

211. Al-Musfir, *United Arab Emirates*, 165–78; Khalifa, *United Arab Emirates*, 99–103.

212. Van der Meulen, *Role of Tribal*, 90–92.

213. Khalifa, *United Arab Emirates*, 65, 91.

214. Heard-Bey, *From Trucial States*, 242, 244.

215. Marchal, "Dubai: Global City," 94–95, 100.

216. On domestic issues, for example, Dubai has been the least willing of the

emirates to permit federal intervention in its educational or health sectors. Al-Musfir, *United Arab Emirates*, 150, 153, 155–56.

217. Ibid., 44–45. For deeper discussion of the development of British relations with tribal powers and rulers in the region in the eighteenth century, and earlier imperialist interventions and conflicts, see ibid., 30–44. For discussion of some of the tribal divisions and conflicts in the early eighteenth century and before, see ibid., 46–47.

218. Ibid., 45–46.

219. Ibid., 47–48.

220. Ibid., 48–49.

221. Khalifa, *United Arab Emirates*, 20–21.

222. Khalifa, *United Arab Emirates*, 21; al-Musfir, *United Arab Emirates*, 48–49; Heard-Bey, *From Trucial States*, 84, 293–94.

223. Khalifa, *United Arab Emirates*, 9, 23.

224. Al-Owais, *Federation of the UAE*, 28, 33.

225. Davidson, "Arab Nationalism," 880.

226. Al-Musfir, *United Arab Emirates*, 50.

227. Al-Owais, *Federation of the UAE*, 17–19; al-Musfir, *United Arab Emirates*, 63–64.

228. al-Musfir, *United Arab Emirates*, 51.

229. Heard-Bey, *From Trucial States*, 294–302, 306–11.

230. Al-Musfir, *United Arab Emirates*, 51–54.

231. Khalifa, *United Arab Emirates*, 11.

232. Ibid., xv, 37–39. Original negotiations included nine emir-led territories, including Qatar and Bahrain, whose leaders withdrew from the process as a result of competitions and conflicts over power and declared their own states. Al-Owais, *Federation of the UAE*, 21–23.

233. Al-Owais, *Federation of the UAE*, 20–22; al-Musfir, *United Arab Emirates*, 67–80.

234. Al-Owais, *Federation of the UAE*, 28–30. At popular levels, however, many people in the region were part of a tribal confederation before imperial rule and there were a number of unsuccessful attempts to create a federal system during the twentieth century. al-Musfir, *United Arab Emirates*, 60–61.

235. Khalifa, *United Arab Emirates*, 11, 14, 28, 91; al-Owais, *Federation of the UAE*, 28.

236. Al-Sayegh, "Domestic Politics," 164.

237. Al-Muhairi, "Development of the UAE Legal System," 120.

238. Al-Owais, *Federation of the UAE*, 42–43; al-Musfir, *United Arab Emirates*, 125–26, 132.

239. Al-Musfir, *United Arab Emirates*, 120.

240. Van der Meulen, *Role of Tribal*, 268–69.

241. Al-Musfir, *United Arab Emirates*, 136–37. Abu Dhabi has historically paid most of the budgetary needs in the areas of "defense, internal security, education and health." Al-Musfir, *United Arab Emirates*, 139.

242. Ibid., 143.

243. Al-Owais, *Federation of the UAE*, 23, 33–34.

244. Heard-Bey, *From Trucial States*, 122, 132.

245. Ibid., 122.

246. Ibid., 121–22, 132.

247. Heard-Bey, *From Trucial States*, 123. *Muṭawwaʿīn* until very recently also played the role of "one-man school," in almost all localities providing the "children of the average household with a foot on the first rung of the ladder of education" through Qur'an study. *Women in the UAE*, 17.

248. Heard-Bey, *From Trucial States*, 122.

249. Ibid., 452–53, and n. 60 and 123.

250. E-mail communication between author and Mohamed Al Roken, October 28, 2006.

251. The Maliki tradition is officially recognized in the emirates of Abu Dhabi and Dubai; Shafi'i in Fujayra; and Hanbali in the remaining emirates of Ra's al-Khayma, 'Ajman, and Umm al-Quwayn. Peck, *United Arab Emirates*, 61.

252. Heard-Bey, *From Trucial States*, 132.

253. Al-Muhairi, "Development of the UAE," 117–18, 127.

254. Heard-Bey, *From Trucial States*, 158.

255. Ibid.

256. Al-Muhairi, "Development of the UAE," 126.

257. "Hindus" were considered British subjects. Heard-Bey, *From Trucial States*, 202.

258. Ibid., 216–17.

259. Ibid., 160.

260. Al Tamimi, *Practical Guide*, 14. UAE judges are likely to be Egyptians, Sudanese, Jordanians, or Saudis trained in their respective universities or shari'a colleges, with experience in their own country's courts and legal system; they are licensed to work in the UAE by the Ministry of Justice. Others are graduates of the Faculty of Shari'a and Law at the University of the United Arab Emirates, in al-'Ayn, Abu Dhabi. E-mail communication between author and Mohamed Al Roken, October 28, 2006.

261. Al-Muhairi, "Shari'a in the Pre-Modern Period," 44.

262. Al-Muhairi, "Development of the UAE Legal System," 119.

263. Ibid., 139–42, 144.

264. Ibid., 146.

265. Al-Muhairi, "Position of the Shari'a," 219.

266. Al-Muhairi, "Development of the UAE Legal System," 147–48.

267. Al-Muhairi, "Position of the Shari'a," 219, 225, 226, 228–30.

268. Ibid., 244.

269. Al-Muhairi, "Development of the UAE Legal System," 134–35.

270. Al-Muhairi, "Position of the Shariʻa," 221.

271. Al-Muhairi, "Development of the UAE Legal System," 126–27.

272. Ibid., 150.

273. Ibid., 138, 141.

274. Ibid., 145.

275. Ibid., 139.

276. Ibid., 150, 153–54.

277. Ibid., 146–47.

278. Ibid., 147–48.

279. Van der Meulen, *Role of Tribal*, 46–48.

280. Ibid., 4–6, 7–8.

281. Ibid., 11, 45–47.

282. Al-Muhairi, "Development of the UAE Legal System," 128–29.

283. Ibid., 130.

284. Ibid., 135–36.

285. Ibid., 148.

286. Ibid., 149.

287. Ibid., 129–34, 137.

288. Al Tamimi, *Practical Guide*, 14.

289. I examine this law in Chapter 4.

290. Interview by author with Dr. Ahmad al-Kubaysi, Dubai, UAE, December 10, 2003.

291. Al Roken interview; Al-Kubaysi interview.

292. Al Roken interview.

293. Darwish interview.

294. Al Tamimi, *Practical Guide*, 11.

295. Ibid., 14–15.

296. Ibid.

297. Ibid., 14.

298. Al-Muhairi, "Development of the UAE Legal System," 136.

299. Al Roken interview.

300. Al-Muhairi, "Position of the Shariʻa," 244.

301. Al-Muhairi, "Shariʻa in the Modern Era," 37, and n. 8.

302. Al-Muhairi, "Development of the UAE Legal System," 137.

303. Al-Muhairi, "Position of the Shariʻa," 230–34.

304. Al-Muhairi, "Federal Penal Code," 197–98.

305. Al-Muhairi, "Shariʻa in the Pre-Modern Period," 287.

306. Ibid., 287–88.

307. Ibid., 288–89.

Chapter 2

1. Shapiro, "Politics of the 'Family,'" 277.

2. Singerman and Amar, "Introduction: Contesting Myths," 32.

3. Nemoto, "Postponed Marriage"; Brewster and Rindfuss, "Fertility and Women's Employment"; Jones, "Delayed Marriage."

4. Drieskens, "Changing Perceptions," 97–98.

5. Ibid., 99–100, 112–13.

6. Peck, *United Arab Emirates*, 85.

7. Rashad and Osman, "Nuptiality in Arab Countries," 24, table 2.

8. Ibid., 25, table 3.

9. Mansur, "Social and Economic Changes," 3, table 1.

10. In 1990, in comparison, the total fertility rate of Emirati women was 4.4 children. UNICEF, "Information by Country."

11. Ibid.

12. *United Arab Emirates Yearbook 2003*, 215.

13. Davidson, *United Arab Emirates*, 252.

14. For an article on the degree to which consumption and tourism structure life in Dubai, considered the "party capital," see Sherwood, "Oz of the Middle East."

15. Davidson, *United Arab Emirates*, 149, figure 3.14. Gulf Cooperation Council statistics estimate a total population of 4.3 million living in the UAE in 2004, with 67.8 percent comprised of females and 32.2 percent of males. According to government data not distinguished by citizenship status, 84.6 percent of the labor force of 2,731,000 people in 2004 was male, while 15.4 percent was female. *Statistical Bulletin*, vol. 15, 2006, chap. 1, "Population and Vital Statistics," tables 1 and 4.

16. UAE, *Yearbook 2003*, 215.

17. 'Ismat, "Charity Money," 48.

18. Rashad and Osman, "Nuptiality in Arab Countries," 25, table 3.

19. Al-Dib, "Some Important Facts."

20. Ibid.

21. Singerman, "Economic Imperatives," 13, figure 2–1.

22. Singerman and Ibrahim, "Cost of Marriage," 82, 86, 102–3; Amin and Al-Bassusi, "Education, Wage Work."

23. Singerman and Ibrahim, "Cost of Marriage," 96.

24. Singerman, *Avenues of Participation*, 80.

25. Osman and Shahd, "Age-Discrepant Marriage," 51, 54, 57, 58, 59.

26. 'Ismat, "Charity Money."

27. 'Ismat, "Charity Money"; Group Interview by author with seven MA prep students (three men and four women) at 'Ayn Shams University; Group Interview by author with three male graduate students, Cairo University, May 26, 2008.

28. Dresch, "Debates on Marriage," 137–38.

29. Interview by author with Faysal Yunis, Cairo University, December 20, 2003.

30. Ibid.

31. 'Ismat, "Charity Money," 48–49.

32. *Women in the UAE*, 51–52.

33. Interview by author with Ms. Samira Gargash, Dubai, UAE, December 8, 2003.

34. Khatib, *Beyond the Mysterious*, 267.

35. Gargash interview.

36. Interview by author with Dr. Ebtisam al-Kitbi, UAE University, December 11, 2003.

37. Group Interview by author with seven women students, one married, at (Arab) Sharjah University women's campus. Sharjah, UAE, December 14, 2003.

38. Group Interview by author with three women professors in the Faculty of Humanities and Social Sciences, UAE University, Abu Dhabi, UAE, December 9, 2003.

39. Khatib, *Beyond the Mysterious*, 207–10.

40. Ibid., 237.

41. Ibid., 266.

42. Group Interview with three women professors, UAE University.

43. Ibid.

44. Ibid.

45. Interview by author with a twenty-seven–year-old Emirati professional woman who preferred not to be identified, Dubai, UAE, December 2003.

46. Khatib, *Beyond the Mysterious*, 190–92.

47. Ibid., 191–92.

48. Ibid., 193.

49. Fakhro, "Changing Role of Women," 396; Ridge, "Hidden Gender Gap," 4.

50. Interview by author with Muhammad 'Abdel Rahim, Dubai, UAE, December 1, 2003.

51. Ridge, "Hidden Gender Gap," 1.

52. Ridge, "Hidden Gender Gap," 1; Ridge, "School Quality and Gender."

53. 'Abdel Rahim interview; Interview by author with a thirty-one–year-old Emirati married man who did not want to be identified, Dubai, UAE, December 2003.

54. Dresch, "Debates on Marriage," 146.

55. Khatib, *Beyond the Mysterious*, 34.

56. Ibid., 160, 104–5.

57. Ibid., 159, 169, 262.

58. Ibid., 194–95, 197, 262, 267–70.

59. Mansur, "Social and Economic Changes," 5, table 4.

60. Group Interview by author with seven women students at (Arab) Sharjah University women's campus; Interview by author with a twenty-seven–year-old Emirati professional woman who did not want to be identified, Dubai, UAE, December 2003.

61. Group Interview by author with seven women students at (Arab) Sharjah University women's campus.

62. Ibid.

63. Group Interview by author with seven MA prep students (three men, four women) at 'Ayn Shams University, Egypt, May 28, 2008; the men were Egyptian, Libyan, and Kuwaiti. Two women were Syrian; and two were Egyptian. Also, Group Interview by author with three Egyptian men graduate students at Cairo University, May 26, 2008; Group Interview by author with nine Egyptian Faculty of Economics and Political Science undergraduate students, Cairo University, May 26, 2008.

64. Group Interview with seven MA prep students at 'Ayn Shams University.

65. Cuno, "Divorce and the Fate," 197–201, 206–7.

66. Ibid., 208.

67. Al-Dib, "Some Important Facts."

68. Al-Korashy interview.

69. Al-Dib, "Some Important Facts." A comparison with data in an Egyptian census table indicates that in 1997, 65 percent of Egyptian women were either illiterate (50 percent) or at the barely reading and writing level (15 percent), and 4 percent had at least completed a college education, indicating that the level of education of divorced women in 1999 was close to proportional to their presence in the population. *The Annual Statistical Report*, 5, table 3-1.

70. *UAE Yearbook 2003*, 240.

71. *Statistical Bulletin*, vol. 12, 2003, chap. 1, "Population and Vital Statistics," table 7; *Statistical Bulletin*, vol. 15, 2006, chap. 1, "Population and Vital Statistics," table 7.

72. Mansur, "Social and Economic Changes," 8, table 6.

73. Ibid., 6, table 5.

74. I do not share the exact statistics provided in the paper because they did not total 100 percent and no explanation of why not is provided by the author. Mansur, "Social and Economic Changes," 7–8.

75. Ibid., 7.

76. Khatib, *Beyond the Mysterious*, 269.

77. Ibid., 293–94.

78. Ibid., 294.

79. Group Interview by author with six men students, one married, at UAE University, December 9, 2003.

80. Interview by author with a thirty-one–year-old Emirati married man who did not want to be identified, Dubai, UAE, December 2003; Group Interview by author with six men students, one married, at United Arab Emirates University; Group Interview by author with seven women students at (Arab) Sharjah University women's campus; Interview by author with Ms. Widad Lutah, Dubai, December 2003.

81. Dresch, "Debates on Marriage," 152–55.

82. Hallaq, *An Introduction*, 25, 26–27.

83. Dresch, "Debates on Marriage," 141. For further discussion on citizenship and "naturalization" practices in the UAE, see Kapiszewski, *Nationals and Expatriates*, 50–51.

84. Because Abu Dhabi "was short of people" when the federation was established, its ruler granted citizenship widely, although families originating from Yemen, who are well represented in the military and other government offices, are distrusted by the Abu Dhabi ruling family. In contrast, Iranian-origin citizens "obsessed on occasion" members of the Dubai ruling family as a potential fifth column, although "so many people have Iranian mothers and grandmothers that a sense of threat is hard to inculcate." Dresch, "Debates on Marriage," 141–42.

85. Ibid., 143–44.

86. Al-Mutairi, *Impact of Federalism*, 44, and n. 6.

87. Dresch, "Debates on Marriage," 151.

88. Ibid., 151, 267, and n. 31.

89. Darwish interview.

90. Kubaysi interview.

91. Bristol-Rhys, "Weddings, Marriage," 29. Dresch similarly reports on an April 1999 "Third Colloquium on the Family" in Ra's al-Khayma in which about sixty to seventy young Emirati women protested restrictions on their marriage options, asking what "foreigner" meant. Dresch, "Debates on Marriage," 152.

92. Kubaysi interview.

93. A 2005 Amnesty International report, for example, discussed the case of an Emirati woman who married a Saudi national in Egypt in October 2001 because her father had refused to consent to the marriage in the Emirates. When they returned to resolve the problem with the woman's family in 2002, the male Saudi national was arrested by security forces, accompanied by the Emirati wife's father, while he was staying in a Dubai hotel. He was released only after divorcing his wife, although he reported to Amnesty in 2004 that he revoked the divorce and registered the revocation in Saudi courts. Shari'a courts in the UAE annulled the marriage upon the woman's father's request, on the basis that it was in violation of Maliki rules, in 2002. State authorities rearrested her husband, who was staying in a hotel in Al-'Ayn, Abu Dhabi, to attend the court proceedings. He was released in October 2002, although he had an international arrest warrant against him issued by the UAE. Amnesty International, *GCC Countries*, 20.

94. Hadid, "United Arab Emirates."

95. Abdul Sattar, *Women in Egyptian*, 139.

96. Ibid., 139–40.

97. Ibid., 141.

98. "315 Foreigners Granted Egyptian Citizenship," 17.

99. United Nations Development Programme, "The Gender and Citizenship Initiative."

100. Similarly, 17 percent of the marriages examined were between national women and "foreign" men, some of whom were probably related to the women (for example, cousins) but who had parents who had not acquired UAE citizenship. Dresch, "Debates on Marriage," 145–46.

101. Darwish interview. There are some restrictions for citizen men who marry women from families with no nationality (*bidūn*). Bidūn, meaning "without" in Arabic, refers to people originally from nearby or bordering places such as Iran, Yemen, or Oman who were never incorporated into the system of bounded territorial nation-states that developed in the twentieth century. Al Roken interview.

102. Bristol-Rhys, "Weddings, Marriage," 27, 28; Dresch, "Debates on Marriage," 146–47, 150–51, 154–56.

103. *Women in the UAE*, 53.

104. Dresch, "Debates on Marriage," 148–49.

105. Interview by author with Ms. Saliha Ghabish. Shariqa, UAE, December 16, 2003.

106. Darwish interview.

107. Bristol-Rhys, "Weddings, Marriage," 20–36, 29.

108. Brennan, *What's Love Got to Do with It?* 96–97.

109. Dresch, "Debates on Marriage," 144.

110. Lutah interview; al Roken interview.

111. Kubaysi interview.

112. Dresch, "Debates on Marriage," 144–45.

113. In addition to hierarchies based on class, family, and which Emirate one is from in the evaluation of a spouse's status, there is a racialized hierarchy for the non-Emirati wives of Emirati men and the children of such couples. Indian mothers and their children are considered the most inferior; non-Emirati Arab mothers and their children have a higher status than Indians; and having a British wife is considered an "accomplishment" [*injaz*]. There is also an ethnic hierarchy among Emiratis regarding Arab women who marry Emirati men: Moroccan women are viewed as "unacceptable," Egyptian women are considered inferior, Lebanese women are "accepted with caution," and Syrian women are the most acceptable. Bachiri and Chahine interview, Dubai; Interview by author with a twenty-seven–year-old Emirati professional woman who did not want to be identified, Dubai.

114. Bristol-Rhys, "Weddings, Marriage," 20–36, 28.

115. Al-Bah interview.

116. Ibid.

117. The assertion about children's adjustment rates refers to research comparing children in Emirati homes with foreign or native mothers. The following are UAE Marriage Fund Institution brochures I collected in 2003, translated, and analyzed: "A

Letter to Young Men"; "A Social Project to Match Those Who Want to Marry"; "Intro-duction Summary"; "Group Weddings: How they are understood . . . their goals . . . their significance"; and "Get to Know Your Other Half: A Special Course on Marriage Relations for those Planning to Marry." All in Arabic.

118. Al-Bah interview; Bristol-Rhys, "Weddings, Marriage," 27.

119. Singerman and Ibrahim, "Cost of Marriage," 83.

120. For example, after discussion of such issues in a classroom, a North African student privately shared with the author that her brother and sister-in-law had a cus-tomary marriage with the families' knowledge in order for the woman not to lose a university fellowship that required students to be unmarried.

121. This state support for widowed women was established because of the large number of Egyptian married men who were killed in the 1962–67 war with Yemen and the 1967 war with Israel. 'Abd al-Jawad and al-Kurdi, "Social Change," 4, 28. Interview by author with Lamya Lutfi, Cairo, Egypt. Beginning in the 1970s, the UAE Ministry of Social Affairs allocated needy divorced Emirati women an income and extra support if they are mothers with custody of Emirati children, although the father remains legal guardian and responsible for children's maintenance. Soffan, *Women of the UAE*, 44. The UAE Social Security Law of 1977 also provides economic support to widows and "spinsters." *Women in the UAE*, 34.

122. Jessica Carlisle provides nuanced evidence of these issues as they surround a contested marital case in the Syrian shari'a courts. Carlisle, "From Behind the Door," 59–74.

123. Kepel, *Muslim Extremism*, 86–89.

124. Yunis interview.

125. Bachiri and Chahine interview.

126. "Friend marriage" is discussed in Jamil Thiyabi, "Patching up Chastity!" "Blood marriage" was discussed in an interview by author with Dr. 'Ali Layla, sociol-ogy professor at 'Ayn Shams University, Egypt. "Gift," "cassette," and "blood" unreg-istered marriages are also discussed in 'Abdallah and Yusif, *Common Law Marriage*, 52–53.

127. 'Abdel Rahim interview.

128. 'Abd al-Jawad and al-Kurdi, "Social Change," 10; 'Abdallah and Yusef, *Com-mon Law Marriage*, 52, 112, 161.

129. Lutah interview.

130. 'Abdallah and Yusef, *Common Law Marriage*, 120–21.

131. Al-Shibil, "For Women Only"; "New Paternity Law"; MacFarquhar, "Paternity Suit"; "New Paternity Suit"; Reem, "Ties Made Better."

132. Darwish interview.

133. Ibid.

134. Bachiri and Chahine interview.

135. Darwish interview.

136. Ibid.

137. Al Roken interview.

138. Darwish interview.

139. Ibid.

140. Amnesty International, *GCC Countries*, 20, 21.

141. Lutah interview.

142. Al-Shibil, "For Women Only" episode.

143. 'Abdallah and Yusef, *Common Law Marriage*, 54–59, 136–39, 146–47, 165.

144. 'Abd al-Jawad, guest on al-Shibil, "For Women Only."

145. 'Abdallah and Yusef, *Common Law Marriage*, 207–9.

146. Interview with Dr. Nadya al-'Afify, Cairo.

147. 'Abdallah and Yusef, *Common Law Marriage*, 95–96, 158, 185.

148. 'Abd al-Jawad and al-Kurdi, "Social Change," 17–18.

149. 'Abd al-Jawad, on al-Shibil, "For Women Only"; 'Abdallah and Yusef, *Common Law Marriage*, 100.

150. 'Abd al-Jawad, on al-Shibil, "For Women Only."

151. Najat al-Qawwas of Yemen, guest on al-Shibil, "For Women Only" program.

152. 'Abdel Rahim interview.

153. Idris, "Underage Mafia," 3; Interview by author with Atef Sa'id, Cairo; Lutfi interview.

154. 'Abd al-Jawad and al-Kurdi, "Social Change," 4–5.

155. 'Abdallah and Yusef, *Common Law Marriage*, 54, 97. This Cairo University study was based on a pretested semistructured survey administered to a nonrandom group of more than one thousand university students and staff at Cairo University, 'Ayn Shams University, and Helwan University (27.3 percent men and 72.2 percent women). The researchers also developed a semistructured questionnaire for a nonrandom selection of seventeen men and eighteen women involved in a customary marriage. Ibid., 74, 86, 136–37. I am grateful to Dr. Ahmed A. Zayed, dean of the Faculty of Arts and Sciences, Cairo University, for generously providing me with a copy of this study in May 2008.

156. Group Interview by author with Egyptian women students, Cairo University, conducted in Professor Hala Kamal's Honda Civic, following the students' final examination. These students, who numbered eight to nine at different points, had taken Professor Kamal's course in English feminist literature. Students referenced by name are given pseudonyms. I am grateful to Professor Kamal for arranging this interview.

157. Ibid.

158. Magdy, "Tears of a Young Face," 14.

159. Group Interview by author with three women professors in the Faculty of Humanities and Social Sciences, UAE University, Abu Dhabi.

160. I briefly interviewed this woman on a mobile phone when she called while I was interviewing her fiancé face-to-face, Dubai, December 1, 2003.

161. Darwish interview.

162. Interview by author with Dr. Al-'Olama, UAE University, Al-'Ayn, Abu Dhabi, December 9, 2003.

163. Ibid.

164. Darwish interview.

165. 'Abd al-Jawad and al-Kurdi, "Social Change," 4; Lutah interview.

166. Abaza, "Perceptions of 'Urfi Marriage," 20–21.

167. 'Abdallah and Yusef, *Common Law Marriage*, 137–39, 146–47.

168. Ibid., 156–58.

169. Ibid., 177.

170. Ibid., 181.

171. Ibid., 175.

172. Ibid., 176.

173. Ibid., 171, table 80. The remainder reported that the contract remained with a lawyer (2), a friend (3), or "other" (2).

174. Abaza, *Changing Consumer Cultures*, 244.

175. Arabi, "Itinerary of a Fatwa," 148.

176. Al-'Olama interview.

177. Ibid.

178. Arabi, "Itinerary of a Fatwa," 149.

179. Jabarti, "Happy Misyar Union."

180. Lutah interview.

181. Al-'Olama interview.

182. Ibid.

183. Arabi, "Itinerary of a Fatwa," 157.

184. Arabi, "Itinerary of a Fatwa," 157; al-Kubaysi interview; Darwish interview; al Roken interview.

185. Darwish interview.

186. Al-Kubaysi interview.

187. Darwish interview.

188. Al-'Olama interview.

189. Darwish interview.

190. Al-'Olama interview.

191. 'Abdel Rahim interview.

192. Ibid.

193. Arabi, "Itinerary of a Fatwa," 159–60, 167.

194. Al Roken interview.

195. Arabi, "Itinerary of a Fatwa," 148, 164–65.

196. Arabi, "Itinerary of a Fatwa," 165–66; Al-'Olama interview.

197. Abaza, "Perceptions of 'Urfi Marriage," 21.

198. Ibid.

199. Ibid.

200. Kosmatopoulos, "In . . . Mall We Trust?" 123, 122.

201. 'Abd al-Jawad and al-Kurdi, "Social Change," 25.

202. Interview by author with Dr. Riad Hamzawi, al-'Ayn, Abu Dhabi, December 9, 2003.

203. Ibid.

204. Ibid.

205. 'Awatef 'Abd al-Rahman, Giza, Egypt. December 30, 2003.

206. 'Abd al-Jawad and al-Kurdi, "Social Change," 15–16, 18–20.

207. 'Abd al-Jawad and al-Kurdi, "Social Change," 3–5, 14, 21–25, 29; Layla interview.

208. Abaza, "Perceptions of 'Urfi Marriage," 21.

209. Group Interview by author with Egyptian women students, Cairo University, December 27, 2003; Group Interview by author with about nine undergraduate students, Faculty of Economics and Political Science, Cairo University, May 26, 2008. All students are referenced with pseudonyms.

210. Group Interview by author with about nine undergraduate students, Cairo University, May 26, 2008.

211. Ibid.

212. Ibid.

213. Ibid.

214. Group Interview by author with Egyptian women students, Cairo University, December 27, 2003; all students referenced with pseudonyms.

215. Group Interview by author with about nine undergraduate students, Cairo University, May 26, 2008. I thank Dr. May Saikaly and Dr. Mona N. Mikhail for discussion of the term "*mabsūslahum*." E-mail correspondence with author, January 28, 2009.

216. Darwish, "Contemporary Changes," 13.

217. Al-Rasheed, "Introduction: Localizing," 3. For the UAE specifically, see Dresch, "Debates on Marriage," 140.

218. Darwish, "Contemporary Changes," 14–15.

219. Hamid, "Cultural Influences."

220. For the most part, he seemed to use the term "youth" (*shabab*) as a reference to boys and young men, unless he specifically mentioned girls. Indeed, I learned over time in interviews that for many (not all) men informants and respondents boys and men were the universal subject when terms such as "youth" or "young people" were used.

221. Another paper presented at the same conference, by 'Issa al-Sari, summarized in order of effect the factors which "studies have shown" create youth deviation: "family disintegration," "social environment and friends," "psychological causes,"

"economic situation," and "educational and child-rearing conditions." "Toward a Complete Preventative Policy," 17.

222. Al-Shaykh, "Self-Esteem and Its Relationship," 12.

223. Interview by author with Ms. Hisa al-Diqqi, December 8, 2003, Dubai, UAE.

224. Ghabish interview.

Chapter 3

1. *Women in the UAE*, 2.

2. Rose, *Powers of Freedom*, 85–89.

3. For example, in the United States, McDonald's or Pepsi Cola's aims with respect to consumption negatively impact the profit maximization goals of the health insurance industry. They also exact great cost from federal and state Medicare and Medicaid budgets given that poor eating leads to negative health outcomes, which becomes costly for states.

4. Inda, "Analytics of the Modern," 10–11.

5. Foucault, "On the Genealogy of Ethics," 351. Foucault was increasingly interested in such "technologies of self," which he believed allow "individuals to effect by their own means or with the help of others a certain number of operations on their own bodies and souls, thoughts, conduct, and way of being, so as to transform themselves in order to attain a certain state of happiness, purity, wisdom, perfection, or immortality." Martin, "Truth, Power, Self," 18. Foucault developed the idea of self-styling as a positive strategy in works such as *The Use of Pleasure*. Foucault assumes, following Nietzsche, that human subjectivity is socially constituted rather than predetermined and this occurs through both discourse and practice: "It is not just in the play of symbols that the subject is constituted. It is constituted in real practices—historically analyzable practices. There is a technology of the constitution of the self which cuts across symbolic systems while using them." Foucault, "On the Genealogy of Ethics," 369.

6. Rose, *Powers of Freedom*, 21.

7. While questioning unproblematized notions of freedom, Rose insists on the human responsibility to take political action on the basis of an ethic that "opposes all that . . . blocks or subverts the capacity of others asserting . . . their own vitalism, their own will to live through the active shaping of their lives." Rose, *Powers of Freedom*, 65, 283–84.

8. The term "transnational" (rather than global or international) acknowledges what Inderpal Grewal and others contend are plural "movements of discourses, things, and practices within specific transnational connectivities and the [complex] histories of these movements." It recognizes that such exchanges occur among and between elite and nonelite, capitalist and noncapitalist, state and nonstate actors and apparatuses. Grewal, *Transnational America*, 24. Also see Bhaskaran, *Made in India*, 6–9; Nagar et al., "Locating Globalization."

9. Watts, "Development and Governmentality," 12, 28.

10. Bhaskaran, *Made in India*, 6.

11. Watts, "Development and Governmentality," 9.

12. Rose, *Powers of Freedom*, 86.

13. Earlier iterations of some material in this chapter can be found in Hasso, "Comparing Emirati and Egyptian Narratives," 59–74; and Hasso, "Shifting Practices and Identities," 211–22.

14. Abaza, *Changing Consumer Cultures*, 167. Nevertheless, when I compared the converted prices of Vodafone (a popular provider in both countries) prepaid SIM cards and phone service I purchased in company stores in both countries in mid-2008, they were more expensive in Egypt in comparison to the Netherlands.

15. These sites included paltalk.com, bravochat.com, arabfun.com.

16. In a 2002 survey that included 250 women students from throughout the nearby Emirates studying at Zayed University in Dubai, more than 90 percent owned a cell phone, 90 percent owned a computer, and 80 percent of the computer owners were hooked up to the Internet at home. L. Walters and T. Walters, "The Transitional Woman," 227.

17. 'Abdel Rahim interview.

18. Khatib, *Beyond the Mysterious*, 319.

19. Harib, "Youth and Social," 12.

20. Jameson, "Notes on Globalization," 58–60.

21. Ibid., 55–56, 64.

22. Yang, "Mass Media," 193–95.

23. Ibid., 205.

24. Abaza, *Changing Consumer Cultures*, 46–47.

25. Ibid., 50–51.

26. Ibid., 105.

27. Ibid., 166, 80.

28. Ibid., 79–80, 82, 236, 238, 294.

29. Abaza, *Changing Consumer Cultures*, 240; Konig, "Café Latte," 226.

30. Konig, "Café Latte," 221.

31. Ibid., 222, 226, 227.

32. Abaza, *Changing Consumer Cultures*, 52, 294.

33. Ibid., 240–41.

34. Also see Konig, "Café Latte," 222–23.

35. Ibid., 229.

36. Davidson, *United Arab Emirates*, 262. 'Abd al-Jawad and al-Kurdi, "Social Change," 3.

37. Al-Awadhi, "Women in the Gulf," 426.

38. Hamid, "Cultural Influences."

39. *Women in the UAE*, 56.

40. Ghabish interview.

41. 'Abd al-Jawad, on al-Shibil, "For Women Only" program.

42. 'Abd al-Jawad and al-Kurdi, "Social Change," 31.

43. Darwish interview.

44. Ghabish interview.

45. Al-Bah interview.

46. "Amin," Group Interview by author with nine undergraduate students, Cairo University, May 26, 2008.

47. Abu-Lughod, *Dramas of Nationhood*, 114.

48. Ibid., 136–37.

49. Ibid., 139.

50. Ibid., 149, 152, 153.

51. Ibid., 195, 199–203, 208–9.

52. Abaza, *Changing Consumer Cultures*, 46.

53. Ibid.

54. Hamzawi interview.

55. Al-Qawwas, on al-Shibil, "For Women Only" program.

56. Al-Duwaysh, "The Sea of Love . . . A Tour of the Dangers of the Meaning of Love . . . and Some Tales of Affection . . . and other Recollections about Longing and Yearning." This undated cassette tape is distributed in the Government of Dubai, Courts Department "Marriage Box" of brochures and other supplies for couples who are marrying. Box generously provided to author by Mr. Darwish in late December 2003. Arabic to English translations completed by the author.

57. Ghabish interview.

58. 'Abd al-Jawad and al-Kurdi, "Social Change," 19, 30–31.

59. Starrett, *Putting Islam to Work*, 160–62.

60. 'Abd al-Jawad, on al-Shibil, "For Women Only" program.

61. Sadek, "Cairo as a Global/Regional," 174.

62. Ibid., 175.

63. Ibid.

64. Ghannam, "Keeping Him Connected," 252.

65. Tucker, *In the House of the Law*, 149–51.

66. Arabi, "Itinerary of a Fatwa," 152.

67. Al-'Afify interview.

68. Ibid.

69. Al-'Olama interview.

70. Al-Diqqi interview.

71. Group Interview by author with three women professors who preferred not to be identified, UAE University, December 9, 2003.

72. Ibid.

73. In *surat al-baqara* in my copy of an Arabic Qur'an, section 2:223, which says: "*nisā'ūkum ḥarthun lakum fā'tū ḥarthakum ānnay shi'tum wa qadimū ilā nafūsikum wa ātaqū allah wa-a'lamū annakum . . . ,*" published in Cairo by Nahdhat Misr Printing, Hijra 1454/1984 AD, 44–45. According to *The Holy Quran, Mashaf al-Madina al-Nabawiyya*, Presidency of Islamic Researches, King Fahd Holy Quran Printing Complex, n.d., page 96, the translation of this sentence is the following: "Your wives are as tilth unto you so approach your tilth when or how you will: but do some good act for your souls [could be selves?] beforehand: and fear Allah, and know that ye are to meet him in the hereafter, and give these good tidings to those who believe." I thank Dr. Amaney Jamal for her assistance and a useful discussion of interpretations and translations of this revelation.

74. Al-Kubaysi interview.

75. Group Interview by author with three women professors, UAE University, December 9, 2003.

76. Ibid.

77. Al-Kubaysi interview.

78. Ibid.

79. I thank In'am 'Obaydi for explaining this phrase for me.

80. Al-Kitbi interview.

81. Mitchell, *Rule of Experts*, 299.

82. Ali, *Planning the Family*, 4–5.

83. Ibid., 1.

84. Ibid., 59.

85. Ibid., 14.

86. Bier, "From Birth Control," 70–72.

87. Eickelmann and Piscatori, *Muslim Politics*, esp. 57–79.

88. Eickelman, "New Media in the Arab Middle East," 39.

89. Starrett, *Putting Islam to Work*, 186.

90. Ibid., 187.

91. Ibid., 219.

92. Rugh, "Reshaping Personal Relations," 151, 163.

93. Ibid., 155.

94. Ibid., 151.

95. Ibid., 176.

96. Jameson, "Notes on Globalization," 64, 67–68.

97. McDaniel, "Measuring Gender Egalitarianism," esp. 68–72; Seguino, "Plus Ça Change?" esp. 9–10.

98. An analysis of a large-scale 1997 survey of Egyptian adolescents, focused on sixteen- to nineteen-year-old boys and girls from throughout Egypt, found that while

boys and girls diverged from their parents in their attitudes toward gender relations and responsibilities in the family, girls were more liberal on most questions, especially if they were enrolled in secondary school or lived in one of the urban governorates. Tawila et al., "Social Change," 159, 160, table 7.3, 164, 166. The *Arab Human Development Report 2005* largely does not break down responses to gender-related measures based on gender with the exception of a question regarding polygamy administered to respondents in Morocco, Lebanon, Egypt, and Jordan. Results indicate that more than half of men and women do not approve of plural marriage in these countries, with much higher rates of disapproval in Lebanon and Egypt. At the same time, each country reflects a gender gap on this question, with the highest in Jordan, where about 39 percent of men supported polygamy in comparison to 10 percent of women. UNDP, *Arab Human Development Report*, 136, Box 5–2 and 272, Annex II. A series of value surveys administered in Egypt, Iran, Jordan, and Saudi Arabia between 2001 and 2003 found Jordan and Egypt to have the highest gender gaps on questions related to working mothers, although all the countries reflected significant gender differences on whether women should always obey husbands and the education of sons in comparison to daughters. Moaddel, "Saudi Public Speaks," 221, table 9.3, and 223, table 9.4.

99. Group Interview by author with six men students at United Arab Emirates University, December 9, 2003.

100. Darwish interview.

101. Ibid.

102. Ibid.

103. Al-'Olama interview.

104. Group Interview by author with Egyptian women students, Cairo University, December 27, 2003.

105. Ibid.

106. Ibid.

107. Group Interview by author with about nine undergraduate students, Cairo University, May 26, 2008.

108. Group Interview by author with seven MA prep students at 'Ayn Shams University, Egypt.

109. Ibid. A large-scale 1997 survey of Egyptian adolescents interestingly found that boys and young men with university schooling were more conservative than boys in secondary school on indicators such as sharing child-rearing responsibilities with wives, taking kids to a physician, and accepting that the wife can be a breadwinner, although both boys and girls were generally conservative on gender allocation of household tasks. Ibrahim et al. *Transitions to Adulthood*, table 8.12, 164–65. The study also found Egyptian boys to be more approving of divorce than girls. Ibid., 173.

110. Al-Shibil, "Secret Marriage."

111. Al-Qawwas, in al-Shibil, "For Women Only" program.

112. Dib, in al-Shibil, "For Women Only" program. A male Emirati citizen interviewed on the same program reported the same reasoning for secret marriage, although he added that he was also afraid of his children's responses. The plan in a situation of secret marriage, according to this Emirati, is that "two, three or four years later, he can gradually start announcing it to the children." Al-Shibil, "For Women Only" program.

113. Darwish interview.

114. Group Interview by author with Egyptian women students, Cairo University, December 27, 2003.

115. Bristol-Rhys, "Weddings, Marriage," 30, 31–32.

116. Interview by author with a twenty-seven–year-old Emirati professional woman who did not want to be identified, Dubai, UAE, December 2003.

117. "Men" is pronounced in this manner in colloquial Arabic in the Arabian Peninsula.

118. Ghabish interview.

119. Al-Shibel, "For Women Only" program.

120. Ibid.

121. Group Interview by author with six men students, United Arab Emirates University, December 9, 2003.

122. Hamid, "Cultural Influences."

123. Ibid.

124. Al-Kubaysi interview.

125. Hamid, "Cultural Influences."

126. Darwish, "Contemporary Changes," 17.

127. Ibid., 18.

Chapter 4

1. Foucault, "Governmentality," 139; Inda, "Analytics of the Modern," 6; Dean, *Governmentality*, 20; Foucault, *History of Sexuality*, 137; Foucault, "Subject and Power," 784, 789.

2. Rose, *Powers of Freedom*, 3.

3. 'Abdallah and Yusif, *Common Law Marriage*, 209.

4. Foucault, *History of Sexuality*, 144; Ewald, "Norms, Discipline," 138–60.

5. Shapiro, "Politics," 278; Danzelot, *Policing of Families*, 25, 36.

6. Biopolitics is concerned with the "detailed administration of daily life" and can be understood as the "power to foster life or disallow it." Dean, *Governmentality*, 138, 139.

7. Almihdar, "Human Rights," 1–15, esp. 13.

8. In Foucault's terms, this would be considered the sovereign, "deductive," and juridical power of states, in MENA typically framed in the pastoral terms of family care.

9. Welchman, *Women and Muslim Family*, 22–23.

10. Ibid.

11. Ibid., 22.

12. Al Roken interview.

13. Ibid.

14. Al-Kubaysi interview.

15. Ibid.

16. Gargash interview.

17. Ibid.

18. Lutah interview.

19. Al-Diqqi interview.

20. Al-Kubaysi interview.

21. Ibid.

22. Ibid.

23. United Arab Emirates, *Law of Personal Status Matters*, Law No. 28. The law addresses, among other issues, state and court jurisdiction, marriage, engagement, maintenance, divorce, guardianship, wills, inheritance, kinship definitions, heirs, relational obligations and their order and priority, and settlements.

24. Ibid.

25. Welchman, *Women and Muslim Family*, 45–46.

26. UAE, *Law of Personal Status Matters*.

27. Welchman, *Women and Muslim Family*, 98.

28. A UAE Ministry of Health press release ("UAE MoH premarriage screening campaign completes 9,389 tests in six months") lists "genetic and contagious" diseases included in the premarriage health screening (arranged with BinSina pharmacies) as thalassemia, AIDS, hepatitis, and tuberculosis. *http://www.ameinfo.com/176631.html* (accessed January 14, 2009). Article 112 of Law No. 28 allows either spouse to request annulment of a marriage in cases of the following "repulsive or harmful" illnesses (insanity, leprosy) or conditions that prevent "sexual pleasure" (impotence, vaginal abnormalities blocking intercourse, or similar conditions) regardless of whether they existed before the contract or developed during marriage. (I thank Moulouk Berry for determining the meaning of *al-qarn*.) Article 114 allows request for separation if a member of the couple has a disease such as AIDS. Article 112 states that court hearings for women suing for divorce from men alleged to have sexual illnesses will occur in "secret hearings," and Article 113 states that if such an illness is deemed to be permanent, "the court will nullify the marriage immediately." UAE, *Law of Personal Status Matters*.

29. Articles 172–179 stipulate that "a person reaches adulthood if he/she completes 21 lunar years," which ends male guardianship except over a "mature" daughter who wants to marry. Ibid.

30. Welchman, *Women and Muslim Family*, 71–72.

31. The article states that "in case of inability to speak, writing will substitute for it, or if that is not possible, then signs that are understood." UAE, *Law of Personal Status Matters*.

32. Welchman, *Women and Muslim Family*, 54–55.

33. As addressed in Chapter 2, *misyār* marriage contracts were completed similarly to regular contracts before personal status codification. Agreements, if any, to give up maintenance or housing were not included in the marriage contract on file with the state, at least in Dubai.

34. Welchman, *Women and Muslim Family*, 103.

35. Ibid., 51.

36. Article 156. This article allows a mother to keep custody (not legal guardianship) of children beyond these ages (boys until they reach eighteen, "come of age," and girls until they marry) if the court determines this to be in the best interests of the child(ren). UAE, *Law of Personal Status Matters*.

37. Al Roken interview; Darwish interview.

38. This woman was of a modest family background in the status scheme among native clans.

39. The new law replaced Law 78 of 1931; part 4 of the Civil and Commercial Code; Articles 868–1032 of Law No. 77 of 1949; and other procedural articles in the personal status laws. Al-Sharmani, "Recent Reforms," 3, and n. 1.

40. Ibid., 18; Interview by author with al-Sharmani, Cairo, May 29, 2008.

41. Al-Sharmani, "Recent Reforms," 10; Welchman, *Women's Rights*, 58.

42. Al-Sharmani, "Recent Reforms," 3, 7.

43. Sa'id interview.

44. Souleiman, "Introduction," 9; Zakareya, "Khol': A Socio-Legal," 68; Al-Sharmani, "Recent Reforms," 69.

45. Al-Sharmani, "Recent Reforms," 10.

46. Ibid., 3, and n. 2. According to Article 20 of the law: "If the couple is not reconciled . . . then divorce will be considered if the wife declares explicitly that: she can no longer endure the situation, married life between them is impossible and that she fears her consequent inability to maintain the 'limit of God' due to her marital circumstances. The consideration for *khul'* may not be the forfeiting [by the mother] of custody of minors, or their maintenance or any of their rights." In Hasan, "Granting *Khul'*," 82. Article 18 of the law is vague regarding how long reconciliation efforts should take, stating that "at least" two efforts at court reconciliation should be undertaken in marriages *with children*, separated by "at least 30 days but no more than 60 days." See articles 18 and 20 of the law, available in Arabic at: *http://www.arab2all.com /vb/t10349.html* (accessed May 14, 2008).

47. 'Abd al-Jawad and al-Kurdi, "Social Change," 10.

48. Al-Sharmani, "Recent Reforms," 10. The outraged response of many Egyptian

male elites to Article 26 is discussed in Welchman, *Women's Rights*, 63, 65, 78–79. The substance of the excised article was made law in a November 2000 ruling by the Egyptian Higher Supreme Court against the Interior Ministry; the court found that restricting the travel of a wife was unconstitutional. Al-Sharmani, "Recent Reforms," 11.

49. Al-Sharmani, "Recent Reforms," 10.

50. Zakareya, "Khol'," 55–58, 70–74, 43.

51. Welchman examines the positions staked out by the religious establishment, progressive Islamists, and political parties and how these played out in the parliamentary debates, including the misogynist nature of the discussions. Welchman, *Women's Rights*, 59–67.

52. Al-Sharmani, "Recent Reforms," 11.

53. Sa'id interview.

54. Al-Sharmani, "Recent Reforms," 11.

55. Ibid.

56. Welchman, *Women's Rights*, 62–63.

57. In the most widely discussed example, the highly respected lawyer and first woman judge (appointed in 2003 by presidential decree to the Supreme Constitutional Court) in Egypt, Tahany al-Gebaly, discussed the case of "Jamila, the wife of [Thabit Ibn Qais]," who disliked her husband and asked the Prophet Muhammad his opinion on her receiving a divorce. The "Prophet Mohammed required that Jamila give back the prompt part of her dower to her husband in return for *khul'*. She was not required to pay her husband any more than that prompt part. . . . By contrast, the present law states that a wife must renounce all her financial rights, even those ensured by [Egyptian state] law according to the husband's social and economic status, such as their *mata'a* [alimony if the husband is at fault based on Law No. 100 of 1985]." Al-Gebaly, "Law of Khol'," 39. Arabi writes that Egyptian lawmakers focused on the hadith reporting that in response to Habiba bint Sahl's (called Jamila in the above) request, the Prophet commanded Thabit to separate from her without his consent and take as compensation the garden he had given her as prompt dower. Arabi, "Dawning," 182–86.

58. Tadrous, "Law of Khol'," 75–77.

59. Zakareya, "Khol'," 46.

60. Abdul Sattar, *Women in Egyptian Legislations*, 51, 124–25; Welchman, *Women's Rights*, 64, 70.

61. Al-Sharmani, "Recent Reforms," 13; Abdul Sattar, *Women in Egyptian Legislations*, 54.

62. Al-Sharmani, "Recent Reforms," 3, 9.

63. This information is taken from a copy of a completed Egyptian marriage contract. This copy had a diagonal line crossed through the blank lines with the phrase "there are no conditions [*lā yūjad shurūṭ*]" written above the line.

64. From a copy of a completed Egyptian marriage contract. Men and women are

instructed by the state that *qānūn*, or state law, has punishments for men who lie about this information. Egypt Republic National Council for Women, "On the Path of Life" series, cassette one.

65. Welchman, *Women and Muslim Family,* 101; Al-Korashy interview; Al-Sharmani interview.

66. Al-Sharmani interview.

67. Abdul Sattar, *Women in Egyptian Legislations,* 90–92.

68. This law elaborated on Article 10 of Law No. 1 of 2000. Al-Sharmani, "Recent Reforms," 3, 12, 15.

69. Abdul Sattar, *Women in Egyptian Legislations,* 125, 126–27.

70. Al-Sharmani, "Recent Reforms," 12–13.

71. Ibid., 13, 15, and n. 18; Abdul Sattar, *Women in Egyptian Legislations,* 132. In *khul'* divorces, the case is filed with the court and the husband is summoned to appear (the wife or her legal representative must assure he receives the summons). The wife returns the advanced dower to the husband and states that "she is resolved to end the marriage"; the judge proposes reconciliation; the court experts meet with the disputants, followed by an arbitration involving either two family relatives or an appointed arbiter. Most women do not want reconciliation and neither disputant trusts relatives to arbitrate, thus they choose a court-appointed arbiter, although the plaintiff must pay the burdensome fee for most women. Al-Sharmani, "Recent Reforms," 40.

72. Welchman, *Women's Rights,* 69.

73. Article 72 of Law No. 1.

74. Al-Sharmani, "Recent Reforms," 3 and 12.

75. Abdul Sattar, *Women in Egyptian Legislations,* 135.

76. Al-Korashy interview.

77. Egypt Ministry of Justice, "Summary Text for Egypt"; Abdul Sattar, *Women in Egyptian Legislations,* 53.

78. Al-Korashy interview.

79. Al-Gebaly, "Law of Khol'," 36; Al-Sharmani, "Recent Reforms," 15–16.

80. Souleiman and Salah, "Legal Aspects of Khol'," 17.

81. Al-Sharmani, "Recent Reforms," 17–18.

82. Ibid., 17, and n. 29.

83. Ibid., 49, 59. The new system also continues to require that the "judge examining the case estimates the harm in view of the circumstances of the action and the social status of the spouses." Abdul Sattar, *Women in Egyptian Legislations,* 100.

84. Al-Sharmani, "Recent Reforms," 56, 67–68; Al-Sharmani interview; E-mail correspondence between author and Dr. al-Sharmani, July 14, 2009.

85. Al-Sharmani, "Recent Reforms," 61. The Center for Egyptian Women Legal Assistance, for instance, contends that the changes do "not represent a solution for women experiencing marital problems, because [they] fall short of granting wives

equal rights with their husbands. . . . The substantive personal status law needs radical reform, as well as the corresponding procedural rules." Souleiman, "Introduction," 10.

86. E-mail correspondence between author and Mulki al-Sharmani, July 14, 2009.

87. Darwiche interview.

88. Al-Sharmani, "Recent Reforms," 61.

89. Souleiman and Salah, "Legal Aspects of Khol'," 18, 20–24, 31–32. The authors also found that many judges "created new rules of their own" in making *khul'* judgments. In Cairo, this included exaggerating the wedding gift the woman had to repay to the husband and obliging women "to return both the prompt and the deferred [or never paid] parts of the dower, despite the fact that the imperative legal term states a woman has to return only the prompt part of the dower and renounce the rest of her financial rights." Ibid., 29, 33.

90. Mulki al-Sharmani, "Recent Reforms," 21.

91. More than half of the "no-fault" divorce cases studied by Halim et al. lasted six to twelve months, whereas more than half of the "prejudicial" divorce cases lasted one to two years, with 28 percent lasting over two years. In al-Sharmani, "Recent Reforms," 21, and n. 36.

92. The focus of the study was court personnel, lawyers, and disputants involved in "maintenance, *khul'* divorce, prejudicial divorce, obedience awards, visitation rights for noncustodial parents, child custody, paternity disputes, destruction of marital furniture, and repossession of conjugal home." Al-Sharmani, "Recent Reforms," 3, 19, 23.

93. Al-Korashy interview.

94. Al-Sharmani, "Recent Reforms," 45, 26.

95. Ibid., 46.

96. Al-Sharmani, "Recent Reforms," 24, 41, 43–44; Al-Sharmani interview.

97. Al-Sharmani interview.

98. Darwiche interview.

99. Al-Sharmani, "Recent Reforms," 63.

100. Ibid., 43.

101. Legal representatives make less money if they resolve a case in mediation and are sometimes incompetent. Al-Sharmani's team found that mediation and enforcement were more effective in rural family court branches, possibly because people in these communities are more accountable to each other. Al-Sharmani, 26, 28, 30, 35–36, 48–50.

102. Al-Sharmani, "Recent Reforms," 27–28.

103. Al-Korashy interview; 'Arafat interview.

104. Al-Sharmani, "Recent Reforms," 38.

105. The mediation specialists employed in these courts were predominantly women and some men who had graduated from faculties of law and social work and departments of psychology and sociology; the majority were in their forties. Al-Sharmani, "Recent Reforms," 25, 30–31.

106. Ibid., 70–71.

107. Al-Sharmani interview.

108. Abdul Sattar, *Women in Egyptian Legislations*, 140–41.

109. Ibid., 141–42.

110. Leila, "Citizens at Last."

111. Abdul Sattar, *Women in Egyptian Legislations*, 52–53, 144–45; Egypt Ministry of Justice, "Summary Text"; Leila, "Citizenship Costs Less."

112. Interview by author with Ahmad ʿArafat, Giza, May 26, 2008.

113. Lutfi interview.

114. Leila, "Ties Made Better."

115. Lutfi interview.

116. El Shakry, "Schooled Mothers," 127. El Shakry points out that while the discourses coming from feminist-secular and Islamist authors in early twentieth-century Egypt differed with respect to the nature of the "uplift" project, they both targeted especially lower-class women for education in rational child-rearing methods. Ibid., 141, 143.

117. Layla interview.

118. Abu-Lughod, *Dramas of Nationhood*, 159.

119. Ibid., 42–43.

120. Ibid., 10, 11. Abu-Lughod also terms this agenda "developmental realism," describing it as an idealization of "education, progress, and modernity within the nation." Ibid., 81.

121. Ibid., 42.

122. Ibid., 63, 82, 83.

123. Ibid., 12–13, 245.

124. Ibid., 96, 103.

125. Sadek, "Cairo as a Global/Regional Cultural Capital?" 166.

126. Abu-Lughod, *Dramas of Nationhood*, 37–38, 52, 63, 141.

127. Ibid., 141–42.

128. Ibid., 143.

129. Ibid., 12, 14, 33, 145.

130. The "On the Path of Life" series of cassettes, according to its introductory brochure, "accomplishes one of the national goals for raising women and incorporating her [*idmājiha*] into the Five-Year National Plans for Economic and Social Development [which is] concerned with erasing legal illiteracy among Egyptian women in all sectors." The series is part of the "Awareness of Women's Legal Rights Through Use of Information Technology" project, produced by Husni Ghunaym for the Egypt Republic National Council for Women in 2007. The tapes were in an elegant brown-and-tan box of Arabic-language materials embossed on top with three logos: Pharaonic statues with a setting sun behind them above the words National Council for Women

in Arabic (middle), a UNDP "ICTDAR" logo (right), and the European Union logo (left). Below this, the project title ("Awareness . . . ") is printed in a larger font, above silhouettes of the heads of two girls and two women, a scale of justice, and images of a CD and two cassette tapes. The box includes a booklet titled *Women's Inheritance*; a CD Rom and booklet listing its contents, which focus on international protocols on women's rights; a booklet on polygamy by Dr. Zaynab al-Radhwan, professor of Islamic philosophy at Cairo University, parliament member, and member of the NCW; a brochure introducing the project, which describes the NCW as "an independent constitutional organization under the President of the Republic that aims to raise [*nuhūd*] the situation of Egyptian women." The project includes Lebanon and Tunisia and was funded by the UN Development Programme, the European Union, and the Arab Program for Information Technology and Communication. I am very grateful to Dr. Huda al-Sharqawi, assistant to the general secretary of the NCW, who generously provided this box of material to me in May 2008.

131. To be considered valid by the state, the divorce must be documented with a state registry within thirty days and the registrar will inform or confirm this with the (former) wife. Egypt Republic National Council for Women, "On the Path of Life" series, cassette tape one.

132. According to these cassettes, premature ejaculation is not a valid basis for judicial divorce because it can be medically treated, while a husband having no penis and smelling poorly in relation to an illness the wife was unaware of (rather than poor grooming habits, which can be changed through retraining) can be bases for divorce. Having sexual relations with other women through Internet "chatting" is not a basis for divorce unless a husband leaves the wife for such a relationship. Being forced to live in a home with a plural wife, being unjustly accused of adultery by the husband, having a greedy husband who steals a wife's money and things, having a husband who tries to force a Christian woman to convert to Islam, having a husband who forces a wife to take birth control pills, having a husband who insists on anal sex, having a husband who watches "sexual deviance" on the Internet and forces her to try things that "violate her dignity," having a husband who insists on photographing their intimacy, having a husband who wants to prostitute his wife to his friends, and having a husband who insists on her serving alcohol to his friends are valid bases for divorce. Having no hymen is not necessarily a basis for divorce, and female virginity is only a valid basis if it was a condition of the marriage. Finding out about a husband's customary marriage is a basis for divorce if a wife can prove it and confirm it harms her. Egypt Republic National Council for Women, "On the Path of Life" series, cassette tapes two and ten.

133. Tapes seven and eight of the series address Christian, Jewish, and other sect differences with regard to family law in Egypt.

134. For example, speakers on the tapes strongly encourage and insist that a male

guardian's presence is necessary, required, and customary for women contracting a marriage, while also conceding that male guardian approval is technically not required for women of majority age. Some information contradicts the law and demonstrates the degree to which even rationalized laws and statutes are interpreted and applied differently.

135. Karam, *Women, Islamisms*, 25.

136. Egypt Republic National Council for Women, "On the Path of Life" series, cassette tape one.

137. Ibid.

138. Interview with Dr. Su'ad Salih, Professor of Comparative Fiqh, Al-Azhar University, Girls' College for Islamic and Arabic Studies, Cairo, Egypt, May 29, 2008.

139. Abdul Sattar, *Women in Egyptian Legislations*, 39.

140. Ibid., 93.

141. Ibid., 95–96.

142. Ibid., 23–24.

143. Ibid., 39.

144. Ibid., 93–94. The situation for Coptic Christians is similar in Egyptian law: the man is considered the head and guardian of the family who must share and provide a home that the wife and children must live in; there is no shared matrimonial regime between the resources of the husband and wife. Although the Coptic religious institution does not recognize divorce and considers marriage "eternal," Copts can be judicially divorced in Egypt if one of the spouses "defects from his/her Christian religion," sexual intercourse does not occur, or any of the following possibilities occur and are demonstrated in family court: adultery, incurable illness, "physical or moral abuse," or long-term imprisonment. The husband must maintain the wife under Coptic rules unless she refuses to live with him; the wife is obligated to spend on the family if he is insolvent and incapable of working or if "she is financially capable of spending on him." Ibid., 114–17.

145. Ibid., 93–94.

146. Egypt Republic National Council for Women, "On the Path of Life" series, cassettes one, two, three.

147. Al-Korashy interview.

148. Egypt Republic National Council for Women, "On the Path of Life" series, cassettes one and two.

149. Egypt Republic National Council for Women, "On the Path of Life" series, cassette ten.

150. Al-Musfir, *United Arab Emirates*, 145.

151. Ibid., 146.

152. "Forced Marriage Is Null."

153. Hamid, "Cultural Influences," 14–15.

154. Al-Shaykh, "Self-Esteem and its Relationship," 12.

155. Darwish interview.

156. Ibid.

157. Al-ʿOlama interview.

158. Ibid.

159. Darwish interview.

160. Al-Diqqi interview.

161. The box is embossed with the slogan of the courts in Arabic: "Pioneering in the Work of Courts [*al-riyāddatun fī ʿamal al-maḥākim*]" above a scale of justice, labeled "Government of Dubai, Courts Department" (Arabic and English) and titled, "Family Guidance and Reconciliation [*al-tuwjiya wal-islāḥ al-usarī*]." Attached blue ribbons can seal the lid to the box. In addition to material I discuss in the chapter, the box contains the following items: (1) a booklet titled "Dowry of the Wives: Between Shariʿa and Custom," by Dr. Saif Rashed al-Jabiri, published by the UAE Marriage Fund (2002). The author stresses that marriage is a social good in God's eyes and remaining unmarried is to be avoided; insists on the necessity of a dowry from the husband to be kept by a wife; discusses its religious history; and warns against dowry inflation, conspicuous consumption, and "showing off" so that men can avoid "debt" and "humiliation." (2) A booklet titled "The Pre-Marriage Health Exam," by the UAE Marriage Fund, undated but published no earlier than late 2001. (3) A book with a picture of the UAE president, Shaykh Zayed bin Sultan al-Nahyan on the cover, titled *Marriage in Islam* and published by the Marriage Fund to mark the twenty-second birthday of the UAE as a state. (4) A small book titled *The Model Marriage*, by M'hmd Rasheed al-ʿAwīd (Jeddah: Saudi Arabia: Dar al-Mahmadi for Publishing and Distribution, 2003). (5) A book titled *The Bases of Marital Relations*, by Judge Shaikh M'hmd Hamad Kanʿaan (Beirut: Lebanon: Dar al-Bashir al-Islamiyya Printing, Publishing and Distribution, 2001), which describes and defines in great detail and matter-of-factly issues and Islamic rules related to marriage, engagement, the marriage contract, the wedding, marital sexual intercourse, including preparing for intercourse, pregnancy and childbirth, nursing and caring for young children, the rights of the two spouses, behaviors that corrupt marital relations (including looking at others freely, associating with other women, employment in mixed-gender environments, media sources . . .), the end of a failed marriage, and acquiring bodily moral disposition (cleanliness, circumcision—Islamically required for boys; reduction of the clitoris is a tribal ritual among some that is not required or recommended by Islam for girls; how to treat men's and women's body hair and nails); each chapter includes a question-and-answer section. I deeply appreciate the willingness of Mr. Darwish, Government of Dubai Courts Department, to give me this box in December 2003.

162. Darwish interview. At this point in the interview, we were interrupted by a Syrian national trying to register a divorce from a Romanian wife. After looking over

his paperwork, Mr. Darwish instructed him to go register the divorce in the Shariqa courts, his location of residence and work.

163. The cover of this 1998 publication has a color picture of two boys, about eight and ten years old, wading on beach, one with his arm lightly around the shoulders of the other; the title of the booklet is written as a question in a cartoonlike bubble above the head of one of the boys; the cover includes the following questions in a smaller font: "What does the man want from the woman? What does the woman want from the man? This is what you will know when you read this book." The "preliminary survey" of four hundred married Kuwaiti people, half men and half women, found that for a wife to "care for the house" ranked as the first priority for the largest group of married men, 21 percent; 16 percent ranked "emotions and expressing feelings" as their first priority; and 15 percent ranked "mutual respect" as their first priority. Among the women surveyed, the largest group, 21 percent, ranked "taking responsibility" as their first priority in terms of expectations from husbands; the second largest group, 17 percent, expressed their first priority as a husband assuring the wife "feel safe"; and the third largest group of women, 13.5 percent, expected as their first priority from husbands "emotions and expressing feelings." Overall, the results of the survey indicate significant differences within gender categories with respect to priorities, although the largest groups of women and men seem to prefer a framework in which women care for the home in return for men "taking responsibility" (financial and social) in the household. Al-Mutawwa', "Do You Know the Priorities," 10–11, 14, 15–table 1, 16–17, 18–table 2, 19, 30, 31–table 1, 32–33, 34–35.

164. Ibid., 7.

165. The tape begins with religious music and singing as background to the introduction of each section by a deep-voiced male.

Conclusion

1. Indeed, the goal of "an analytics of government" is not "to show how humans can be liberated from or, indeed, by government." Dean, *Governmentality*, 34.

2. Ms. Heba Kotb, an Egyptian sex therapist who runs an "Islam-oriented" clinic and had a "satellite television show on sexual and marital issues" between 2006 and 2008, is also interviewed in the article. Worth, "Challenging Sex Taboos."

Bibliography

Print and Multimedia Sources

'Abd al-Jawad, Layla. Guest on Luna al-Shibil, "For Women Only" program. Al-Jazeera satellite television channel. December 27, 2004. (Arabic)

'Abd al-Jawad, Layla, and Maha al-Kurdi. "Social Change and the Customary Marriage." Unpublished paper (38 pp.) Presented in April 2003 at the Fifth Conference of the National Center for Social and Criminal Research, "Social Change and Egyptian Society in the Past Fifty Years," Cairo, Egypt. Kindly provided to the author. (Arabic)

'Abdallah, Mu'taz Sayyid, and Jum'a Sayyid Yusif. *Common Law Marriage: Its Reality and Psychological and Social Effects*. Heritage and Social Change Research Report Series. Cairo: Cairo University Center for Research and Social Studies Publications. 2004. Kindly provided to the author by Dr. Ahmed A. Zayed, Dean of the Faculty of Arts and Sciences, Cairo University. (Arabic)

'Ismat, Asma'. "Charity Money Dedicated Towards Facilitating Marriage: How Do We Face the Problem of Spinsterhood?!" *Al-Shaqa'iq* [Sisters], no. 76 (December 2003): 48–49. (Arabic)

'Umar, Samir. Field report on Luna al-Shibil, "The Secret Marriage in our Arab World: Its Reasons and Precariousness." Episode of "For Women Only [li-l-nisā' faqad]" Program on al-Jazeera satellite television channel. December 27, 2004. (Arabic)

Abaza, Mona. *The Changing Consumer Cultures of Modern Egypt: Cairo's Urban Reshaping*. Cairo: American University in Cairo Press, 2006.

———. "Perceptions of 'Urfi Marriage in the Egyptian Press." *ISIM Newsletter 7*, no. 1 (March 2001): 20–21.

Abdal-Rehim, Abdal-Rehim Abdal-Rahman. "The Family and Gender Laws in Egypt during the Ottoman Period." In *Women, the Family, and Divorce Laws in Islamic History*, edited by Amira El Azhary Sonbol, 96–111. Syracuse, NY: Syracuse University Press, 1996.

Abdul Sattar, Fawziya. *Women in Egyptian Legislations.* Translated 3rd edition. Cairo: National Council of Women, Arab Republic of Egypt, 2007.

Abou El-Magd, Nadia. "Single Mother Shocks and Divides Egyptians by Keeping Baby, Pushing Actor to Recognize His Daughter." *Associated Press*, February 27, 2005. Lexis Nexis Academic Universe (accessed July 6, 2007).

Abrams, Philip. "Notes on the Difficulty of Studying the State." In *The Anthropology of the State: A Reader*, edited by Aradhana Sharma and Akhil Gupta, 112–30. Malden, MA: Blackwell Publishing, 2006.

Abu Dhabi Tourism Authority. http://www.visitabudhabi.ae/en/uae.facts.and.figures/ language.religion.aspx (accessed June 9, 2009).

Abu-Lughod, Lila. "Dialects of Women's Empowerment: The International Circuitry of the *Arab Human Development Report 2005." International Journal of Middle East Studies* 41, no. 1 (February 2009): 83–103.

———. *Dramas of Nationhood: The Politics of Television in Egypt.* Chicago: University of Chicago Press, 2005.

———. "The Marriage of Feminism and Islamism in Egypt: Selective Repudiations as a Dynamic of Postcolonial Cultural Politics." In *Remaking Women: Feminism and Modernity in the Middle East*, edited by Lila Abu-Lughod, 243–69. Princeton, NJ: Princeton University Press, 1998.

El Alami, Dawoud Sudqi. *The Marriage Contract in Islamic Law: In the Shari'ah and Personal Status Laws of Egypt and Morocco.* London, Dordrecht, and Boston: Graham and Trotman/Kluwer, 1992.

Ali, Kamran Asdar. *Planning the Family in Egypt: New Bodies, New Selves.* Austin: University of Texas Press, 2002.

Al-Ali, Nadje. *Secularism, Gender and the State in the Middle East: The Egyptian Women's Movement.* Cambridge: Cambridge University Press, 2000.

Almihdar, Zainah. "Human Rights of Women and Children Under The Islamic Law of Personal Status and Its Application in Saudi Arabia." *Muslim World Journal of Human Rights* 5, no. 1 (2008, published 2009): 1–15.

Amin, Sajeda, and Nagah H. al-Bassusi. "Education, Wage Work, and Marriage: Perspectives of Egyptian Working Women." *Journal of Marriage and Family* 66, no. 5 (December 2004): 1,287–99.

Amnesty International. *Gulf Cooperation Council (GCC) Countries: Women Deserve Dignity and Respect.* London: Amnesty International International Secretariat, 2005. www.amnesty.org. AI Index: MDE 04/004/2005.

The Annual Statistical Report: The Situation of Women and Men in Egypt. Egypt Central Agency for Public Mobilization and Statistics. Cairo: CAPMAS, January 2002. (Arabic)

Appadurai, Arjun. "Disjuncture and Difference in the Global Cultural Economy." In *The Anthropology of Globalization: A Reader*, edited by Jonathan Xavier Inda and Renato Rosaldo, 46–64. Malden, MA: Blackwell Publishing, 2002.

"Arab Gays Face Forced Hormone Treatment: UAE Mulls Punishment Against Dozens Arrested at Mass Gay Wedding." *Associated Press*, November 26, 2005. http://www.msnbc.msn.com/id/10218234 (accessed April 3, 2009).

The Arab Republic of Egypt. "Egyptian Personal Status Law No. 1 of 2000." http://www.arab2all.com/vb/t10349.html (accessed May 14, 2008). (Arabic)

The Arab Republic of Egypt National Council for Women. "On the Path of Life." Series of ten cassette tapes focused on "Awareness of Women's Legal Rights Through Use of Information Technology. Produced by Husni Ghunaym. Cairo: National Council for Women, 2007. Kindly provided to the author by Huda al-Sharqawi, Assistant to the General Secretary, NCW. (Arabic)

Arabi, Oussama. "The Dawning of the Third Millennium on Shari'a: Egypt's Law No. 1 of 2000, or Women May Divorce at Will." *Arab Law Quarterly* 16, no. 1 (2001): 2–21.

———. "The Itinerary of a Fatwa: Ambulant Marriage (al-Zawaj al-Misyar), or Grass Roots Law-Making in Saudi Arabia of the 1990s." In *Studies in Modern Islamic Law and Jurisprudence*, by Oussama Arabi, 147–67. The Hague, London, and New York: Kluwer Law International, 2001.

Asad, Talal. "Ethnographic Representation, Statistics and Modern Power." *Social Research* 61, no. 1 (spring 1994): 55–88.

———. *Formations of the Secular: Christianity, Islam, Modernity*. Stanford: Stanford University Press, 2003.

Al-Awadhi, Badria Abdullah. "Women in the Gulf and Globalization: Challenges and Opportunities." In *The Gulf: Challenges of the Future*, 423–40. Abu Dhabi: The Emirates Center for Strategic Studies and Research, 2005.

Baalbaki, Dr. Rohi. *Al-Mawrid: A Modern Arabic-English Dictionary* (al-Mawrid: Qamus 'Arabi-Inqlizi). 16th edition. Beirut: Dar al-'Ilm li-l-Malayin, 2002.

Baron, Beth. "The Making and Breaking of Marital Bonds in Modern Egypt." In *Women in Middle Eastern History*, edited by Nikki R. Keddie and Beth Baron, 275–91. New Haven, CT: Yale University Press, 1991.

Bhaskaran, Suparna. *Made In India: Decolonization, Queer Sexualities, Tran/National Projects*. New York: Palgrave MacMillan, 2004.

Bier, Laura. "From Birth Control to Family Planning." In *Family in the Middle East: Ideational Change in Egypt, Iran, and Tunisia*, edited by Kathryn M. Yount and Hoda Rashad, 55–79. New York: Routledge, 2008.

Brennan, Denise. *What's Love Got to Do with It? Transnational Desires and Sex Tourism in the Dominican Republic*. Durham, NC, and London: Duke University Press, 2004.

Brewster, Karin, and Ronald R. Rindfuss. "Fertility and Women's Employment in Industrialized Nations." *Annual Review of Sociology* 26 (2000): 271–96.

Bristol-Rhys, Jane. "Weddings, Marriage and Money in the United Arab Emirates." *Anthropology of the Middle East* 2, no. 1 (spring 2007): 20–36.

Butler, Judith. *The Psychic Life of Power: Theories in Subjection*. Stanford: Stanford University Press, 1997.

Carlisle, Jessica. "From Behind the Door: A Damascus Court Copes with an Alleged Out of Court Marriage." In *Les Métamorphoses du Mariage au Moyen-Orient*, edited by Barbara Drieskens, 59–74. Beirut: Institut Français du Proche-Orient, 2008.

Carnegie Endowment for International Peace. *Arab Political Systems: Baseline Information and Reforms—UAE*. Washington, DC. www.carnegieendowment.org/arabpolit icalsystems; www.fride.org/eng/Publications/Publication.aspx?Item=787 (accessed July 17, 2007).

Charrad, Mounira M. *States and Women's Rights: The Making of Postcolonial Tunisia, Algeria, and Morocco*. Berkeley and Los Angeles: University of California Press, 2001.

Collins, Patricia Hill. "Black Feminist Epistemology." In *Contemporary Sociological Theory*, edited by Craig Calhoun et al., 323–31. Oxford: Blackwell, 2002.

Cuno, Kenneth M. "Divorce and the Fate of the Family in Modern Egypt." In *Family in the Middle East: Ideational Change in Egypt, Iran, and Tunisia*, edited by Yount and Rashad, 196–216. New York: Routledge, 2008.

Cuno, Kenneth M., and Michael J. Reimer. "The Census Registers of Nineteenth-century Egypt: a New Source for Social Historians." *British Journal of Middle Eastern Studies* 24, no. 2 (1997): 193–216.

Darwish, 'Abdul Salam Muhammad. "Contemporary Changes and Their Impact on Youth." Unpublished paper presented at the "Youth in the Face of a More Challenging World" conference, December 9–10, 2003, sponsored by the Ajman (UAE) women's association (December 2003): 1–23. (Arabic)

Davidson, Christopher M. "Arab Nationalism and British Opposition in Dubai, 1920–66." *Middle Eastern Studies* 43, no. 6 (November 2007): 879–92.

———. *The United Arab Emirates: A Study in Survival*. Boulder, CO, and London: Lynne Rienner Publishers, 2005.

Dean, Mitchell. *Governmentality: Power and Rule in Modern Society*. London: Sage Publications, 1999.

Dib, Hala 'Ahed. Guest on Luna al-Shibil, "For Women Only" program. Al-Jazeera satellite television channel. December 27, 2004. (Arabic)

Al-Dib, Buthayna. "Some Important Facts Regarding Marriage and Divorce in Egypt During the Recent Era (1981–2001)." Unpublished report kindly shared with author by Dr. al-Dib, Head of the Central Administration for the Affairs of the Population Research Center, at the Central System of Mobilization and Statistics, Cairo. n.d., received in 2003. (Arabic)

Donzelot, Jacques. *The Policing of Families*. Foreword by Gilles Deleuze. Translated from French by Robert Hurley. New York: Pantheon Books, 1979.

Dresch, Paul. "Debates on Marriage and Nationality in the United Arab Emirates." In

Monarchies and Nations: Globalisation and Identity in the Arab States of the Gulf, edited by Paul Dresch and James Piscatori, 136–57. London: I.B. Tauris, 2005.

Drieskens, Barbara. "Changing Perceptions of Marriage in Contemporary Beirut." In *Les Métamorphoses du Mariage au Moyen-Orient*, edited by Barbara Drieskens, 97–118. Beirut: Institut Français du Proche-Orient, 2008.

"Dubai 'Sex-on-Beach' Couple Escape Jail Term." *CNN*, November 25, 2008. www.cnn.com /2008/WORLD/meast/11/25/dubai.sex.couple/index.html (accessed April 23, 2009).

Al-Duwaysh, al-Shaykh Ibrahim Ibn 'Abd-illah. "The Sea of Love . . . A Tour of the Dangers of the Meaning of Love . . . and Some Tales of Affection . . . and other Recollections about Longing and Yearning." Cassette tape distributed in the Government of Dubai, Courts Department, "Marriage Box." Riyadh: Rawasin Institute for Media Production, n.d. Kindly provided to the author by Mr. Mohammad Darwish in December 2003. (Arabic)

Egypt Ministry of Justice. "Summary Text for Egypt." Department of International and Cultural Co-operation. Document approved by Cherifa Kalaoui, family lawyer, El Kalaoui Law Firm, Cairo, July 26, 2005: 1–6, unnumbered pages. Available on Reunite International website, Leicester, UK. www.reunite.org/pages/egypt.asp (accessed October 23, 2008).

"Egyptian Appeals Court Rules that Baby Is Movie Star's Daughter." *Deutsche Presse-Agentur*, May 24, 2006. Lexis Nexis Academic Universe (accessed July 6, 2007).

"Egyptian Court Nixes Recognizing Paternity of 'Extramarital' Baby." *Deutsche Presse-Agentur*, January 26, 2006. Lexis Nexis Academic Universe (accessed July 6, 2007).

Eickelman, Christine. *Women and Community in Oman*. New York: New York University Press, 1984.

Eickelman, Dale F. "New Media in the Arab Middle East and the Emergence of Open Societies." In *Remaking Muslim Politics: Pluralism, Contestation, Democratization*, edited by Robert W. Hefner, 37–59. Princeton, NJ: Princeton University Press, 2005.

Eickelman, Dale F., and James Piscatori. *Muslim Politics*. Princeton, NJ: Princeton University Press, 1996.

Esposito, John L., with Natana J. DeLong-Bas. *Women in Muslim Family Law*, 2d ed. Syracuse, NY: Syracuse University Press, 2001.

Ewald, François. "Norms, Discipline, and the Law." In *Law and the Order of Culture*, edited by Robert Post, 138–60. Translated and adapted by Marjorie Beale. Berkeley: University of California Press, 1991.

Fakhro, Munira Ahmed. "The Changing Role of Women in the Gulf Region." In *The Gulf: Challenges of the Future*, 391–422. Abu Dhabi: The Emirates Center for Strategic Studies and Research, 2005.

Fargues, Philippe. "Family and Household in Mid-Nineteenth-Century Cairo." In *Family History in the Middle East: Household, Property, and Gender*, edited by Beshara Doumani, 23–50. Albany: State University of New York Press, 2003.

———. "State Policies and the Birth Rate in Egypt: From Socialism to Liberalism." *Population and Development Review* 23, no. 1 (March 1997): 115–38.

Al-Fishawy, Ahmad. Interview with Ahmad al-Fishawy on *al-Bayt Baytak* program, al-Misriyya Egyptian satellite television station. November 22, 2008. http://www.youtube.com/watch?v=AbTSIqeWhMs (accessed April 1, 2009). (Arabic)

"Forced Marriage Is Null . . . the Girls' Agreement Is Necessary." *Kul al-Usra* magazine, no. 529 (December 3, 2003): 162–64. Published by Dar al-Khalij, Sharjah, United Arab Emirates. (Arabic)

Foucault, Michel. *The Birth of Biopolitics: Lectures at the College de France, 1978–79*. Michel Senellart, edited by François Ewald and Alessandro Fontana. Translated from French by Graham Burchell. New York: Palgrave Macmillan, 2008.

———. "On the Genealogy of Ethics: An Overview of Work in Progress." In *The Foucault Reader*, edited by Paul Rabinow, 340–72. New York: Pantheon Books, 1984.

———. "Governmentality." In *The Anthropology of the State: A Reader*, edited by Sharma and Gupta, 131–43. Malden, MA: Blackwell Publishing, 2006.

———. *The History of Sexuality*, Volume 1: *An Introduction*. Translated from French by Robert Hurley; originally published in French in 1976. New York: Vintage Books, Random House, 1978, 1990.

———. "The Political Technology of Individuals." In *Technologies of the Self: A Seminar with Michel Foucault*, edited by Luther H. Martin, Huck Gutman, and Patrick H. Hutton, 145–62. Amherst: University of Massachusetts Press, 1988.

———. "The Subject and Power." *Critical Inquiry* 8 (summer 1982): 777–95.

———. *The Use of Pleasure: The History of Sexuality*, Volume 2. Translated from French by Robert Hurley; originally published in French in 1984. New York: Vintage Books, Random House, 1985, 1990.

Al-Gazali, L.I., A. Bener, Y.M. Abdulrazzaq, R. Micallef, A.I. Al-Khayat, and T. Gaber. "Consanguineous Marriages in the United Arab Emirates." *Journal of Biosocial Science* 29 (1997): 491–97.

Al-Gebaly, Tahany. "The Law of Khol': Between Text and Application." In *The Harvest: Two Years After Khol': An Analytical Study*, edited by Azza Souleiman, Azza Salah, Huda Zakareya, and Mariz Tadrous. Translated by Seham Abd el Salam, 36–40. Cairo: The Center for Egyptian Women Legal Assistance, 2003.

Ghannam, Farha. "Keeping Him Connected: Globalization and the Production of Locality in Urban Egypt." In *Cairo Cosmopolitan: Politics, Culture, and Urban Space in the New Globalized Middle East*, edited by Diane Singerman and Paul Amar, 251–66. Cairo and New York: American University in Cairo Press, 2006.

Gimbel, Barney. "The Richest City in the World." *Fortune Magazine*, March 12, 2007. money.cnn.com/magazines/fortune/fortune_archive/2007/03/19/8402357/index.htm (accessed April 28, 2009).

Golder, Ben, and Peter Fitzpatrick. *Foucault's Law*. London: Routledge, 2009.

Grewal, Inderpal. *Transnational America: Feminisms, Diasporas, Neoliberalisms*. Durham, NC: Duke University Press, 2005.

Gupta, Akhil. "Blurred Boundaries: The Discourse of Corruption, the Culture of Politics, and the Imagined State." In *The Anthropology of the State: A Reader*, edited by Sharma and Gupta, 211–42. Malden, MA: Blackwell Publishing, 2006.

Hadid, Diaa. "United Arab Emirates: UAE National Women Gather to Demand Citizenship for Their Husbands and Children." Women Living Under Muslim Laws. http://www.wluml.org/english/newsfulltxt.shtml?cmd%5B157%5D=x-157-537009 (accessed July 2, 2006).

Haeri, Shahla. *Law of Desire: Temporary Marriage in Shi`i Iran*. Syracuse, NY: Syracuse University Press, 1989.

Hallaq, Wael B. *An Introduction to Islamic Law*. Cambridge: Cambridge University Press, 2009.

———. *The Origins and Evolution of Islamic Law*. Cambridge: Cambridge University Press, 2005.

Hamid, 'Abd al-Rahman Dhakir. "Cultural Influences and their Relationship to Values and the Concept of Freedom." Unpublished paper presented at the "Youth in the Face of a More Challenging World" conference, December 9–10, 2003, sponsored by the Ajman (UAE) women's association (December 2003): 1–15, unnumbered. (Arabic)

Hanna, Nelly. "Marriage Among Merchant Families in Seventeenth-Century Cairo." In *Women, the Family, and Divorce Laws in Islamic History*, edited by Amira El Azhary Sonbol, 143–54. Syracuse, NY: Syracuse University Press, 1996.

Haraway, Donna. "Situated Knowledges: The Science Question in Feminism and the Privilege of Partial Perspectives." *Feminist Studies* 14, no. 3 (fall 1988): 575–99.

Harib, Sa'id 'Abdullah Harib. "Youth and Social, Political, and Economic Development." Unpublished paper presented at the "Youth in the Face of a More Challenging World" conference, December 9–10, 2003, sponsored by the Ajman (UAE) women's association (December 2003): 1–33. (Arabic)

Hasan, Aznan. "Granting Khul' For a Non-Muslim Couple in Egyptian Personal Status Law: Generosity or Laxity?" *Arab Law Quarterly* 18, no. 1 (2003): 81–89.

Hasso, Frances S. "Comparing Emirati and Egyptian Narratives On Marriage, Sexuality, and the Body." In *Global Migration, Social Change, and Cultural Transformation*, edited by Emory Elliott, Jasmine Payne, and Patricia Ploesch, 59–74. New York: Palgrave Publishers, 2007.

———. "Narratives of Marriage, Sexuality, and the Body/Self among Egyptians and Emiratis." Translated into Arabic by Rehab el-Qubtan. *Taybah*, "Women in the Private Sphere," journal published by the New Woman Research Centre, Cairo. 5 (September 2004): 48–64. (Arabic)

———. *Resistance, Repression, and Gender Politics in Occupied Palestine and Jordan*. Syracuse, NY: Syracuse University Press, 2005.

———. "Shifting Practices and Identities: Nontraditional Relationships Among Sunni Muslim Egyptians and Emiratis." In *Family, Gender, and Law in a Globalizing Middle East and South Asia*, edited by Kenneth M. Cuno and Manisha Desai, 211–22. Syracuse, NY: Syracuse University Press, 2009.

Heard-Bey, Frauke. *From Trucial States to United Arab Emirates: A Society in Transition*. London and New York: Longman, 1996.

Hoodfar, Homa. *Between Marriage and the Market: Intimate Politics and Survival in Cairo*. Berkeley: University of California Press, 1997.

Hourani, Albert. *A History of the Arab Peoples*. New York: Warner Books, Inc., 1991.

Hunt, Alan, and Gary Wickham. *Foucault and Law: Towards a Sociology of Law as Governance*. London: Pluto Press, 1994

Hurreiz, Sayyid H. *Folklore and Folklife in the United Arab Emirates*. London: Routledge Curzon, 2002.

Ibrahim, Barbara, et al. *Transitions to Adulthood: A National Survey of Egyptian Adolescents*, 2d ed. New York: Population Council, 2000.

Idris, Khalid. "Underage Mafia in Circulation: Rich Old Arabs Hunt for Poor Girls in an Attempt to Take Advantage of their Harsh Circumstances." *Insaf*, magazine published by the Center for Women's Studies Research, Media Department, Cairo University (May 2003): 3. (Arabic)

Inda, Jonathan Xavier. "Analytics of the Modern: An Introduction." In *Anthropologies of Modernity: Foucault, Governmentality, and Life Politics*, edited by Inda, 1–20. Malden, MA: Blackwell Publishing, 2005.

Inhorn, Marcia C. *Local Babies, Global Science: Gender, Religion, and In Vitro Fertilization in Egypt*. New York and London: Routledge, 2003.

Jabarti, Somayya. "A Happy Misyar Union." *Arab News*, June 5, 2005. http://www.arabnews.com/?page=9&section=0&article=64892&d=5&m=6&y=2005 (accessed June 21, 2008).

Jameson, Fredric. "Notes on Globalization as a Philosophical Issue." In *The Cultures of Globalization*, edited by Jameson and Masao Miyoshi, 54–77. Durham, NC: Duke University Press, 1998.

Jones, Gavin. "Delayed Marriage and Very Low Fertility in Pacific Asia." *Population and Development Review* 33 (September 2007): 453–78.

Joseph, Suad, ed. *Gender and Citizenship in the Middle East*. Syracuse, NY: Syracuse University Press, 2000.

Kanaaneh, Rhoda Ann. *Birthing the Nation: Strategies of Palestinian Women in Israel*. Berkeley and Los Angeles: University of California Press, 2002.

Kanna, Ahmed. "Dubai in a Jagged World." *Middle East Report Online*, summer 2007, no. 243. http://www.merip.org/mer/mer243/kanna.html (accessed October 27, 2009).

Kanna, Ahmed Ismail. *"Not Their Fathers' Days": Idioms of Space and Time in the Urban Arabian Gulf*. PhD dissertation. Department of Anthropology, Harvard University, 2006.

Kapiszewski, Andrzej. *Nationals and Expatriates: Population and Labour Dilemmas of the Gulf Cooperation Council States*. Reading, UK: Garnet Publishing, Ltd., 2001.

Karam, Azza M. *Women, Islamisms and the State: Contemporary Feminisms in Egypt*. New York: St. Martin's Press, 1998.

Kechichian, Joseph A. "Unity in the Arabian Peninsula." In *Iran, Iraq, and the Arab Gulf States*, edited by Joseph A. Kechichian, 281–302. New York: Palgrave, 2001.

Kepel, Gilles. *Muslim Extremism in Egypt: The Prophet and the Pharaoh*. Berkeley and Los Angeles: University of California Press, 1986.

Khalifa, Ali Mohammed. *The United Arab Emirates: Unity in Fragmentation*. Boulder, CO: Westview Press, 1979.

Khatib, Maha K. *Beyond the Mysterious and Exotic: Women of the Emirates (And I) Assess Their Lives and Society*. PhD dissertation. Department of Anthropology, Brown University, 1994.

Kholoussy, Hanan. "The Nationalization of Marriage in Monarchical Egypt." In *Re-Envisioning Egypt, 1919–1952*, edited by Arthur Goldschmidt, Amy J. Johnson, and Barak A. Salmoni, 317–51. Cairo and New York: American University in Cairo Press, 2005.

El-Kholy, Heba. *Defiance and Compliance: Negotiating Gender in Low-Income Cairo*. New York and Oxford: Berghahn Books, 2002.

Konig, Anouk de. "Café Latte and Caesar Salad: Cosmopolitan Belonging in Cairo's Coffee Shops." In *Cairo Cosmopolitan: Politics, Culture, and Urban Space in the New Globalized Middle East*, edited by Singerman and Amar, 221–33. Cairo and New York: American University in Cairo Press, 2006.

Kosmatopoulos, Nicolas. "In . . . Mall We Trust? Young Employees, Space and Power in a Cairo Shopping Mall." In *Youth, Gender and the City: Social Anthropological Explorations in Cairo*, edited by Thomas Husken, 119–41. Cairo: Goethe-Institut Egypt, 2007.

Kozma, Liat. "Negotiating Virginity: Narratives of Defloration from Late Nineteenth-Century Egypt." *Comparative Studies of South Asia, Africa and the Middle East* 24, no. 1 (2004): 55–65.

Krane, Jim. "Arab Police Arrest 22 at Mass Gay Wedding." *The Cleveland Plain Dealer* (Associated Press report), November 27, 2005, A8.

Lay, Alexis R. "Interpretations of Islamic Practices Among Non-Qatari Students Living in the University of Qatar's Ladies Hostel." *Dialectical Anthropology* 29, no. 2 (June 2005): 181–219.

Leila, Reem. "Citizens at Last: The Long Awaited, Revised Egyptian Nationality Law Has Become a Reality." *Al-Ahram Weekly Online* (Cairo), 1–7 July, no. 697. http://weekly.ahram.org.eg/2004/697/eg10.htm (accessed October 23, 2008).

———. "Citizenship Costs Less." *Al-Ahram Weekly Online* (Cairo), 3–9 August 2006, no. 806. http://weekly.ahram.org.eg/2006/806/eg4.htm (accessed October 23, 2008).

————. "Ties Made Better." *Al-Ahram Weekly Online* (Cairo), 22–28 February 2007, no. 833. http://weekly.ahram.org.eg/2007/833/eg12.htm (accessed January 21, 2009).

Lombardi, Clark B. *State Law as Islamic Law in Modern Egypt: The Incorporation of the Shari'a into Egyptian Constitutional Law.* Leiden, Boston: Brill, 2006.

Long, Scott. "Raped By The State: Reflections on Sexuality and Democracy in the Middle East." *Index on Censorship* 3 (2005): 122–29.

MacFarquhar, Neil. "Paternity Suit Against TV Star Scandalizes Egyptians." *New York Times*, January 25, 2005. Lexis Nexis Academic Universe (accessed January 31, 2005).

Magdy, Sara Ahmed. "The Tears of a Young Face." *Potpourri* magazine, Department of English, Faculty of Arts, Cairo University, no. 2 (May 2002): 14.

Mansur, Muhammad Ibrahim. "Social and Economic Changes and their Impact on Youth in United Arab Emirates Society." Unpublished paper presented at the "Youth in the Face of a More Challenging World" conference, December 9–10, 2003, sponsored by the Ajman (UAE) women's association (December 2003): 1–20. (Arabic)

Marchal, Roland. "Dubai: Global City and Transnational Hub." In *Transnational Connections and the Arab Gulf*, edited by Madawi al-Rasheed, 93–110. London: Routledge, 2005.

Marston, Sallie A., and Neil Smith. "States, Scales and Households: Limits to Scale Thinking? A Response to Brenner." *Progress in Human Geography* 25, no. 4 (2001): 615–19.

Martin, Rux. "Truth, Power, Self: An Interview with Michel Foucault, October 25, 1982." In *Technologies of the Self: A Seminar with Michel Foucault*, edited by Martin, Gutman, and Hutton, 7–15. Amherst: University of Massachusetts Press, 1988.

McDaniel, Anne E. "Measuring Gender Egalitarianism: The Attitudinal Difference Between Men and Women." *International Journal of Sociology* 38, no. 1 (2008): 58–80.

Merry, Sally Engle. "Governmentality and Gender Violence in Hawai'i." *Social and Legal Studies* 11, no. 1 (2002): 81–111.

Messick, Brinkley. *The Calligraphic State: Textual Domination and History in a Muslim Society.* Berkeley: University of California Press, 1993.

Mir-Hosseini, Ziba. *Marriage on Trial: A Study of Islamic Family Law, Iran and Morocco Compared.* London: I.B. Tauris and Co. Ltd., 2000.

Mitchell, Timothy. *Colonising Egypt.* Berkeley: University of California Press, 1991.

————. *Rule of Experts: Egypt, Techno-Politics, Modernity.* Berkeley: University of California Press, 2002.

————. "State, Economy, and the State Effect." In *The Anthropology of the State: A Reader*, edited by Sharma and Gupta, 168–86. Malden, MA: Blackwell Publishing, 2006.

Moaddel, Mansoor. "The Saudi Public Speaks: Religion, Gender, and Politics." In *Values and Perceptions of the Islamic and Middle Eastern Publics*, edited by Mansoor Moaddel, 209–46. New York: Palgrave Macmillan, 2007.

Molyneux, Maxine. "The Law, the State and Socialist Policies with Regard to Women: the Case of the People's Democratic Republic of Yemen 1967–1990." In *Women, Islam and the State*, edited by Deniz Kandiyoti, 237–71. Philadelphia, PA: Temple University Press, 1991.

Moors, Annelies. "Debating Islamic Family Law: Legal Texts and Social Practices." In *A Social History of Women and Gender in the Modern Middle East*, edited by Margaret L. Meriwether and Judith E. Tucker, 141–75. Boulder, CO: Westview Press, 1999.

Al-Muhairi, Butti Sultan Butti Ali. "The Development of the UAE Legal System and Unification with the Judicial System." *Arab Law Quarterly* 11, no. 2 (1996): 116–60.

———. "The Federal Penal Code and the Aim of Unification." *Arab Law Quarterly* 12, no. 2 (1997): 197–210.

———. "Islamisation and Modernisation within the UAE Penal Law: Shari'a in the Pre-Modern Period." *Arab Law Quarterly* 10, no. 4 (1995): 287–309.

———. "Islamisation and Modernisation within the UAE Penal Law: Shari'a in the Modern Era." *Arab Law Quarterly* 11, no. 1 (1996): 34–49.

———. "The Position of the Shari'a Within the UAE Constitution and the Federal Supreme Court's Application of the Constitutional Clause Concerning Shari'a." *Arab Law Quarterly* 11, no. 3 (1996): 219–44.

Al-Musfir, Muhammad Salih. *The United Arab Emirates: An Assessment of Federalism in a Developing Polity*. PhD dissertation. The Graduate School of the State University of New York at Binghamton, 1984.

Al-Mutairi, Abaid. *The Impact of Federalism Over the Formation of Personal Jurisdiction Rules in Two Different Legal Traditions: Limited Comparison to the Civil Law Model of the United Arab Emirates and the Common Law Model of the United States*. Doctorate of judicial science dissertation. Washington College of Law of the American University, Washington, DC, 2005.

Al-Mutawwa', Ahmad Jasim M'hmd. "Do You Know the Priorities of Married Life?" Jeddah: Dar al-Balagh Publishing, 1998. (Arabic)

Nagar, Richa, Victoria Lawson, Linda McDowell, and Susan Hanson. "Locating Globalization: Feminist (Re)readings of the Subjects and Spaces of Globalization." *Economic Geography* 78, no. 3 (July 2002): 257–84.

Al-Naggar, Mona. "Egypt: Actor is Father, Court Rules." *New York Times*. May 25, 2006. Lexis Nexis Academic Universe (accessed July 6, 2007).

Naveh, Immanuel. "The Tort of Injury and Dissolution of Marriage at the Wife's Initiative in Egyptian Mahkamat al-Naqd Rulings." *Islamic Law and Society* 9, no. 1 (2002): 16–41.

Nemoto, Kumiko. "Postponed Marriage: Exploring Women's Views of Matrimony and Work in Japan." *Gender and Society* 22, no. 2 (April 2008): 219–37.

Neumann, Roderick P. "Political Ecology: Theorizing Scale." *Progress in Human Geography* 33, no. 3 (2009): 398–406.

"New Paternity Law Stipulating DNA Testing Proposed." *IRIN*, April 13, 2006. http://www.IRINnews.org (accessed July 3, 2006).

Osman, Magued, and Laila S. Shahd. "Age-Discrepant Marriage in Egypt." In *Cairo Papers in Social Science* 24, edited by Nicholas S. Hopkins, 51–61. "The New Arab Family," nos. 1–2 (spring–summer 2001). Cairo: American University in Cairo Press, 2003.

Al-Owais, Hadif Rashid. *The Federation of the United Arab Emirates and the Legislative Power of the Federal Government Compared with the Legislative Power of the Federal Government of the United States.* LLM dissertation. Harvard Law School, 1984.

Owen, Roger. "The Population Census of 1917 and its Relationship to Egypt's Three 19th Century Statistical Regimes." *Journal of Historical Sociology* 9, no. 4, (December 1996): 457–472.

Peck, Malcolm C. *The United Arab Emirates: A Venture in Unity.* Boulder, CO: Westview Press, 1986.

Pollard, Lisa. *Nurturing the Nation: The Family Politics of Modernizing, Colonizing, and Liberating Egypt, 1805–1923.* Berkeley and Los Angeles: University of California Press, 2005.

Al-Qawwas, Najat 'Ali Saleh. Guest on Luna al-Shibil, "For Women Only" program. Al-Jazeera satellite television channel. December 27, 2004. (Arabic)

Rashad, Hoda, and Magued Osman. "Nuptiality in Arab Countries: Changes and Implications." In *Cairo Papers in Social Science* 24, edited by Hopkins, 20–50. "The New Arab Family," nos. 1–2 (spring–summer 2001). Cairo: American University in Cairo Press, 2003.

Al-Rasheed, Mawadi. "Introduction: Localizing the Transnational and Transnationalizing the Local." In *Transnational Connections and the Arab Gulf*, edited by al-Rasheed, 1–18. London: Routledge, 2005.

Rebello, Poroma. "Politics of Fashion in Dubai." *ISIM Newsletter*, no. 1 (October 1998): 18.

Ridge, Natasha. "The Hidden Gender Gap in Education in the UAE." *Dubai School of Government Policy Brief*, no. 12 (August 2009): 1–7. http://www.dsg.ae/LinkClick.aspx?link=Policy+Brief+12+Ridge+English.pdf&tabid=308&mid=826 (accessed October 27, 2009).

———. "School Quality and Gender in the Gulf: A Comparative Study of Girls' and Boys' Secondary Schools in the United Arab Emirates." Paper under journal review, kindly provided by the author (November 2009).

Rose, Nikolas. *Powers of Freedom: Reframing Political Thought.* Cambridge: Cambridge University Press, 1999.

Roseberry, William. "Hegemony and the Language of Contention." In *Everyday Forms of State Formation: Revolution and the Negotiation of Rule in Modern Mexico*, edited by Gilbert M. Joseph and Daniel Nugent, 355–66. Durham, NC: Duke University Press, 1994.

Rugh, Andrea B. 1993. "Reshaping Personal Relations in Egypt." In *Fundamentalisms and Society: Reclaiming the Sciences, the Family, and Education*, edited by Martin E. Marty and R. Scott Appleby, 151–80. Chicago and London: University of Chicago Press, 1993.

Sadek, Said. "Cairo as a Global/Regional Cultural Capital?" In *Cairo Cosmopolitan: Poli-*

tics, Culture, and Urban Space in the New Globalized Middle East, edited by Singerman and Amar, 153–90. Cairo and New York: American University in Cairo Press, 2006.

Saleh, Heba. "Paternity Scandal Divides Egypt." *BBC News*, February 24, 2005. http://newsvote.bbc.co.uk (accessed July 6, 2007).

Al-Sari, 'Issa Ma'dad. "Toward a Complete Preventative Policy for Youth Problems." Unpublished paper presented at the "Youth in the Face of a More Challenging World" conference, December 9–10, 2003, sponsored by the Ajman (UAE) women's association (December 2003): 1–27. (Arabic)

Al-Sayegh, Fatma. "Domestic Politics in the United Arab Emirates: Social and Economic Policies, 1990–2000." In *Iran, Iraq, and the Arab Gulf States*, edited by Joseph A. Kechichian, 161–75. New York: Palgrave, 2001.

Sayer, Derek. "Everyday Forms of State Formation: Some Dissident Remarks on 'Hegemony.'" In *Everyday Forms of State Formation: Revolution and the Negotiation of Rule in Modern Mexico*, edited by Joseph and Nugent, 367–77. Durham, NC: Duke University Press, 1994.

Sayre, Nathan F. "Ecological and Geographical Scale: Parallels and Potential for Integration." *Progress in Human Geography* 29, no. 3 (2005): 276–90.

Schvaneveldt, Paul L., Jennifer L. Kerpelman, and Jay D. Schvaneveldt. "Generational and Cultural Changes in Family Life in the United Arab Emirates: A Comparison of Mothers and Daughters." *Journal of Comparative Family Studies* 36, no. 1 (2005): 77–91.

Seguino, Stephanie. "Plus Ça Change? Evidence on Global Trends in Gender Norms and Stereotypes." *Feminist Economics* 13, no. 2 (2007): 1–28.

Shadid, Anthony. "The Towering Dream of Dubai." *Washington Post*, April 30, 2006. www.washingtonpost.com/wp-dyn/content/article/2006/04/29/AR2006042901457.html (accessed May 1, 2006).

Shaham, Ron. *Family and the Courts in Modern Egypt: A Study Based on Decisions by the Shari'a Courts, 1900–1955*. Leiden, New York, and Koln: Brill, 1997.

———. "State, Feminists and Islamists—The Debate Over Stipulations in Marriage Contracts in Egypt." University of London *Bulletin of the School of Oriental and African Studies* 62, no. 3 (1999): 462–83.

El Shakry, Omnia. *The Great Social Laboratory: Subjects of Knowledge in Colonial and Postcolonial Egypt*. Stanford: Stanford University Press, 2007.

———. "Schooled Mothers and Structured Play: Child Rearing in Turn of the Century Egypt." In *Remaking Women: Feminism and Modernity in the Middle East*, edited by Lila Abu-Lughod, 53–76. Princeton, NJ: Princeton University Press, 1998.

Shapiro, Michael J. "The Politics of the 'Family.'" In *Cultural Studies and Political Theory*, edited by Jodi Dean, 269–84. Ithaca, NY: Cornell University Press, 2000.

Sharma, Aradhana, and Akhil Gupta. "Introduction: Rethinking Theories of the State in an Age of Globalization." In *The Anthropology of the State: A Reader*, edited by Sharma and Gupta, 1–41. Malden, MA: Blackwell Publishing, 2006.

Al-Sharmani, Mulki. "Recent Reforms in Personal Status Laws and Women's Empowerment: Family Courts in Egypt." Cairo: American University in Cairo, Social Research Center, February 2008. Report kindly provided to the author by Dr. al-Sharmani.

Al-Shaykh, Muhammad Mahmud. "Self-Esteem and Its Relationship to the Level of Ambition Youth Have." Unpublished paper presented at the "Youth in the Face of a More Challenging World" conference, December 9–10, 2003, sponsored by the Ajman (UAE) women's association (December 2003): 1–14. (Arabic)

Sherif, Bahira. "The Prayer of a Married Man is Equal to Seventy Prayers of a Single Man: The Central Role of Marriage Among Upper-Middle-Class Muslim Egyptians." *Journal of Family Issues* 20, no. 5 (September 1999): 617–32.

Sherwood, Seth. "The Oz of the Middle East." *New York Times.* http://travel.nytimes.com/2005/05/08/travel/08dubai.html?pagewanted=3&ei=5070&en=69464081038b8f69&ex=1187928000 (accessed August 22, 2007).

Al-Shibil, Luna. "Secret Marriage in our Arab World: Its Reasons and Precariousness." Episode of "For Women Only [*li-l-nisā' faqad*]" Program on al-Jazeera satellite television channel. December 27, 2004. (Arabic)

Singerman, Diane. *Avenues of Participation: Family, Politics, and Networks in Urban Quarters of Cairo.* Princeton, NJ: Princeton University Press, 1995.

———. "The Economic Imperatives of Marriage: Emerging Practices and Identities Among Youth in the Middle East," no. 6 (September 2007). The Modern Middle East Initiative, Working Paper, Wolfensohn Center for Development, Dubai School of Government.

Singerman, Diane, and Paul Amar. "Introduction: Contesting Myths, Critiquing Cosmopolitanism, and Creating the New Cairo School of Urban Studies." In *Cairo Cosmopolitan: Politics, Culture, and Urban Space in the New Globalized Middle East,* edited by Singerman and Amar, 3–43. Cairo and New York: American University in Cairo Press, 2006.

Singerman, Diane, and Barbara Ibrahim. "The Cost of Marriage in Egypt: A Hidden Variable in the New Arab Demography." In *Cairo Papers in Social Science* 24, edited by Hopkins, 80–116. "The New Arab Family," nos. 1–2 (spring–summer 2001). Cairo: American University in Cairo Press, 2003.

Skovgaard-Petersen, Jakob. *Defining Islam for the Egyptian State: Muftis and Fatwas of the Dar al-Ifta.* Leiden, New York, and Koln: Brill, 1997.

Soffan, Linda Usra. *The Women of the United Arab Emirates.* London and New York: Croom Helm and Barnes and Noble Books, 1980.

Sonbol, Amira El Azhary. "Adults and Minors in Ottoman Shari'a Courts and Modern Law." In *Women, the Family, and Divorce Laws in Islamic History,* edited by Sonbol, 236–56. Syracuse, NY: Syracuse University Press, 1996.

———. "History of Marriage Contracts in Egypt." *Hawwa* 3, no. 2 (2005): 159–96.

————. "Law and Gender Violence in Ottoman and Modern Egypt." In *Women, the Family, and Divorce Laws in Islamic History*, edited by Sonbol, 277–89. Syracuse, NY: Syracuse University Press, 1996.

————, ed. *Women, the Family, and Divorce Laws in Islamic History*. Syracuse, NY: Syracuse University Press, 1996.

Souleiman, Azza. "Introduction." In *The Harvest: Two Years After Kholʿ: An Analytical Study*, edited by Souleiman, Salah, Zakareya, and Tadrous, 9–12. Translated by Seham Abd el Salam. Cairo: The Center for Egyptian Women Legal Assistance, 2003.

Souleiman, Azza, and Azza Salah. "The Legal Aspects of Kholʿ and its Application." In *The Harvest: Two Years After Kholʿ: An Analytical Study*, edited by Souleiman, Salah, Zakareya, and Tadrous, 13–35. Translated by Seham Abd el Salam. Cairo: The Center for Egyptian Women Legal Assistance, 2003.

Statistical Bulletin. The Cooperation Council for the Arab States of the Gulf, Secretariat General, Information Center, Statistical Department. Volume 12, 2003. Chapter 1: "Population and Vital Statistics," table 7 ("Marriage and Divorce Cases"). http:// www.gcc-sg.org/gccstatvol12/genstat/G7.htm (accessed July 11, 2006).

Statistical Bulletin. The Cooperation Council for the Arab States of the Gulf Secretariat General, Information Center, Statistical Department. Vol. 15, 2006. Chapter 1: "Population and Vital Statistics," table 7 ("Marriage and Divorce Cases"). http://library .gcc-sg.org/gccstatvol15/genstat/g7.htm (accessed July 17, 2007).

Statistical Bulletin. The Cooperation Council for the Arab States of the Gulf, Secretariat General, Information Center, Statistical Department. Vol. 15, 2006. Chapter 2: "Education Statistics," table 11 ("Students in Secondary by Sex and Nationality, Governmental Education") http://www.gcc-sg.org/gccstatvol12/educstat/ed11.htm; table 15 ("Students in Secondary By Sex and Nationality, Private"). http://www.gcc-sg.org /gccstatvol12/educstat/ed15.htm; table 32 ("Students in Secondary By Sex and Nationality, Technical and Vocational") http://www.gcc-sg.org/gccstatvol12/educstat /ed26.htm; and table 38 ("Students in University by Sex and Nationality") http:// www.gcc-sg.org/gccstatvol12/educstat/ed31.htm (accessed July 17, 2007).

Statistical Bulletin. The Cooperation Council for the Arab States of the Gulf Secretariat General, Information Center, Statistical Department. Vol. 15, 2006. Chapter 1: "Population and Vital Statistics," table 1 ("Total Number of Population") and table 4 ("Labour Force"). http://library.gcc-sg.org/gccstatvol15/genstat/G1.htm and http:// library.gcc-sg.org/gccstatvol15/genstat/G4.htm (accessed July 17, 2007).

Starrett, Gregory. "The Anthropology of Islam." In *Anthropology of Religion: A Handbook*, edited by Stephen D. Glazier, 279–303. Westport, CT: Greenwood Press, 1997.

————. *Putting Islam to Work: Education, Politics, and Religious Transformation in Egypt*. Berkeley: University of California Press, 1998.

Stowasser, Barbara Freyer. "Women and Citizenship in the Qurʾan." In *Women, the*

Family, and Divorce Laws in Islamic History, edited by Sonbol, 23–38. Syracuse, NY: Syracuse University Press, 1996.

———. *Women in the Qur'an, Traditions, and Interpretation*. New York: Oxford University Press, 1994.

Tadrous, Mariz. "The Law of Khol' in the Egyptian Press." In *The Harvest: Two Years After Khol': An Analytical Study*, edited by Souleiman, Salah, Zakareya, and Tadrous, 75–84. Translated by Seham Abd el Salam. Cairo: The Center for Egyptian Women Legal Assistance, 2003.

Al Tamimi, Essam. *Practical Guide to Litigation and Arbitration in the United Arab Emirates*. The Hague, London, and New York: Kluwer Law International, 2003.

Al-Tawila, Sahar, Barbara Ibrahim, and Hind Wassef. "Social Change and Adolescent-Parent Dynamics in Egypt." In *Cairo Papers in Social Science* 24, edited by Hopkins, 214–46. "The New Arab Family," nos. 1–2 (spring–summer 2001). Cairo: American University in Cairo Press, 2003.

El Tawila, Sahar, Barbara Ibrahim, and Hind Wassef. "Social Change and Parent-Adolescent Dynamics in Egypt." In *Family in the Middle East: Ideational Change in Egypt, Iran, and Tunisia*, edited by Yount and Rashad, 151–70. New York: Routledge, 2008.

Thiyabi, Jamil. "Patching up Chastity!" *Dar al Hayat*, February 19, 2007. www.daralhayat .net/actions/print2.php (accessed January 31, 2009). (Arabic)

"[Three Hundred Fifteen] 315 Foreigners Granted Egyptian Citizenship." *Khaleej Times*, December 8, 2003, 17.

Tucker, Judith E. *In the House of the Law: Gender and Islamic Law in Ottoman Syria and Palestine*. Berkeley and Los Angeles: University of California Press, 1998.

UNICEF. "Information by Country." http://www.unicef.org/infobycountry/ (accessed July 29, 2006).

United Nations Development Programme. *Arab Human Development Report 2005: Towards the Rise of Women in the Arab World*. New York: Regional Bureau of Arab States, cosponsored with the Arab Fund for Economic and Social Development and the Arab Gulf Programme for United Nations Organizations, 2006.

———. "The Gender and Citizenship Initiative: Country Profiles: United Arab Emirates." Programme on Governance in the Arab Region, http://gender.pogar.org/ countries/gender.asp?cid=21 (accessed July 17, 2007).

United Arab Emirates. *Census 2005*. Abu Dhabi: Ministry of Economy. www.tedad.ae/ english/about_census/background.html (accessed January 14, 2007).

———. *Law of Personal Status Matters 2005, Federal Law No. 28, with Explanatory Memos*. Published by UAE Jurists Association. Al-Shariqa, UAE: Dar al-Fatah Press for Publication and Distribution, January 2006. This text was kindly provided to the author by Dr. Mohamed al-Roken. (Arabic)

———. *United Arab Emirates Yearbook 2003.* Abu Dhabi: UAE Ministry of Information and Culture, 2003. Published by London: Trident Press.

Van der Meulen, Hendrik. *The Role of Tribal and Kinship Ties in the Politics of the United Arab Emirates.* PhD dissertation. The Fletcher School of Law and Diplomacy, Tufts University, 1997.

Visweswaran, Kamala. *Fictions of Feminist Ethnography.* Minneapolis: University of Minnesota Press, 1994.

Walby, Kevin. "Contributions to a Post-Sovereigntist Understanding of Law: Foucault, Law as Governance, and Legal Pluralism." *Social and Legal Studies* 16, no. 4 (2007): 551–71.

Walters, Lynne, and Timothy N. Walters. "The Transitional Woman: A Case Study of Values in the Context of an Arabic/Islamic Society." *Hawwa* 3, no. 2 (2005): 216–44.

Watts, Michael. "Development and Governmentality." *Singapore Journal of Tropical Geography* 24, no. 1 (2003): 6–34.

Welchman, Lynn. *Women and Muslim Family Laws in Arab States: A Comparative Overview of Textual Development and Advocacy.* Amsterdam: Amsterdam University Press, 2007.

———. *Women's Rights and Islamic Family Law: Perspectives on Reform.* London: Zed Books, 2004.

Wickham, Carrie Rosefsky. *Mobilizing Islam: Religion, Activism, and Political Change in Egypt.* New York: Columbia University Press, 2002.

Wikan, Unni. *Behind the Veil in Arabia: Women in Oman.* Chicago: University of Chicago Press, 1982.

———. *Tomorrow, God Willing: Self-Made Destinies in Cairo.* Chicago and London: University of Chicago Press, 1996.

Williams, Daniel. "Gay Men Face Jail in Egypt, Kuwait in Bid to Appease Islamists." *Bloomberg.com*, April 8, 2009. http://www.bloomberg.com/apps/news?pid=20670001 &sid= . . . (accessed April 3, 2009).

Women in the UAE. Abu Dhabi: United Arab Emirates Women's Federation, 1995.

Worth, Robert F. "Challenging Sex Taboos, With Help from the Koran." *New York Times*, June 6, 2009. http://www.nytimes.com/2009/06/06/world/middleeast/06dubai.html (accessed June 6, 2009).

Yang, Mayfair Mei-hui. "Mass Media and Transnational Subjectivity in Shanghai: Notes on (Re)Cosmopolitanism in a Chinese Metropolis." In *Media Worlds: Anthropology on a New Terrain*, edited by Faye D. Ginsburg et al., 189–210. Berkeley: University of California Press, 2002.

Zakareya, Huda. "Khol': A Socio-Legal Study." In *The Harvest: Two Years After Khol': An Analytical Study*, edited by Souleiman, Salah, Zakareya, and Tadrous, 41–74. Translated from Arabic by Seham Abd el Salam. Cairo: The Center for Egyptian Women Legal Assistance, 2003.

Zeidan, David. "The Copts—Equal, Protected or Persecuted? The Impact of Islamiza-
tion on Muslim-Christian Relations in Modern Egypt." *Islam and Christian-Muslim
Relations* 10, no. 1 (1999): 53–67.

Zubaida, Sami. *Islam, the People and the State: Political Ideas and Movements in the
Middle East*. London: I.B. Tauris, 1993.

Zulfiqqar, Muna. "Equality and Equal Opportunities." *Hagar on Women's Issues*, no. 2,
Sina' Publishing (1994): 49–58. (Arabic)

Interviews Conducted by Author

'Abd al-Rahman, 'Awatef. Faculty of Mass Communications, Cairo University. Giza,
Egypt. December 30, 2003.

'Abdel Rahim, Muhammad. Dubai, UAE. December 1, 2003.

'Arafat, Ahmad. Lawyer. Giza, Egypt. May 26, 2008.

Al-'Afify, Nadya Abdel Wahab. Director of Geriatrics Department, Palestine Hospital;
member of the New Woman Research and Study Center. Cairo, Egypt. December
28, 2003.

Al-'Olama, Dr. al-Shaykh Mohammad 'Abdul Rahim Sultan. Professor and Assistant
Dean for Scientific Research, Head of Basic Studies Department, Faculty of Shari'a
and Law, United Arab Emirates University. Abu Dhabi, UAE. December 9, 2003.

Bachiri, Amal, and Ahmed Chahine. Journalists, intellectuals. Dubai, UAE. December 4, 2003.

Al-Bah, Jamal Bin Obaid. Assistant Undersecretary for the Managing Director, The
Marriage Fund. Dubai, UAE. December 7, 2003.

Darwiche, Nawla. Director, New Woman Research Center. Cairo, Egypt. December 22,
2003.

Darwish, 'Abdul Salam Muhammad. Head of Family Guidance and Reconciliation,
Government of Dubai, Courts Department. Dubai, UAE. December 7, 2003.

Al-Diqqi, Hisa. Executive Committee Member, Women's Renaissance Association—
Dubai (Dubai Women's Association in organization's English translation); Director,
Renaissance Center for Counseling and Training. Dubai, UAE. December 8, 2003.

Gargash, Samira 'Abdullah. Advocate and Legal Consultant before the United Arab
Emirates Courts. Dubai, UAE. December 8, 2003.

Ghabish, Saliha 'Obayd. Cultural Affairs Manager, Shariqa Girls' Clubs, referred to on
organizational letterhead as the Sharjah Women's Club. Shariqa, UAE. December 16,
2003.

Group Interview with eight women students, seniors (pseudonyms). Cairo University.
Giza, Egypt. December 27, 2003. Interview arranged with the kind assistance of Professor Hala Kamal, professor of English literature, Cairo University.

Group Interview with nine men and women students, largely seniors (pseudonyms).
Faculty of Economics and Political Science (FEPS), Cairo University. Giza, Egypt.

May 26, 2008. Interview arranged with kind assistance of Dr. Heba Rauf 'Ezzat, professor of political science; Dina Magdi Taha, senior and FEPS class representative; Dr. 'Abdul-Mon'em Al-Mashat, professor and director, FEPS.

Group Interview with seven MA prep students (three men and four women) (pseudonyms). 'Ayn Shams University. 'Ayn Shams, Egypt. May 28, 2008. Interview arranged with kind assistance of Dr. 'Ali Layla, professor of sociology, 'Ayn Shams University.

Group Interview with seven women students (pseudonyms). Arab Sharjah University, women's campus. Shariqa, UAE. December 14, 2003. Interview arranged with the kind assistance of Sulayman Khalaf, professor of sociology, Shariqa University.

Group Interview with six men students (pseudonyms). UAE University. Abu Dhabi (al-'Ayn), UAE. December 9, 2003. Interview kindly arranged by Mohammad 'Obayd Ghubash.

Group Interview with three men graduate students (pseudonyms). Faculty of Arts and Sciences, Cairo University. Giza, Egypt. May 26, 2008. Interview arranged with kind assistance of Dean of Faculty of Arts and Sciences, Ahmed A. Zayed and 'Ali Muhammad al-Makawwi, professor of sociology.

Group Interview with three women professors (pseudonyms). Faculty of Humanities and Social Sciences, United Arab Emirates University. Abu Dhabi (al-'Ayn), UAE. December 9, 2003. Interview kindly arranged by Mona Al-Bahr and Maryam Sultan Lutah.

Hamzawi, Riad Amin. Professor, UAE University. Al-'Ayn, Abu Dhabi, UAE. December 9, 2003.

Al-Kitbi, Ebtisam Suhayl. Political science professor, UAE (Al-'Ayn) University. Dubai, UAE. December 11, 2003.

Al-Korashy, Mona 'Abd al-Raouf Ibrahim. Lawyer in the High Appeals Court, active in the Republic of Egypt National Council for Women, member of the Arab Lawyers Union. Giza, Egypt. May 26, 2008.

Al-Kubaysi, Ahmad. Dubai, UAE. December 10, 2003.

Layla, 'Ali. Sociology professor, 'Ayn Shams University. 'Ayn Shams, Egypt. May 24, 2008.

Lutah, Widad Naser. Family advisor, Government of Dubai Courts Department. Dubai, UAE. December 6, 2003.

Lutfi, Lamya. New Woman's Research Center. Cairo, Egypt. May 25, 2008.

Mostafa, Magdy. School of social work professor, UAE University (al-'Ayn). Abu Dhabi, UAE. December 9, 2003.

Redha, Abdul-Redha Ali Bin. Dubai, UAE. December 11, 2003.

Al Roken, Mohamed Abdallah Mohamed. Busit, Al Roken and Associates, Advocates and Legal Consultants; Faculty of Shari'a and Law, Associate Professor—Public Law, United Arab Emirates University. Dubai, UAE. December 6, 2003.

Sa'id, Atef Shahat. Researcher, Hisham Mubarak Law Center. Cairo, Egypt. December 22, 2003.

Salih, Su'ad. Professor of Comparative Fiqh. Girls' College for Islamic and Arabic Studies, Al-Azhar University. Cairo, Egypt. May 29, 2008.

Al-Sharif, Anisa. Dubai, UAE. December 8, 2003.

Al-Sharmani, Mulki. Cultural anthropologist, research assistant professor, Social Research Center, American University in Cairo. Cairo, Egypt. May 29, 2008.

Yunis, Faysal 'Abd al-Qadir. Chair, Psychology Department, Cairo University. Cairo, Egypt. December 20, 2003.

Index

Abaza, Mona, 88, 94, 103, 104–6, 110, 209n14

'Abd al-Jawad, Layla, 107, 112

Abdal-Rehim, Abdal-Rehim Abdul-Rahman, 5, 46

'Abdel Rahim, Muhammad, 103

Abduh, Muhammad, 37, 47

abortion, 1, 86, 107, 130. *See also* individual choice

Abrams, Philip, 27

Abu Dhabi: citizenship, 202n84; civil courts, 58; nationality viewpoints, 73; personal status law (PSL) codification, 136; power differential, 52; role as seat of federation government, 52; shari'a tradition, 59; significance, 49. *See also* UAE (United Arab Emirates)

Abu-Lughod, Lila, 37, 109–10, 154, 219n118

Adli, Habib Al, 76

'Afify, Nadia al-, 115

'ā'ila. See family (*usra, 'ā'ila*)

'Ajman, 19, 48, 52, 71, 96, 251n197. *See also* UAE (United Arab Emirates)

Ali, Kamran, 119

alimony (*mut'a*), 5, 40, 43, 44, 92, 140, 143, 146, 157, 194n167, 216n57

ambulant marriage contracts (*misyār*), 12–13, 74, 76, 88–92, 118, 124, 139, 215n33

Americanization, 110

American University in Cairo, 147, 149

annulment, 4, 138, 139, 140, 143, 158, 178n27, 214n28

Arabi, Oussama, 91–92, 114, 182n111, 216n57

Arabian peninsula states, 89, 134–35

Arab nation-state differentiations, 16–20

Arabness, 17–18

'Arafat, Ahmad, 152

arbitration. *See* mediation

Asad, Talal, 28, 37

Association for the Union of Egyptian Women Lawyers, 146

authenticity, 14, 15, 17, 40, 60, 74, 96, 101, 120, 129, 132, 153

Azhar, Shaykh al-, 47, 143

al-Azhar University, 143, 155–56

Bah, Jamal Bin Obaid al-, 80, 108, 109